The Existentialism of
Jean-Paul Sartre

Routledge Studies in Twentieth-Century Philosophy

1. The Story of Analytic Philosophy
Plot and Heroes
Edited by Anat Biletzki and Anat Matar

2. Donald Davidson
Truth, Meaning and Knowledge
Edited by Urszula M. Zeglén

3. Philosophy and Ordinary Language
The Bent and Genius of Our Tongue
Oswald Hanfling

4. The Subject in Question
Sartre's Critique of Husserl in
The Transcendence of the Ego
Stephen Priest

5. Aesthetic Order
A Philosophy of Order, Beauty and Art
Ruth Lorland

6. Naturalism
A Critical Analysis
Edited by William Lane Craig and
J P Moreland

7. Grammar in Early Twentieth-Century Philosophy
Richard Gaskin

8. Rules, Magic and Instrumental Reason
A Critical Interpretation of Peter Winch's Philosophy of the Social Sciences
Berel Dov Lerner

9. Gaston Bachelard
Critic of Science and the Imagination
Cristina Chimisso

10. Hilary Putnam
Pragmatism and Realism
Edited by James Conant and
Urszula Zeglen

11. Karl Jaspers
Politics and Metaphysics
Chris Thornhill

12. From Kant to Davidson
The Idea of the Transcendental in
Twentieth-Century Philosophy
Edited by Jeff Malpas

13. Collingwood and the Metaphysics of Experience
A Reinterpretation
Giuseppina D'Oro

14. The Logic of Liberal Rights
A Study in the Formal Analysis of
Legal Discourse
Eric Heinze

15. Real Metaphysics
Edited by Hallvard Lillehammer and
Gonzalo Rodriguez-Pereyra

16. Philosophy After Postmodernism
Civilized Values and the Scope
of Knowledge
Paul Crowther

17. Phenomenology and Imagination in Husserl and Heidegger
Brian Elliott

18. Laws in Nature
Stephen Mumford

19. Trust and Toleration
Richard H. Dees

20. The Metaphysics of Perception
Wilfrid Sellars, Critical Realism and the Nature of Experience
Paul Coates

21. Wittgenstein, Austrian Economics, and the Logic of Action
Praxeological Investigations
Roderick T. Long

22. Ineffability and Philosophy
André Kukla

23. Cognitive Metaphor and Continental Philosophy
Clive Cazeaux

24. Wittgenstein and Levinas
Ethical and Religious Thought
Bob Plant

25. Philosophy of Time
Time before Times
Roger McClure

26. The Russellian Origins of Analytic Philosophy
Bertrand Russell and the Unity of the Proposition
Graham Stevens

27. Analytic Philosophy Without Naturalism
Edited by A. Corradini, S. Galvan and E.J. Lowe

28. Modernism and the Language of Philosophy
Anat Matar

29. Russell vs. Meinong
One Hundred Years after "On Denoting"
Edited by Nicholas Griffin and Dale Jacquette

30. The Existentialism of Jean-Paul Sartre
Jonathan Webber

The Existentialism of Jean-Paul Sartre

Jonathan Webber

New York   London

First published 2009
by Routledge
270 Madison Ave, New York, NY 10016

Simultaneously published in the UK
by Routledge
2 Park Square, Milton Park, Abingdon, Oxon OX14 4RN

Routledge is an imprint of the Taylor & Francis Group, an informa business

© 2009 Jonathan Webber

Typeset in Sabon by IBT Global.
Printed and bound in the United States of America on acid-free paper by IBT Global.

All rights reserved. No part of this book may be reprinted or reproduced or utilised in any form or by any electronic, mechanical, or other means, now known or hereafter invented, including photocopying and recording, or in any information storage or retrieval system, without permission in writing from the publishers.

Trademark Notice: Product or corporate names may be trademarks or registered trademarks, and are used only for identification and explanation without intent to infringe.

Library of Congress Cataloging in Publication Data
Webber, Jonathan (Jonathan Mark)
 The existentialism of Jean-Paul Sartre / Jonathan Webber.
  p. cm.—(Routledge studies in twentieth-century philosophy ; 30)
 Includes bibliographical references (p.) and index.
 1. Sartre, Jean-Paul, 1905–1980. I. Title.
 B2430.S34W43 2009
 194—dc22
                2008032501

ISBN10: 0-415-41118-1 (hbk)
ISBN10: 0-203-88317-9 (ebk)

ISBN13: 978-0-415-41118-9 (hbk)
ISBN13: 978-0-203-88317-4 (ebk)

To Suzi

Contents

Preface xi

1. Understanding Ourselves 1
2. The Reality of Character 16
3. Situations 30
4. Freely Chosen Projects 44
5. Radical Freedom 59
6. Anguish, Bad Faith, and Sincerity 74
7. The Project of Bad Faith 88
8. God and the Useless Passion 104
9. One Another 118
10. The Virtue of Authenticity 132
11. Being One Self 146

Bibliography 161
Index 165

Preface

The existentialism of Jean-Paul Sartre is an account of the way that we humans exist, in contrast to the ways in which such things as chairs and tables, flowers and trees, rocks and planets, and cats and dogs exist. It aims to elaborate the central structures of our lives, around which all the things that we do are built. This topic is interesting in its own right and Sartre's consideration of it is among the most thorough and systematic available. But there is more reason than this to study it. For answering the question of exactly what we are is also central to addressing some of the pressing issues that we all face. This is what motivated Sartre. He intended his philosophy to be much more than an abstract theory to be studied in libraries. He wrote about it in the popular press and illustrated it in his fiction because he saw the questions of how we should treat one another, how we should organise our societies, and how we should each think about our own plans and hopes and dreams as simply unanswerable unless we consider them within the framework of a theory of human existence and as receiving only disastrously wrong answers when the framework itself is wrong.

The theory that he developed, however, has been interpreted in a variety of different ways. This is partly because he does not always express himself as clearly as he might. He seems to have found it necessary to develop a new conceptual repertoire in which to express his thought, but he could have been more careful to explain his terminology. But it is also partly because most commentators on his existentialist work focus on one aspect of it or another, or at least one aspect at a time, at the expense of the overall picture. It then often turns out that one commentator's reading of one part does not sit easily with their own or someone else's reading of another part. The aim of this book is to present a single coherent picture of the central themes of Sartrean existentialism. We will see that this philosophy is the elaboration of one basic idea, one that is rarely identified as being even a part of it, and that this idea has much to offer to current debates over issues that we all face. The idea at the centre of Sartrean existentialism is simply that an individual's character consists in the projects that person pursues.

We should not understand this as claiming that actions result from nothing more than a decision about what to do, as though there were no such thing as spontaneous action and as though one's decisions did not anyway reflect deeper facts about oneself. This is important because one common caricature of Sartre has him claiming that everything we experience and do is something we just choose there and then. It is sometimes even said that he thinks we can decide how something will look to us and what emotions to feel about it. This caricature comes about because Sartre likes to say that all of our experiences and actions are in some sense chosen, but he does not mean that when we are confronted with something we decide how it will look to us, how we will feel about it, what we will think about it, and what we will do about it. He uses the language of choice in this way to emphasise his view that we have reflective control over the deeper aspects of ourselves that in turn determine how things will look to us, how we will feel in response to things, and the relative importance each consideration will have for us when we deliberate about what to do.

Each person's spontaneous and considered responses to their environment fall into patterns that we have come to describe in the language of character traits. Sartrean existentialism is basically the claim that these patterns result from the set of projects the individual pursues. If this is right, then a person's character, their traits such as honesty and dishonesty, courage and cowardice, kindness and meanness, and so on, are rooted in the projects that they have adopted and that they can alter. This is not to say that each trait is something that the individual deliberately and knowingly adopts, as though one cannot be a petty or bitter person without wanting to be. Neither is it to say that we are always very well aware of our character traits, as if one could not discover after careful reflection that one is rather insensitive. It is just to say that the overall patterns in a person's behaviour are determined by the overall set of projects that they are pursuing. It is to say that our characters are neither physically necessary effects of our genetic structures nor inescapable outcomes of formative experiences nor simply habits that have become entrenched by repetition, but rather manifest the purposive and goal-directed projects that we are engaged in and that we can change.

This lack of solidity at the core of the individual, this dependence of one's identity on merely contingent and changeable factors, this lightness of human being, is something that Sartre thinks we have covered over. We prefer to think of ourselves as having fixed natures that determine our thoughts, feelings, behaviour, and thereby ultimately our destinies, he claims. In this way, we can evade the feelings of responsibility that come with recognising that we do not have to see things this way, we do not have to think along these lines, we do not have to behave like this. So we deceive ourselves about the true structure of our own existence. This is what Sartre calls 'bad faith', and as we will see in the second half of this book he considers it to be a socially pervasive phenomenon that accounts not only for the way people think about themselves and others, but also for much of our treatment of one another, and even for some aspects of the way in which we have ordered our world. He sees this attitude as lying at the heart of such widespread social ills as racial hatred.

Although his philosophy is often portrayed as gloomy and pessimistic, this is a misrepresentation he complained about ever since it started circulating soon after the publication of *Being and Nothingness*. Sartrean existentialism is an optimistic theory, which teaches that we can learn to accept the way we really are, to see one another as we really are, and thereby get away from the basic problem underlying many of our ills. Not only that, but it also argues that the values we each already hold should lead us to embrace this alternative to bad faith, which he calls authenticity, as we will see towards the end of this book. As well as unpacking the idea that character consists in projects and considering the value of this idea as a contribution to contemporary discussions of the nature of agency, character, and the self, we will investigate the ethical claim that we ought to recognise this truth about our existence rather than accept the illusion that we have learned to find comforting.

The picture of Sartrean existentialism presented in this book is based entirely on *Being and Nothingness* and Sartre's published works preceding and immediately following it. For it is in these works that Sartre formulates the basic theory of character that this book analyses. His work over the subsequent three and a half decades continues to refine this theory, but tracing that further development is a large and separate task. Even within these few early works, the details of Sartre's theory change in important ways, as we will see, which is something that many commentators have overlooked. We will not be concerned with Sartre's posthumously published notebooks either, even those from the same period of his life as the published works we are considering. This is partly because it can be misleading to read a philosopher's publications in the light of other ideas that they sketched but never fully worked out or put into print, ideas that were then selected and ordered decades later by someone else, but mainly because we will find all that we need without having to take this controversial step.

This book aims to contribute not only to the understanding of Sartrean existentialism itself, but also to various current debates in moral philosophy by highlighting the distinctive advantages of this theory of character over its rivals and by distinguishing between a broadly Sartrean view of character and the details of Sartre's own position. It supersedes my article 'Sartre's Theory of Character'. Although some basic aspects of that article have found their way into the first few chapters of this book, others have been substantially revised or even jettisoned in order to make better sense of the bigger picture that this book discusses. The first few chapters also draw occasionally on some recent work of mine concerning psychological experiments into the nature of character and the attribution of traits, so for full justification of the points made in these areas, please see my articles listed in the bibliography.

Earlier versions of parts of this book have been presented at a conference of the UK Society for Sartrean Studies and to the philosophy departments of Bristol and Cardiff Universities. I am grateful to the audiences on those occasions and to three cohorts of philosophy students at Sheffield and Bristol for their searching questions. I am also grateful to Jules Holroyd, Suzi Wells, and an anonymous referee for their feedback on the first draft. Finally, I am grateful to many scholars of Sartre's writings, especially those whose works are listed in the bibliography. Dispute is no less germane to textual interpretation than to philosophy, with the effect that I have cited other works on Sartre largely in a critical tone. This is unfortunate. Sartre has not made himself easy to understand, and the position elaborated in this book could never have been formulated without consideration of the insightful explanations and criticisms presented in those scholarly works. Just as Josef Zawinul said, we always solo and we never solo.

1 Understanding Ourselves

Character is central to our thinking about ourselves and one another. We find patterns in the thoughts, feelings, and actions of each individual that we deal with, we see these patterns differ from person to person, and we understand these differing patterns in terms of underlying properties or traits. Thus we understand ourselves and one another as being honest, cowardly, kind, selfish, prudent, spiteful, upbeat, arrogant, and so on. These terms are applied on the basis of experience and help us predict future behaviour and hence to decide how to deal with one another. Not all of our explanations of the ways in which people react to situations are given in terms of character traits, of course, since some point instead to physical or social aspects of those situations. We might say that somebody ran away because there was a lion on the loose, for example, or remained quiet because their family expected them to. But the idea that each person possesses a portfolio of character traits, which are a subset of the huge range of traits possessed by the population at large, is nonetheless fundamental to our common-sense psychological understanding of people.

This idea of character is therefore a very good place to begin an intellectual critical enquiry into the nature of our lives. We should investigate what this type of description really amounts to and whether we would be better off with a different approach. If we find that it picks out a real aspect of ourselves, then we should consider what kinds of things character traits are, how they are formed, how we find out which ones we have, and how much control we have over them. Improving our understanding of ourselves has often been recommended for its potential to enrich our lives. It has sometimes been claimed to be intrinsically good, but more often it is encouraged for the positive consequences it could have. The better we know ourselves and the better we understand one another, the thought runs, the more successful we are likely to be in our relationships with one another and in the fulfilment of our hopes and dreams in general. This is what drives the practice and development of psychoanalysis, for example: the idea is that people who are troubled by aspects of their own behaviour can be helped to either accept or alter that behaviour by coming to understand the underlying traits that it manifests. Such positive consequences need not require the specialist uncovering of hidden traits, since it may well be that a good understanding of the nature, origins, and knowledge of character is enough.

It is not only one's happiness that could be served by advances in one's understanding of character, moreover, since the notion of character plays a significant role in ethical discourse. Questions about how we should live our lives, which kinds of behaviour should be encouraged and which discouraged, what we should praise and what we should condemn, are often answered with some reference to character traits. For one reason or another, many philosophers recommend that ethical practice be concerned with reflecting on one's own character and aiming to develop good traits in place of any bad ones. This recommendation can also be extended, as we will see, to matters of social policy.

Some philosophers recommend this approach to ethical practice by arguing that character is at the very heart of our ethical concerns. Honest behaviour, according to this view, is good only when it manifests an underlying trait of honesty, which in turn is a good thing in itself. Within this theory, philosophers disagree over just what makes traits good or bad. Some argue that honesty is good because it is likely to have good consequences for everyone: the more honest people there are in society, the happier all members of that society are; actions that are honest but done for some other reason, such as self-interest, are not good, because they do not manifest an underlying trait that is good for society at large. Others agree that actions are good only if they manifest good traits but deny that the goodness of traits is a matter of their consequences for society. Good traits, on this view, are rather those that contribute to the flourishing of the person whose traits they are. Given the nature of human existence, that is, we can identify ways in which people can excel at living a distinctively human life and see traits as good or bad according to whether they contribute to or mitigate against such excellence. Honesty is good, on this view, because being good at being human requires, among other things, being honest with one's fellow humans.

Against this idea that character is at the heart of ethics stand those philosophers who see ethics as essentially concerned with action and therefore claim that any value character traits have is the result of their relation to good and bad actions. One form of this view evaluates actions according to the intentions with which they are performed, and the opposing form evaluates actions according to their consequences. But each can be coupled with the further idea that the best way to maximise the right kinds of actions and minimise the wrong ones is to develop certain character traits rather than others. Honesty is good, on this view, because an honest person will behave in the right way more often than will somebody similar in all other respects but lacking in honesty. Honesty is good, that is, because it inclines one to act with the right intentions or because it inclines one to actions that have good consequences. Either way, the ethical evaluation of character traits is dependent upon the ethical evaluation of the actions they dispose one towards.

The phrase 'virtue ethics' often used in discussions of moral philosophy is therefore very misleading if it is supposed to refer to a particular approach to ethics, since we can easily distinguish four very different kinds of mainstream ethical theory that praise some character traits as good and condemn some as bad. There are two that evaluate actions in terms of the traits they manifest and disagree over how to evaluate traits. And there are two that evaluate traits in terms of the actions they lead to and disagree over how to evaluate those actions. All four of these theories have the right to the traditional labels of 'virtues' for good traits and 'vices' for bad traits. What is more, within each of these four camps there is plenty of room for disagreement over just which traits are to be considered virtues and vices. If any of these views is to be accepted and translated into action, however, then we need to understand what character traits are, how we can identify our traits, and whether or how we can change them.

We also need a good understanding of character if we are to make properly informed decisions about certain social and political issues. Many educational theorists recommend that we pay close attention to character development in the formulation of the school curriculum and the methods used to deliver it, for example. Many legal theorists similarly recommend that the state should aim at rehabilitating offenders rather than, or as well as, punishing them. Aiming seriously at improving the characters of children and adults requires a clear idea of whether and to what extent this is possible. Perhaps it is the case that although we can foster the right kinds of traits among children, adults are set in their ways. Perhaps, on the contrary, adults can develop their traits. Or perhaps neither children nor adults can do so. Perhaps the issue is more complicated, and some kinds of traits are set from birth or early life whereas others are not. If it is possible to deliberately inculcate any kind of character traits, moreover, then we need also to know how best to go about doing this, and this will depend on exactly what character is, how it is formed, and how it is best determined.

Similar issues arise on an international scale. One influential Aristotelian thought is that if we are to aim to promote opportunities for human flourishing around the world, then we need to understand the nature of character in order to understand what human flourishing consists in. Moreover, the promotion of peace and prosperity around the world requires decisions about which political and economic systems to encourage in which areas, how best to encourage those systems, and how best to oppose the forces that lead to violence, poverty, and injustice. These decisions need to be informed by many areas of thought, of course, but among these is thought about the nature, origin, and knowledge of character. For it may be important whether there genuinely are such things as national or ethnic characters, whether such traits as greed or selfishness are widespread, perhaps even universal, the extent to which political and economic systems need to reflect the characters of those within their ambit, and the extent to which those characters are partly formed by such political and economic systems.

It is not just character itself that is relevant here, but also the ways in which people tend to think about character. It has been argued that people generally possess the trait of misconstruing their own character traits and those of others. There are various forms of this claim, but if there is indeed a significant gap between the traits people possess and those that most people ascribe to them, then this widespread error in trait-ascription needs to be acknowledged in our social and political outlook. We might find, for example, that racism is sometimes grounded in the idea that behavioural traits are partly a matter of ethnicity, and we might find that this idea is empirically false. But if we also found that people would inevitably hold this false idea, because it follows from erroneous but universally employed heuristics for ascribing character traits, then we would need to recognise the inevitability of such forms of racism. Alternatively, we might find that such forms of racism were consequences of common, though by no means necessary, thought patterns. In which case, fostering more rational approaches to understanding the characters of those around us may seem the most effective way of reducing the prevalence of such attitudes, indirect though this strategy might seem.

These issues surrounding the notion of character and its place in our ethical, social, and political thought are central concerns of Sartre's philosophy. The account he provides in *Being and Nothingness* is one that developed out of various difficulties with his earlier writing on issues in philosophical psychology, as we shall see over the next couple of chapters, and one that he continued to refine and apply until his death nearly four decades later. Character is not a given that determines our actions and destiny, according to this theory, and is therefore neither the inevitable result of one's genetic make-up nor the outcome of the contingencies of one's formative years. An individual's character rather consists in the projects that individual has freely chosen to pursue. This does not mean that each character trait is itself a project, as if someone could only be jealous or cowardly by aiming to be so, but rather that the distinctive patterns in the ways in which that individual sees, thinks about, feels about, and behaves in the world are due to the total set of projects that they are pursuing and need not be pursuing, whether or not they acknowledge these projects to themselves.

Sartre is not content merely to provide a theory of what character is, however. He aims also to show that the reason why people in our culture do not already hold this theory is no accident: we are motivated, he claims, to pretend that our characters are fixed aspects of ourselves beyond our control. We are already in some way aware, that is, that our character consists in projects that we can change, but we hide this truth from ourselves so effectively that our thought and talk about ourselves and one another is at odds with it. We have covered over the truth through our strategies of bad faith. This leads us, he claims, to conflictual and frustrated relations with one another, the only escape from which involves embracing the honest attitude towards character that he calls 'authenticity'.

Commentators interpret Sartre's writings on these topics in a wide variety of ways, however, and most of them tend to underplay his theory of character, present an account of his philosophy that leaves no room for it, or even claim that he thinks there is no such thing as character. As a result, the theories of bad faith and interpersonal relations that he develops in *Being and Nothingness* are widely misunderstood and his recommendation of the virtue of authenticity seems at best rather puzzling or at worst entirely unjustified. We will see that these accounts of Sartrean existentialism are mistaken. The central aspects of this philosophy are all rooted, as we will see, in a general theory of the nature of character and of our aversion to facing the truth about it, even though he rarely uses the terms 'personality', 'character', or 'trait'. This philosophy of character in *Being and Nothingness*, moreover, underpins his voluminous writings across a wide range of literary genres for the rest of his career.

Philosophical debates over character and virtue do occasionally refer to Sartre's idea that people are commonly in 'bad faith' about their own traits but because the larger theory of character of which this is a part has been overlooked by commentators on Sartre's works, this larger theory has not made an impact on philosophical debates over character, and the notion of bad faith that is borrowed from it is not fully understood. Indeed, the very idea that character might be rooted ultimately in projects freely undertaken simply does not feature in these debates, with or without Sartre's name or other ideas attached. This book aims not only to uncover the true structure of Sartrean existentialism, but in so doing aims to make this theory of character and the distinctive perspectives it affords available to the general debate over the nature and knowledge of character, with the aim of considerably enriching that debate.

We should distinguish at the outset between the broad outline of Sartre's theory and its details. The broad outline is presented in *Being and Nothingness* and remains unchanged in subsequent work, although the details evolve within this outline. What is more, the logical space enclosed by the outline is not replete with Sartre's own ideas: further Sartrean positions can be formulated, just as there are Aristotelian theories of character and virtue other than Aristotle's own. Debates about character could benefit from Sartre's work in either of two ways. One is to investigate the development of his own ideas over the decades after *Being and Nothingness*. The other is to think independently within the broad framework of Sartrean existentialism. This book will facilitate both projects, by detailing Sartre's own philosophy of character and sketching ways in which further theories can be developed within the Sartrean picture, while drawing out the distinctive contributions that these projects can make to debates over character and virtue.

If Sartre really has so much to offer the debates over character, one might well ask, then why are participants in that debate not already drawing on his work? There are a number of reasons for this. One is Sartre's idiosyncratic vocabulary of 'being' and 'nothingness', 'in-itself' and 'for-itself', 'facticity' and 'transcendence', 'possibility' and 'potentiality', and so on. Like many European philosophers of the twentieth century, Sartre takes ordinary language to have developed a set of meanings that are insufficient for expressing his new and innovative philosophy. So he uses new and unfamiliar terms. He also uses terms that might seem familiar, but are thereby misleading because he does not use them with meanings that we ordinarily associate with them. The complexity of this terminology means that somebody picking up *Being and Nothingness* for the first time may well find whole swathes of it impenetrable. The more time one spends with Sartre's texts the more familiar these terms become, of course, but this can just mean that one has become better at using them rather than that one has come to understand them well enough to define them accurately. In these respects, Sartre's terminology is like any language, though with a restricted application. We would do well to think of it as such, to keep it at arm's length, and dub it *sartrais*.

Sartre's applications of his theory of character, such as his discussion of anti-Semitism, for example, or his analysis of the bizarre personality of Baudelaire, although written within a few years of *Being and Nothingness*, are refreshingly free of sartrais. But understanding these applied works requires understanding the theory they apply and the motivations for holding it, and these are provided in abstract theoretical works largely written in sartrais. This may well lead to bafflement on the part of people interested in theories of character when they pick up Sartre's theoretical writings for the first time. And it certainly does lead to differences of opinion over exactly what Sartre's view is among those who have spent a considerable amount of time reading and discussing his works, disputes which further complicate the difficulties faced by someone reading Sartre for the first time. The strategy of this book is to avoid sartrais as much as possible and to provide translations of key terms of it where necessary.

Sartrean terminology is not the only barrier to the use of this theory in mainstream philosophical debates over character and virtue, however. Another is that certain misconceptions of Sartre's philosophy are widespread. These misconceptions are due in part to the sheer scale of the philosophical system that Sartre develops in *Being and Nothingness*, which need not be too problematic were it not for his tendency to present any given aspect of it against the backdrop of many other aspects of it and his fondness for weaving together his treatments of a variety of related issues. These strategies are presumably intended to highlight the systematic nature of his theory, but can give the misleading impression that one cannot accept his comments on character without accepting certain other aspects of his philosophy too. This impression can be encouraged, moreover, by his habit of exaggerating the importance or range of some strand of his philosophy when discussing that strand. This impression generates two major obstacles to using Sartre's philosophy in debates over character and virtue. One of these obstacles is quite general, the other more specific.

The general obstacle is due to Sartre's presentation of his philosophy within the confines of his general ontology of being and nothingness, object and consciousness, being in-itself and being for-itself: his writing can easily give the impression that one cannot consider his theory of character without also accepting his vast and abstruse metaphysical system. Philosophers concerned with character and virtue might simply not want to unravel this system just to see whether it holds within it anything of use to their debates. Or they might even actively resist the suggestion that any theory based on such a system can be of any use to anyone who does not accept that kind of metaphysics. Although this ontology is part of the way Sartre motivates and presents his philosophy of character, however, there is no reason for us to consider it a necessary condition of the truth of that theory. This book aims to show that Sartrean existentialism is essentially a philosophy of the nature and knowledge of character that is acceptable and indeed valuable entirely independently of the metaphysical system within which Sartre presents it.

The more specific obstacle to using Sartre's philosophy in debates over character and virtue is that his work might give the impression that his comments on character are inextricable not from his metaphysics in general, but from his theory of 'radical' freedom and responsibility. Since many philosophers find Sartre's theory of freedom and responsibility either extremely obscure or simply unacceptable, this would provide a reason to ignore his work on character. In his early philosophy, Sartre denies all deterministic theories of human action and so faces the problem that if action is undetermined, then it seems it must be random. Since we seem to find intelligible patterns in our own and each other's behaviour, it seems that action is not random. And since moral responsibility seems to require that people have control over their actions, it seems that agents cannot be responsible for actions that are random. Sartre therefore faces the conundrum of explaining how action can be neither determined nor random. Many philosophers think such an explanation cannot be given, and Sartre's own attempt to explain this is rarely considered as a candidate solution to the problem (see B&N: 474–86).

His theory of freedom, therefore, may seem obscure and at the very least in need of further development. The fact that Sartre later distanced himself from his early theory of freedom and responsibility, moreover, might be taken as evidence for something stronger: that whatever this obscure theory of freedom is, it is probably unacceptable anyway, since the person best placed to understand it ended up rejecting it (see IT: 44). As we will see in chapter 5, however, we can accept Sartre's theory that character consists in freely chosen projects without also accepting his notion of 'radical' freedom. We do not need to resolve the conundrum of how actions can be neither determined nor random, that is, to accept the Sartrean theory of character. It might even be the case that the development of Sartre's philosophy in the decades after the works we are concerned with here is best understood as involving the realisation that the theory of character itself is independent of, and perhaps even better off without, the theory of 'radical' freedom, but the exegetical work required to assess this idea is outside the scope of this book.

A further reason to resist the idea that Sartre's philosophy has much to offer the current discussion of character might be due to his oft-repeated claim that 'existence precedes essence', which he links to his theory of freedom and responsibility in his early works. This slogan expresses two related ideas: that individuals do not have natures or essences that determine their behaviour and that there is no such thing as human nature or a human essence. A person 'first exists: he materialises in the world, encounters himself, and only afterwards defines himself' (EH: 22; see also B&N: 490). This means that the character trait terms that we use to describe people should not be understood as designating fixed properties. Honesty and dishonesty, courage and cowardice, should not be understood as unchangeable parts of our nature that force us to behave in this way or that in response to external stimuli.

This aspect of existentialism can certainly look like the claim that there are no such things as character traits. Such a view might seem to be of interest to philosophers engaged in the debate over character traits, since by denying the terms of the debate entirely it might open up and recommend wholly new approaches to understanding ourselves and one another and therefore to ethical and social theory. This idea that there really is no such thing as character is not currently part of philosophical discussion. Even works with such radical sounding titles as *Lack of Character* and 'The Nonexistence of Character Traits' do not propound such a view. In the former, John Doris argues that we should understand character traits as being far more numerous and restricted in behavioural application than has generally been thought, so that while there is no such trait as sociability there might be such traits as sociability-at-parties and sociability-towards-colleagues. In the latter, Gilbert Harman argues that we should abandon the language of character because trait-ascription is systematically erroneous, and so our characterisations of individuals are almost always mischaracterisations of them. Were Sartre to be arguing that there are no traits at all, not even ones common to all or most people, then he certainly would be occupying a novel position in the debate.

But such a radical position faces a problem parallel to that faced by the denial of determinism, a problem that might explain why nobody else advocates it. If there are no character traits at all, then what explains the consistency of an individual's behaviour? Why is it not just random? And why do these patterns of behaviour differ from person to person? The very fact that we have developed the terminology of character traits indicates that we find such patterns. It is difficult to see how these patterns could exist were behaviour not regulated by relevant dispositional properties of those people, properties that we call character traits. The outright denial that there are any such things as character traits will be extremely implausible, that is, precisely because such a denial will be left with the difficult task of explaining the origin of our common-sense psychological notion of character.

Sartre's view is neither as simple nor as radical as the denial of character traits, however. As we will see, Sartre's early view is rather that character *does not fully determine behaviour* and *is within the agent's control*. One's character, on this view, consists in one's projects. The patterns in the ways in which one sees the world, thinks about it, feels about it, and behaves in it, that is to say, result from the collection of projects one has chosen to pursue in life. Since one can change these projects, one can change these patterns. Changing the projects in which one's character consists just is changing one's character. One could not choose to change one's projects, moreover, if each project simply determined relevant behaviour, since discarding a project itself involves behaviour contrary to the behaviour recommended by that project. This is the theory we will be investigating in some detail. It is not the denial of character traits, but rather the view that the intelligible patterns in people's behaviour are a function of their inclinations to behave in one way rather than another, inclinations that they need not act upon but can instead replace.

The relation between inclinations, projects, and character traits will be clarified across the next few chapters. But it is worth noticing that the slogan 'existence precedes essence' claims only that character traits result from the choices one has made and are neither fixed at birth nor the mechanical effect of upbringing: a coward 'is not like that because he has a cowardly heart, lung, or brain' but rather he is a coward 'because he has made himself a coward through his actions' (EH: 38). In his early work, Sartre claims that the projects one undertakes are freely chosen responses to the human condition and one's own particular circumstances. Sartre's later attenuation of this terminology of choice, freedom, and responsibility is based on increasing consideration of the social and economic pressures that lead people to respond to their conditions and environments in the ways that they do. He considers his earlier language inappropriate as a description of the ways in which projects are adopted and revised, but does not reject his theory that character consists in those projects (e.g. IT: 43–5).

Sartre's famous discussions of bad faith and our relationships with one another might provide the basis for one further argument against the idea that his philosophy overall contains an interesting account of character. For these discussions might be taken as claiming that we like to pretend to ourselves that we have character traits and inevitably view one another as having character traits even though, in fact, nobody possesses any such traits. Such a reading involves imputing to Sartre a view that we have already seen in this chapter to be rather implausible, the view that there is no such thing as character. What is more, it also renders his philosophy vulnerable to a charge of inconsistency: if we do indeed possess dispositions to think of ourselves and one another in certain erroneous ways, then these very dispositions must count as character traits; and if either of these traits is an inevitable aspect of being human, then it would seem to count as at least part of human nature.

We will see in the course of this book, however, that Sartre does not claim that we misunderstand ourselves and one another by ascribing character traits where there are none. He thinks rather that we prefer to pretend to ourselves that we have fixed natures, whether this involves seeing the traits we do possess as fixed or pretending that we do not have those traits at all. This preference, moreover, is itself a project that affects the ways in which we see the world, think about it, feel about it, and behave in it. It forms part of the character of all those who adopt this project. It also therefore affects the ways in which we see one another, which he claims inevitably leads to conflict between us. But this is not tantamount to a pessimistic theory of human nature, because he thinks of bad faith as a contingent project that we can abandon in favour of authenticity, albeit one that thoroughly pervades our culture.

Although mistaken, these various motivations for believing that Sartre has nothing to contribute to the philosophy of character are rooted in aspects of his thought that could have been expressed more clearly. They may well be informed, moreover, by the work of commentators on Sartre's philosophy, who tend not to discuss his view of character and who sometimes claim that he denied there was any such thing. This tendency might seem absurd when one considers the aims of his applied writings. His biography of Charles Baudelaire, for example, aims to uncover the poet's personal characteristics that explain his writings and lifestyle. The traits discussed include his avoidance of solitude, his seeking of moral condemnation and punishment, and his horror of and indeed contempt for all that is crudely natural and unsophisticated by human hand. Sartre ultimately traces these back to the aim of being unique (see B: throughout). This account of what appear to be Baudelaire's character traits strongly suggests that Sartre had a theory of character at work here. Nonetheless, commentators on his philosophical writings do tend to overlook or deny his theory of character, and in the next chapter we will investigate their reasons for doing so in more detail. This investigation will not only show these reasons to be mistaken, but will also help to illuminate the detail of Sartre's theory.

Resistance to this project might yet come from another source: since character is now a subject of experimental psychological research, painstaking exegesis of the works of philosophers past has no important role to play in debates over the nature of traits, it might be argued. While there may be some historical interest in discerning Sartre's understanding of character, and it may help us to better understand his fictional, political, and other writings, the argument would run, there is no longer any place in character research for poring over his work as if over some religious text and attempting to discern its message. Should we not abandon the old, pre-experimental literature on moral psychology and base our theory of character solely on the more reliable information now available and the ideas derived from it? Why bother with Sartre when we have science?

Sartre's theory of the nature and knowledge of character, however, is not impugned simply because it is not based on reliable data provided by successfully repeated experiments. One reason for this is that behavioural data relevant to understanding character traits can be drawn from sources other than experimental reports, such as crime statistics, for example. Another, more relevant to this case, is that non-experimental psychologists can base their characterological views on longitudinal studies of individuals that are simply unavailable to experimental psychologists. For ethical and logistical reasons, the long-term surveillance of individuals going about their daily lives cannot be used to provide professional psychologists with information, so formal studies of individuals across situations are very rare. Experimental psychologists rely almost entirely on latitudinal studies of many individuals in the same situation for their information in this area. Yet these latitudinal studies do not seem to tell us about people's dispositions through time and across differing situations, whereas informal observation of those closest to us might seem perfectly suited to that task.

We all informally observe and consider the behaviour of a few individuals, those nearest and dearest to us, across a multitude of real-world situations, and we all attempt to discern and understand patterns in this behaviour. But it does seem reasonable to think that some of us are better at this than others: some are more observant than others, some of us keep records in the form of diaries while others rely on memory, some of us have better memories than others, some of us take more interest in character than others, only some of us read published diaries or correspondence in this way, and so on. Sartre kept copious reflective diaries (though he often lost them) and among the works he refers to in his discussions of character in *Being and Nothingness* are the psychoanalytic reports and theories of Sigmund Freud and Max Scheler (e.g. B&N: 70–8) and the letters and novels of Fyodor Dostoyevsky (B&N: 56, 497–8). His biographical writings are based on large bodies of information about each of their subjects. So although his theories are not rooted in the formulation and controlled testing of hypotheses, they should not be rejected as unjustified purely because of that.

Opponents of non-experimental characterological psychology might object that the kind of reasoning that Sartre employs is notoriously flawed. It is often claimed, that is, that the unreliability of non-experimental psychology has been demonstrated repeatedly since the advent of experimental social psychology more than half a century ago. Psychologists have found systematic errors in people's predictions of the results of various experiments, errors which some have claimed to be evidence of deep-rooted problems with our common-sense categorisation of people around us. A good illustration is provided by Stanley Milgram's famous experiments detailed in his book *Obedience to Authority*, though these are by no means the only experiments to show this feature.

The subject of this experiment is asked to administer a memory test to someone seeming to be another volunteer. Each time this 'learner' gives the wrong answer or no answer at all, the subject is to press a button and so deliver an electric shock to the 'learner'. The shocks seem to start at 15 volts, and increase by 15 volts each time. In fact, of course, there are no shocks, but the behaviour of the 'learner' makes it seem as though there are: he responds to shocks from 75 volts upwards, first by groaning, then by complaining that they are becoming painful, then by exclaiming 'Experimenter, get me out of here! I won't be in the experiment any more! I refuse to go on!' at 150 volts, 'I can't stand the pain!' at 180 volts, screaming at 270 volts, refusing to provide any more answers at 300 volts and at 315 volts, screaming again at 330 volts, and remaining silent after that. The subject is instructed at the beginning of the experiment by the 'experimenter', a man wearing a technician's coat and holding a clipboard. If the subject questions the procedure, the 'experimenter' politely responds in ways that encourage compliance. The experiment ends either when the subject questions the procedure for the fifth time or when the shock level has reached its maximum of 450 volts.

Milgram asked groups of psychiatrists, academic staff and graduate students in behavioural sciences, college sophomores, and middle-class adults to predict the results of this experiment if it were performed on one hundred Americans of diverse ages and occupations. The various groups responded with remarkably similar answers: they predicted that only a pathological minority of one or two per cent would reach the maximum shock level, that almost everyone would have refused to comply before reaching the 300-volt level, and that most would not go beyond the 150-volt level, when the 'learner' first explicitly requests that the experiment end. This experiment has been performed many times, however, and on average around 65 per cent of subjects continue to administer the shocks all the way up to the maximum of 450 volts, the majority go beyond 300 volts, and almost all reach 150 volts.

The difference between the actual results and those predicted is due to a common tendency to assume that only people with little or no regard for the pain of others would obey the 'experimenter' and to assume that such people are rare. The key factor in the actual experiment, of course, is the widespread trait of obedience, or perhaps of deference, to authority figures. But this tends not to be noticed. We have a tendency to exaggerate the importance of unusual psychological traits when explaining or predicting behaviour and to ignore common traits and the corresponding situational features that strongly influence us all. So in predicting the results of this experiment, we focus not on whether people are likely to obey or defer to authority, but on whether they are likely to do something that they think will inflict severe pain on an innocent person.

This tendency has been noticed in a wide variety of contexts and discussions of its nature have been central to social psychology since its inception in the 1930s. It is one of the most widely agreed phenomena in social psychology. But this data does not in itself show that all non-experimental characterological psychology is flawed. Milgram asked people to predict the behaviour of a random sample of the population, not the behaviour of those nearest and dearest to them. His data is perfectly compatible with the idea that we are quite good at predicting the behaviour of those we know well in situations that elicit traits of theirs that we have observed before. Since there is no reason to believe that we are all equally good at doing this, moreover, the data is compatible with the idea that certain non-experimental thinkers such as Sartre might be able to provide us with genuine insights into the nature and development of character.

The rejection of all non-experimental characterological psychology, however, is not usually rooted directly in this kind of data but rather in a particular explanation of it, proposed by Lee Ross in his seminal article 'The Intuitive Psychologist and His Shortcomings'. Harman's rejection of the language of character, mentioned above, is based on this explanation. The mismatch between prediction and actuality, according to Ross, is due to a 'fundamental attribution error': a single erroneous heuristic employed when we attribute character traits. This is itself rooted in the figure-ground structure of perception: we naturally explain the behaviour of a figure by reference to properties of that figure rather than properties of its context, and when we are explaining human action the figure is always the agent. If this explanation is right, then it does indeed seem that we should abandon the use of non-experimental characterological literature, since all of that literature must be grounded in the observations of authors shaped by this erroneous heuristic, and so must be nothing more than complicated illusions.

There are two basic problems with this claim, however. The first is that the explanation Ross proposes simply fails to explain the relevant data. The relevant experiments do not show that people tend to explain behaviour in terms of character traits rather than situational features as such, but rather that people tend to focus on unusual traits rather than common ones when asked to explain or predict the behaviour of strangers. We want to know why people assume that anyone obeying the experimenter in Milgram's obedience experiment has the uncommon trait of sadism or indifference to the pain of others, rather than the common trait of obedience or deference to authority. The idea that we naturally explain behaviour with reference to traits of the agent cannot explain why we prefer some kinds of traits to others.

The second problem is that there is no good reason to believe that we do in fact explain human behaviour in terms of properties of the figure rather than properties of the ground, as Daniel Gilbert and Patrick Malone make clear in their article 'The Correspondence Bias', which surveys the experiments in which trait-attributions are shown to be erroneous and the theories that aim to explain these errors. The search for a single error underlying our false attributions has proved fruitless, they claim, and we should rather think of mistaken trait-attributions as arising from four distinct factors, any combination of which can be in play in any given situation. First, plenty of evidence supports the view that when we do not know someone very well, we tend to assume that they see each situation in the same way that we do, which of course is a mistake. Second, we tend to think we know how most people will respond to a given situation even though most of us have not observed a sufficient cross-section of the population to justify this confidence. Third, unrealistic expectations colour our perception of actual behaviour: if we expect most people to disobey Milgram's experimenter out of compassion, then we will see obedient subjects as lacking in common compassion. Finally, it seems that we explain behaviour by first attributing any trait at all that will serve to explain it and then revising this attribution in the light of other knowledge about or further observation of the subject, but other cognitive demands may preclude the revision process and leave us with the initial attribution however unwarranted it may actually be.

Gilbert and Malone have shown that these four factors can explain all the data on false trait-attribution. The data therefore provides us with no reason to reject non-experimental characterological psychology rooted in informal longitudinal studies of a few individuals and comparison of such studies with one another. For none of the factors applies when we have time to consider in detail how someone well known to us has responded in a series of situations whose details are available to us, even if the relevance of those details is not immediately obvious. The data does seem to show that questions about the distribution of traits across the population, and related questions concerning correlations between traits, are to be answered experimentally. But it allows nonetheless that deeper questions about the nature and development of traits might be answered with reference to non-experimental as well as experimental literature.

Until an explanation of erroneous trait-attribution is provided that can be shown to be superior to that offered by Gilbert and Malone and that shows all non-experimental characterological observations to be poorly grounded, therefore, we should accept that non-experimental literature involving longitudinal observation of individuals can be illuminating. Since we should accept, as we have seen, that some people are better than others at such informal characterological study, we should accept that the pre-experimental tradition in moral psychology, of which Sartre's work is a part, can have genuine insights to offer to debates over character and virtue. This is not to say, of course, that we should simply agree with whatever claims we find in that literature. Theories arrived at in this way can be analysed for their coherence, assessed for their explanatory and predictive power, tested for their plausibility in the light of our own experience of people around us, and of course tested experimentally. It is only to say that it is a mistake to reject them purely for not being based on formal experimentation.

Careful exegesis of Sartre's philosophy of character, therefore, is not simply an exercise in the history of ideas or in understanding his literary output. Such exegesis should not be thought of as displaying inappropriate reverence for the works or assigning some kind of guru status to their author, for it need not conflate the idea of discerning someone's views with the idea of discerning the truth. It should rather be based on the recognition that careful consideration of the writings of a thinker who has paid close attention to a particular set of issues, where that thinker's work in other areas shows great ability, is apt to lead us to formulate sophisticated and well-grounded theories that might not otherwise have been brought to the debate. Discussions of virtue and character, for example, have benefited greatly over the last few decades from exegesis of the writings of Aristotle, and to a lesser extent of David Hume and Immanuel Kant, on these issues. This book is intended to show that these and related debates can also benefit from careful attention to this central theme in Sartre's life's work.

2 The Reality of Character

Why is it that some people will act compassionately in certain situations when others will not? Why do some people lie or cheat or steal while others are honest in one, two, or all three of these ways? One way of answering these questions is to explain the aetiology of character traits, to point to the origins of character in nature or nurture or some combination of the two. But another, more fundamental kind of answer tries to explain the constitution of traits, to point to current facts about some people that make them behave compassionately or honestly in those situations. This is more fundamental because it identifies more precisely the state of affairs whose origins the aetiological answer attempts to identify. It aims to tell us what character consists in. Once we know this, we can know what we need to change about ourselves in order to change our characters. We can also ask about the basis and reliability of our everyday beliefs about our own character traits and those of other people. Sartre's famous theory of bad faith is an answer to this epistemic question, as we will see later on in this book. But he has also formulated a theory in answer to the constitutive question, and this is more fundamental in his philosophy than his account of bad faith, as we will also see, because he thinks of bad faith itself as something that character traits can consist in. Our investigation of Sartre's philosophy of character will therefore begin with the constitutive question. But first we need to clarify that question itself.

Before trying to work out what character consists in, we need to define the thing we are asking about. What does the language of character refer to? We can start by defining a trait as a relatively stable disposition to behave in a certain way when in situations with certain features. That this disposition must be relatively stable seems beyond doubt. Just as one swallow does not make a spring, one cowardly act does not make a coward. This does not mean that traits must be fixed, however, since there is nothing contradictory in the idea of character development. This idea that character traits explain our behaviour but are nonetheless aspects of ourselves that we can change is central to Sartre's philosophy. We must be careful, furthermore, not to confuse the notion of a character trait with something *characteristic* of a person: a trait can be widespread or even universal, and so not serve to characterise anyone in particular. But of course a trait might equally be relatively uncommon or even entirely idiosyncratic, and therefore be characteristic of a few individuals or even just of one.

Refining this initial definition, we are presented with two options. One is to require that someone cannot possess a particular trait without reliably behaving in certain ways in certain kinds of situations. One cannot be honest, on this view, unless one usually acts honestly in situations in which one could act dishonestly, and a brave person rarely shrinks from danger. An influential argument that people do not have character traits as traditionally conceived is based on a version of this view, according to which character traits 'are reliably manifested in trait-relevant behaviour across a diversity of trait-relevant eliciting conditions that may vary widely in their conduciveness to the manifestation of the trait in question' (Doris, *Lack of Character*, 22). Our other option is to understand traits purely in terms of inner mental events. We can define a trait, on this view, simply as a disposition to see the world in certain ways, to think and feel in certain ways in response to certain kinds of situation. Such perceptions, thoughts, and feelings will generally incline the bearer of the trait towards the relevant kind of behaviour, but nonetheless this behaviour might not be forthcoming, due to the presence of countervailing traits. Somebody might be honest but insecure, for example, so be inclined to tell the truth on a particular occasion, but end up lying for fear of being disliked. The more compassionate someone is, the more they will think about the suffering of others and the more upset they will be by news of such suffering, but whether they are more likely to try to avert or alleviate such suffering will depend on their other traits.

To see more clearly the difference between the two options, consider again Milgram's experiments described in the last chapter. Did any of those who continued to obey the experimenter right up to the maximum shock level, only stopping when the shocks could not get any stronger, manifest the trait of compassion in that experiment? If we insist that traits are generally manifested in the relevant actions, then the fact that hardly any of these subjects behaved compassionately points to the conclusion that few of them possessed the trait of compassion. But if we take our second option, we can say that all those who protested against the experiment and who were clearly upset by their role in it displayed the trait of compassion to some extent, even if this was outweighed by other traits so that they went on to behave in an apparently uncompassionate way.

So which of these two understandings of traits should we adopt? There can be no empirical answer to this question, because in this area empirical data can record only the subjects' responses to their situations, whereas what we want to know is how such responses should be classified. Theoretical considerations, however, seem to support the idea that we need not build behavioural response into the definition of character traits. This is essentially because including behavioural response in our understanding of a particular trait requires us to understand each individual as possessing a vast array of traits, each of which disposes the individual to a specific kind of action in response to a situation specified in great detail. Subjects in the Milgram experiment who failed to show disobeying-an-authority-figure-compassion might well show compassion-in-the-absence-of-an-authority-figure. But if we exclude behavioural response, we can talk about general compassion.

This more general notion of a trait has greater explanatory power, as it allows us to explain an individual's behaviour in a vast range of situations by referring to the same limited set of traits. This brings with it a greater predictive power: we can predict someone's mental and behavioural responses to a novel situation so long as we know enough about that situation and enough about that person's general traits. What is more, the task of keeping track of our own traits and those of the people around us becomes vastly more complicated if we understand traits to be more limited in scope and hence more numerous. We would no longer be able to reflect that we are somewhat too timid among strangers or too keen to blurt out the truth, for example, but would have to think of ourselves as having displayed a wide variety of traits on a wide variety of highly specified occasions and would be unable to prescribe any remedy for the future. The moral purposes of thinking in terms of character would therefore be hamstrung.

Not only is it preferable to think of character in terms of mental events, moreover, but this understanding fits more squarely with Sartre's account. Character influences our perceptions, thoughts, and feelings, on this view, not in the sense that we explicitly try to decide how to see things, think about them, and feel about them, taking our character into account, but rather in the simpler sense that these mental events reflect the underlying dispositions that we describe in the language of character. 'Consciousness does not know its own character', Sartre writes, 'except in determining itself reflectively from the standpoint of another's point of view'. Instead, consciousness 'exists its character in pure indistinction non-thematically and non-thetically . . . in the nihilation by which it recognizes and surpasses its facticity' (B&N: 372). Character accounts for the ways an individual tends to experience the world and tends to think and feel about it, that is to say. We will investigate this account of the structure of conscious mental events in more detail in the next chapter. For present purposes, what matters is that we should understand an individual's character as the set of relatively stable dispositions to experience, think, and feel in certain kinds of ways, which thereby generally inclines that person to behave in related ways.

Notice that not all of our character trait terms actually pick out such dispositions, however. An inconsiderate person, for example, seems best described as someone whose perceptions, thoughts, and feelings noticeably lack consideration of other people, rather than someone who sees, thinks, and feels inconsiderately. It seems better, that is, to say that inconsiderate people lack a disposition that considerate people possess than to say that there are two dispositions here and that one person cannot have both. We can distinguish, therefore, between positive trait terms that name dispositions and negative trait terms that are applied when someone lacks a disposition.

Given that we apply positive and negative character trait terms in this way, it seems that we should understand them as functional terms: they refer to properties of the individual concerned only by reference to the functions those properties have in influencing the ways in which the individual perceives, thinks, and feels. Calling somebody an honest person is merely to claim that they have some property or set of properties that are responsible for certain patterns in their experiences, thoughts, and emotions. The language of character, therefore, leaves it entirely open just what these properties are. We are still left with the constitutive question that we began with: what is it that makes the brave person brave, the coward cowardly, and so on? This question, we can now see, is to be answered by pointing to whatever properties play the functional roles that our characterological language indicates, whatever it is about a person that explains why they behave in these ways. John McDowell rightly says that the concept of a virtue that it is 'the concept of a state whose possession accounts for the actions which manifest it' ('Virtue and Reason', § 2). We can extend this point to cover all character traits, not just virtuous ones.

Sartre argues that the patterns in the way an individual sees, thinks, feels, and behaves reflect the projects that individual has chosen to pursue and could choose not to pursue. Our projects therefore warrant the ascription of character traits. Despite the centrality of this theory of character to Sartre's work as a whole, most commentators have failed to draw attention to it or to analyse it in any great detail. They usually ignore the issue of character altogether, but when they do not they tend to read him as claiming that there is not really any such thing as character. We will see in the next few chapters how this has distorted their readings of Sartre and hence the understanding of Sartre among the intellectual community in general. But first, in order to see that this really is Sartre's view, we will consider precisely why commentators have so often gone wrong here and the ways that they should have gone instead.

The problem seems to arise from two aspects of Sartre's philosophy. One is his account of human existence as comprised of 'transcendence' and 'facticity'. The other is his theory that the self or ego is a 'transcendent' object. Terminology plays its role in generating these difficulties, as we will see. These two aspects of Sartre's philosophy involve two distinct senses of the term 'transcendent', both of which are derived from its root meaning of 'going beyond'. An individual's facticity is the set of facts true of them at a given time. Imagining that things were otherwise, wanting them to be otherwise, and acting to make them otherwise are ways in which we all transcend our facticities all of the time. In describing the ego or self as transcendent, Sartre means only that it is external to consciousness rather than contained within it, something that has more to it than we can be aware of at any given time. Transcendence of this sort is contrasted with immanence: the ego is not in consciousness. Ordinary worldly objects like chairs and tables are also transcendent in this sense, according to Sartre, as are certain non-physical objects like melodies and mathematical formulae.

Commentators often take Sartre's discussion of our existence in terms of facticity and transcendence to exclude character. In his book *Using Sartre*, for example, Gregory McCulloch equates 'transcendence' with 'freedom' and understands 'the doctrine about freedom' as being 'opposed to the idea that we have a nature or essence which determines how we should act or live' (57). This latter claim is unclear: it can be read as the denial that one's 'nature or essence' determines how one ought to behave, the denial that one's 'nature or essence' in fact determines one's behaviour, or the denial that we have a 'nature or essence' at all. His discussions of the relation between freedom and the lack of a nature elsewhere in his book are similarly vague (43, 56–64). But since his definitions of facticity make no reference to character traits, he seems to take Sartre to deny that we have a 'nature or essence' at all. Facticity, he writes, is made up of 'the body, and its material history and environment' (4) or 'our material surroundings, our own bodily form of existence, [and] our past decisions and choices that have brought us to where we are now' (57).

This interpretation can also be found in Joseph Catalano's influential work, *A Commentary on Jean-Paul Sartre's Being and Nothingness* (see 82–4), Gary Cox's recent *Sartre: A Guide for the Perplexed* (66, 96), Peter McInerney's article 'Self-Determination and the Project' (674), and many other works. Phyllis Sutton Morris presents a variant of it in her book *Sartre's Concept of a Person* (ch. 4), one that has recently been echoed by Nik Farrell Fox and T. Storm Heter (*The New Sartre*, 15–16; *Sartre's Ethics of Engagement*, 29–30). According to this variant, Sartre considers one's character to be the same as one's pattern of past actions so that one is a thief just if one has stolen things often enough in the past. The difference between this and the explicit denial of character is merely verbal. Since character traits are defined functionally as dispositions towards certain types of behaviour, the theory Morris describes is equivalent to denying that there is any such thing as character, since the patterns of one's past behaviour can hardly be thought to play this functional role (see *Sartre's Concept of a Person*, 99–100). Heter sees this problem and sees that the outright denial of character is implausible, so suggests that we revise Sartre's theory to allow that we form habits through our behaviour (*Sartre's Ethics of Engagement*, 32–3). Neither Morris nor Heter allow, therefore, that Sartre has any account of what it is that plays the functional roles picked out by character terms.

This reading of Sartre seems to be based on various comments in *Being and Nothingness*. One of the most important is the phrase, 'Essence is what has been' (B&N: 59; see also B&N: 461, 472, 518). McCulloch refers to this phrase when he describes Sartre's case of the guilt-ridden homosexual who denies his sexuality as a man denying that his past sexual behaviour fits a homosexual pattern rather than as a man denying that he has a character trait of homosexuality (*Using Sartre*, 59–60). We will consider what Sartre means in his discussion of this case in chapter 6. What is important here is that this description of the essence of an individual as 'what has been' (*ce que a été*) need not be understood in the way that McCulloch, Catalano, Cox, McInerney, Morris, and Heter seem to understand it. In one place where Sartre uses the phrase, he goes on to say that:

> Essence is everything in the human being that we can indicate by the words—that *is*. Due to this fact it is the totality of characteristics which *explain* the act. But the act is always beyond that essence; it is a human act only in so far as it surpasses every explanation which we can give of it, precisely because the very application of the formula 'that is' to man causes all that is designated, *to have-been*. (B&N: 59)

If essence is to explain an action, it could not be composed simply of past actions: there needs to be some explanation of how these past actions connect with the action to be explained. If essence is to be everything about a person that can be indicated by the words 'that is', moreover, it must include the body. It is not difficult to see how the body enters into the explanation of action, but it is difficult to see how it might be, at the time of action, something that 'has been' in the past. We should rather interpret this passage as claiming that a person's essence inclines them towards certain courses of action, but does not determine those courses of action. Action surpasses the inclinations that explain it. So describing a person in terms of body and character traits provides an explanation of that person's past behaviour, but not a definitive prediction of their future behaviour, since that person could always behave in ways contrary to their inclinations. The language of character, on this view, is not simply shorthand for patterns of past behaviour. It is genuinely explanatory of behaviour, but it is not fully predictive: it indicates only what one has been and done so far, not what one must continue to be and do.

This reading is supported by Sartre's subsequent discussion of what he terms 'psychological determinism', a view of human beings that 'provides us with a *nature* productive of our acts' and thereby 'denies that transcendence of human reality which makes it emerge beyond its own essence' (B&N: 64). In this passage, Sartre contrasts the notion of an essence with the deterministic notion of a nature. He objects not to the idea that humans have characters that explain their behaviour, which he calls 'essences', but to the idea that these characters are fixed and determine their behaviour, which he calls 'natures' (see also B&N: 461–2, 465–6). It is therefore a mistake to take Sartre's terms 'nature' and 'essence' to be synonymous, as McCulloch does, for example. Failure to see this distinction in sartrais, that 'nature' names a particular kind of essence, is one central reason why people mistakenly read Sartre as excluding essence, and hence character, from his theory altogether.

Sartre's discussion of bad faith provides further support for the claim that his notion of facticity includes character traits that can explain but do not determine courses of action. His discussion hinges on his claim that any form of bad faith 'must affirm facticity as *being* transcendence and transcendence as *being* facticity' (B&N: 79). It must affirm that there is no more to one's ability to go beyond one's situation than is provided by one's facticity. Bad faith, that is, is the view that one's actions in a given situation are determined by one's facticity. This would require that facticity include character traits where these are understood as determining actions, as constituting a nature. One of Sartre's most famous illustrations of this is his example of a waiter who wishes to deny that he has a choice about how to behave, wishes to identify wholly with his role as a waiter, and so can be seen 'trying to imitate in his walk the inflexible stiffness of some kind of automaton while carrying his tray with the recklessness of a tightrope walker' and so on (B&N: 82). The waiter is pretending to have a set of waiterly character traits that determine his behaviour.

For Sartre, the waiter's bad faith involves an erroneous view of the relation between transcendence and facticity: one's ability to go beyond one's situation is not restricted to the abilities and inclinations embodied in one's facticity, but involves the freedom to behave in ways other than those one's character inclines one towards. One's transcendence, that is, is not the same as one's facticity: it is limited but not determined by that facticity. This mistaken view of the relation between transcendence and facticity is not an honest mistake, but a motivated choice. We will return to this and other issues surrounding Sartre's notion of bad faith in chapters 6, 7, and 8. But here it is worth noticing that Sartre considers his claim that one *freely* transcends one's situation to be a substantial point, not a pleonasm: the terms 'transcendence' and 'freedom' are not synonyms in sartrais, and those who take them to be so will thereby have trouble understanding the discussion of bad faith in *Being and Nothingness*.

A person's essence, for Sartre, therefore includes character traits that incline that person towards certain types of behaviour but do not determine that behaviour. It is not simply restricted to a pattern of past behaviour, or to such a pattern plus bodily facts. Sartre's apparently contradictory definition of 'the human reality' as 'a being which is what it is not and which is not what it is' should be read in the light of this (B&N: 81). Commentators have usually read the second part of this formula to mean that a person cannot be wholly captured by a description of their past behaviour, or a description of their past behaviour and their current bodily and environmental condition (see, e.g., Catalano, *Commentary*, 84; McCulloch, *Using Sartre*, 59). This phrase should rather be understood as the claim that a person is not wholly identical with the character traits they possess, since these traits consist only in the set of projects that the person can change. It is more a claim about the future than about the past: the current set of facts true of that person does not determine how that person will continue to behave (see B&N: 90). We will consider this formula in more detail in chapter 4.

Given this wealth of evidence in favour of reading Sartre as holding that our facticity includes character traits that incline us towards but do not determine certain patterns of behaviour, it might seem odd that commentators have generally taken him to be claiming otherwise. But the idea that Sartre rejects any notion of character may have been motivated by his discussion of the nature of the self in his early essay *The Transcendence of the Ego*. Sartre argues in this work that there is no such thing as a 'transcendental ego' or subject underlying or inhabiting consciousness. His basic strategy is to argue against the position Edmund Husserl held in his later, but not his earlier writings. This is the view that when we reflect on our own previous conscious episodes in the right way, we find a metaphysical subject or transcendental ego underlying or inhabiting them. This subject is understood as a substantial entity that is not part of the public world, much like the immaterial ego postulated by Descartes (see, e.g., Husserl's *Cartesian Meditations*, § 11).

Sartre opposes this view partly by arguing that Husserl is wrong to suggest that such an ego is required to unify consciousness and partly by arguing that such an ego is incompatible with the nature of consciousness. But the lion's share of the book, and the most important for our purposes, is Sartre's argument that the only ego or self discovered in reflecting on our own conscious experiences is not 'transcendental', does not underlie or inhabit consciousness, but is rather 'transcendent', external to consciousness just as physical objects are. The ego or self in question is not, of course, the self understood as the subject of consciousness, nor is it the portion of reality in which this subject inheres. His claim is about the self or ego understood simply as an integrated set of dispositions underlying the experiences, thoughts, and feelings of an individual. His view is that this object is part of the world rather than hidden away in some transcendental realm. He reaffirms this in *Being and Nothingness*, explicitly demurring only from the earlier claim that this point provides a solution to the problem of solipsism (127, 259).

McCulloch takes this to mean that, for Sartre, 'the self is a kind of construct only' (*Using Sartre*, 7). Catalano concurs, claiming that Sartre understood the self to be 'nothing but the *object* formed by reflecting on our past behaviour' (*Commentary*, 75). In her concluding essay in *The Cambridge Companion to Sartre*, Christina Howells similarly talks of 'the self as an imaginary construct and an unrealizable limit' and as 'a fictional synthesis' (see 327–30). Hazel Barnes agrees when she describes the ways in which the Sartrean ego is 'fabricated' by consciousness ('Sartre's Ontology', 27–36), as does David Jopling when he writes that for Sartre 'the ego is an object of conscious experience, but not a real structure' ('Sartre's Moral Psychology',

113). But why should the claim that the ego or self is outside consciousness rather than within or underlying it be taken to mean that the ego or self is a fictional construct rather than a real object? After all, the physical world is outside of consciousness for Sartre, but he is not taken to hold that this depends for its existence on our awareness of it.

There might seem to be an important difference in Sartre's system between the kind of transcendent existence had by physical objects and the kind had by the ego. The sense that our surroundings have for us, the patterns of salience and significance we experience in the world, are a function of the ways in which we are aware of our surroundings, the ways in which we 'constitute' objects, as we will see in the next chapter. But the physical world nonetheless exists independently of consciousness: in sartrais, it has 'being in-itself'. This is why, he claims, there is a 'resistance of things' or 'coefficient of adversity' in the world (B&N: 348), why the world 'does not depend on my whim' (B&N: 3). Sartre considers this point fundamental to understanding our metaphysical relation to the world, which is why his introduction to *Being and Nothingness* is designed to establish it and why he reiterates it in various ways throughout the book (e.g. 220, 240, 351). The ego, on the other hand, is more like a melody: just as we construct melodies from the sequences of notes that we hear, so we construct egos or selves from the sequences of actions and states that we observe in ourselves and others; just as a melody is not a being in-itself underlying the notes, he is often taken to say, the self or ego does not exist independently of our 'constitution' of it (see TE: 29–30).

Sartre's theory of the constitution of the ego is subtle, complex, intriguing, and largely tangential to the present issue. But it is as mistaken to read Sartre as claiming that the self or ego does not really exist as it is to read him as saying that melodies do not really exist. Of course melodies exist! To say that a melody is a sequence of notes and not a substantial object of which notes are properties or effects is not to say that there are no melodies, but to say what kind of thing a melody is. It is to say that the sounding of each successive note cannot be explained by the existence of the melody, but only by the intentions of composer and player to produce that melody, although our access to melodies is not through direct awareness of those intentions but through awareness of the notes. The analogy with melodies, therefore, should not be taken to express the idea that egos do not exist, but rather to express a theory of the kind of existence they have and of our epistemic access to them. After all, Sartre does claim that we encounter egos in the world and that psychologists study them; he does not call the validity of this branch of psychology into question, as we would expect of somebody who thought it to be studying something that is in fact imaginary, but rather makes a claim about which methods are proper to it (TE: 28, 45).

To say that an object is constituted, for Sartre, is therefore not to deny that it is real. If he did think these were equivalent, he could not draw the distinction that he draws in *The Transcendence of the Ego* between actions and states on the one hand and qualities on the other. His view here is that a self or ego is usually thought of as a totality of actions, states, and qualities, when in fact it is only a totality of actions and states. Qualities do not really exist, but actions and states do. He considers all three to be constituted nonetheless, just as the ego is constituted. The state of hating a particular person, for example, is manifested in a variety of thoughts, feelings, and actions, but it is not wholly contained in any of them; it 'is given, *in* and *by* each movement of disgust, revulsion, and anger, but at the same time it *is not* any of them, it goes beyond them and affirms its permanence' (TE: 22). Hatred is real, but composed of rather than causing the events of disgust, revulsion, and anger that manifest it (see TE: 21–6). Similarly, 'action requires time in which to be carried out' and involves a sequence of mental and physical events (TE: 26). The action itself is a transcendent object, constituted from these various events (see TE: 26–7). Just as a melody is not a substantial object causing the notes that compose it, so an action is not a substantial object causing the events that compose it. But this does not mean that there are not really any actions.

Sartre describes qualities as 'optional unities of states' (TE: 27). By 'optional unities' (*unités facultatives*) he means that while we can and tend to think of ourselves and others as having qualities that unify and explain our states, we need not think in this way. Indeed, in *The Transcendence of the Ego*, he thinks that this way of thinking is mistaken. To think of hatred for different people or deep-rooted rancour or long-lasting anger as indicative of being a hateful, rancorous, or angry person, to constitute such qualities as the sources from which the states and actions emanate, is to add something to the self or ego that it does not really contain; 'states and actions can find directly in the Ego the unity that they require' (TE: 28; see also TE: 28–41).

In calling the ego a constituted transcendent object, and in comparing it to a melody, therefore, Sartre is not claiming that it does not really exist, or that it is imaginary. His view is rather that it is a real part of the world, like actions and states, and can be studied scientifically, though our access to this ego is only through surmise on the basis of actions and states, which can be apprehended more directly (see also TE: 15–16, 31). Notice, however, that this is not enough to show that Sartre has a theory of character. For while it shows that he thinks there really is a self or ego, his claim that qualities do not really exist is itself equivalent to the claim that character is an illusion: qualities include 'failings, virtues, tastes, talents, tendencies, instincts, etc.' (TE: 28) and therefore include character traits such as courage or cowardliness, honesty or dishonesty. In the inventory of the ego given in *Being and Nothingness*, moreover, Sartre describes one's set of qualities as 'the ensemble of virtues, latent traits, potentialities which constitute our character and our habits' (185), and he defines a quality as 'an innate or acquired disposition' (185).

There is a subtle shift, however, between the theory of the ego in *The Transcendence of the Ego* and the parallel theory in *Being and Nothingness*, which he also calls a theory of the psyche, and he does not draw attention to this shift. Where the earlier text draws a distinction between the reality of actions and states and the non-reality of qualities, the later makes no such distinction: the three are treated as equally real throughout the relevant passage (B&N: 184–90; see esp. 186–7). This passage can give the impression that Sartre thinks of the three as equally *unreal*, however, and one particular sentence taken in isolation can give the impression that he distinguishes between the reality of states and actions and the unreality of qualities. These impressions are mistaken and arise from unfortunate translation of some key terms.

The first difficulty is due to the translation of *virtuel* as 'virtual' rather than 'potential'. Thus we are told that the whole of the psyche—ego, states, qualities, and acts—is a 'unity' of 'virtual beings' and 'a virtual and transcendent in-itself' (B&N: 184). It is difficult to see what 'virtual' could mean here unless it is to be contrasted with 'actual' and therefore taken to indicate the unreality of the ego or psyche. This seems to be the way that David Reisman, for example, understands it (*Sartre's Phenomenology*, 61–2). But it cannot mean this, since we are soon told that among the acts that are to count as 'virtual' are 'the boxer's training . . . the research of the scientist . . . the work of the artist . . . the election campaign of the politician' (B&N: 185). It would be extremely odd to claim that such things do not really exist. Soon after this, we are told that states, qualities, and acts 'though virtual are not abstract' but each is rather present as 'concrete in-itself' and 'in person' (B&N: 186). It is difficult to see how such a thing could be concrete rather than abstract or could exist 'in-itself' or be present 'in person' unless it really existed.

If we translate *virtuel* as 'potential', on the other hand, we can see that these are all things that are never complete when they exist or occur, and on completion pass into the past. Ongoing training, research, artistry, and campaigning are necessarily unfinished training, research, artistry, and campaigning. Sartre is claiming that the same is true of states such as annoyance and qualities such as irritability. This claim can be taken in either an epistemic or an ontological sense, and Sartre means it in both. In the epistemic sense, the evidence that indicates that I am annoyed is necessarily incomplete, since my current state of annoyance is differentiated from a past state of annoyance only by the fact that it is continuing into the future and I can have no evidence of my future states. Similarly, the evidence that I possess the quality of irritability can only be evidence of its having been manifested in the past: its continuation and manifestation in the future is only probable, so the evidence I have is equally compatible with my having been irritable but being irritable no longer.

Since Sartre thinks that the future is itself undetermined, he holds that this uncertainty about the future infects not just our knowledge of states and qualities but also their very existence: they exist as only potential, or probable, because their existence as actual requires continuation into the future and it is undetermined whether they will so continue; once that continuation is no longer required, they are actual but past. This is why he says that 'the organized psychic ensemble with its future remains only *probable*' and that this probability is not 'an external quality which would come from a relation with my knowledge' but is 'an ontological characteristic' (B&N: 187). Sartre's conception of time is not immediately to the point here, even though the central discussion of the nature of the psyche in *Being and Nothingness* occurs as part of a larger discussion of temporality. What is important is that this discussion makes sense only if *virtuel* is translated as 'potential' rather than 'virtual' and that doing so removes the sense that the ego and its actions, states, and qualities are unreal. Reading the term in this way is also in line with Sartre's use of it in *The Transcendence of the Ego*, where he describes the notion of a quality as the notion of a '*potentialité*' and a '*virtualité*' in a way that makes clear that he takes these terms to be synonymous (TE: 27–8).

This same passage of *Being and Nothingness* also includes the following confusing sentence: 'States—in contrast with qualities, which exist "potentially"—give themselves as actually existing' (B&N: 185). This might seem to endorse the theory of *The Transcendence of the Ego* that states are real but qualities are not, and so to deny that there is any such thing as character. But once *virtuel* is understood to mean 'potential' in the larger passage in which this occurs, this sentence appears to contradict the rest of that passage, which describes both states and qualities as being potential. This problem arises, however, as a result of the translation of '*en puissance*' here as 'potentially'. This phrase is better rendered 'as a power'. The contrast in this sentence is between actual present psychological states such as annoyance and the background condition of a power or potency to bring about such a state in response to certain stimuli. Qualities, or traits, such as irritability are clearly powers or potencies in this sense. They are dispositions. This is all that Sartre means by saying that they exist *en puissance*.

By the time Sartre wrote *Being and Nothingness*, therefore, he no longer endorsed the claim he made in *The Transcendence of the Ego* that qualities are not real aspects of the ego. He had come to the view that actions, states, and qualities are all equally real. 'After my anger yesterday, my "irascibility" survives as a simple latent disposition to become angry', he writes (B&N: 185). One way to explain this shift is to assume that Sartre had noticed, or had been brought to notice, that the earlier theory leaves mysterious the intelligible patterns that we can find in people's behaviour. If our postulation of qualities is motivated by these patterns but is mistaken, then what does explain those patterns? Why aren't your states and actions just random?

In her article 'Self-Deception', Morris argues that while character-trait attributions refer only to 'a series of past actions that have taken place within certain kinds of circumstance', Sartre explains the relative coherence of a person's behaviour over time by reference to that person's 'fundamental project' (35–6). The patterns we discern in an individual's behaviour result, on this view, from the basic project that individual has chosen to pursue in response to that individual's particular situation and the human condition in general. Morris is essentially right that Sartre considers the patterns in our behaviour to result from our projects. But this simply could not be the case were behaviour not genuinely regulated by character. Or rather, it could be the case only if we explicitly considered our projects whenever we acted. But we generally do not do this: we simply act spontaneously in ways that manifest the patterns in question. Brave people respond bravely in dangerous situations without first stopping to explicitly consider whether being brave is part of what they want or how they see themselves. But even if we did explicitly consider our projects when we act, moreover, this would still not explain why an individual's thoughts and feelings in response to situations fall into certain patterns, for it could hardly be maintained that we deliberate about what to think or how to feel, given that thought and feeling are themselves already involved in any deliberation.

Character exerts its influence silently. Sartre himself makes this point when he says that we become aware of our characters only when reflectively considering ourselves as if from the outside, never when we are engaged in attending to the world (B&N: 372–3). Morris is aware that in unreflective action 'we may not become explicitly aware of' our projects (36), but does not realise that this very fact requires the reality and influence of traits, or qualities (see also *Sartre's Concept of a Person*, 102.) We will look at Sartre's accounts of just how character exerts its influence in the next chapter. What matters here is that in order to explain the shift from denying the reality of qualities in *The Transcendence of the Ego* to affirming that reality in *Being and Nothingness*, it seems sensible to point out that the earlier theory cannot explain the patterns we find in people's behaviour, and to assume that Sartre noticed this. After all, as Morris points out, Sartre introduces the notion of projects in the later work precisely for the purpose of accounting for these patterns, a move that fails unless it is coupled with an affirmation of the reality of character traits. (Perhaps this is why, in a later article, 'Sartre on the Transcendence of the Ego', Morris continues to hold that Sartre introduces projects for this purpose, but no longer claims that he takes character trait terms to refer only to past actions.)

Sartre's earlier opposition to the reality of qualities does not disappear altogether: as we have seen, Sartre remains opposed to the idea that such qualities are fixed and determine behaviour, holding instead that they only incline us towards certain types of behaviour and can therefore be revised. The earlier work may have been motivated partly by the erroneous assumption that the rejection of psychological determinism requires the rejection of character, in which case his revision of his theory would be explained not only by the realisation that character is required to explain the patterns in each individual's states and actions over time, but also by the realisation that such character need not be fixed and deterministic, that an essence need not be a nature. It is therefore importantly imprecise to read the theory of the psyche in *Being and Nothingness*, as Reisman reads it, as claiming that constituting the ego is itself 'a part of the project of limiting one's freedom' (*Sartre's Phenomenology*, 64). It is only understanding the ego to embody a fixed nature that is part of this project: the ego itself, with its unfixed character traits, really is part of our makeup.

In *Being and Nothingness*, then, Sartre understands behaviour to manifest qualities, or character traits, that explain why one sees things in certain ways, thinks and feels as one does about these things, and behaves in certain ways as a result, even though these qualities are not fixed aspects of oneself and the explanations they provide are not deterministic ones. These qualities consist in the overall set of projects that each person freely chooses to pursue and has the power to change. This theory addresses both the aetiological and the constitutive questions posed at the beginning of this chapter: character is constituted by projects, on this view, and comes about as a result of free choice. There are many further questions that could be raised about these answers. Over the next three chapters, we will consider in more detail what Sartre's theory of character amounts to.

3 Situations

If we want to know why cowards run away from even the slightest danger when others do not, it is not enough to be told that they would not be cowards otherwise. The question is not about our ways of classifying people, but about the reasons why an individual displays certain patterns of behaviour rather than other ones. It is not much less facetious to say that all cowards have a disposition towards running away from even the slightest danger. This answer, though not entirely uninformative, fails to explain why certain people have this disposition and equally fails to explain how the property that realises this disposition translates into cowardly behaviour. Sartre holds our dispositions to consist in the projects we pursue, as we have seen, but this theory remains somewhat obscure until we have understood exactly how it is that our projects are supposed influence our behaviour. So long as we think of projects in terms of goals that we deliberate about and work knowingly to achieve, moreover, taking as our paradigms the kinds of goals that characterise our careers or family lives, then the theory will seem entirely implausible. Surely these goals are set as a result of the ways in which people see things, think about them, and feel in response to them, which in turn manifest their characters, and so cannot be used to explain their characters. But this is a distortion of the Sartrean theory of character. In order to see why, we need to investigate just how Sartre thinks that our projects explain the ways in which we see things, think about them, and feel about them.

First we need to appreciate just how Sartre construes the functional roles that define character traits, roles that are collectively fulfilled by an individual's set of projects. His understanding of these functional roles is part of his general theory of the motivation of behaviour. Sartre couches this theory in terms of the *mobile* and the *motif* cited in immediate explanations of action. The former term denotes a set of facts about the agent, whereas the latter denotes a set of facts about that agent's environment. To explain why I tidied the room, for example, you might refer to a *motif* such as the room being untidy or at least looking so to me, or you might refer to a *mobile* such as my wanting the room to be tidy. The *motif* is 'the reason for the act' and 'the ensemble of rational considerations which justify it', whereas the *mobile* is 'the ensemble of the desires, emotions, and passions which urge me to accomplish a certain act' (B&N: 467–8).

It is therefore unfortunate that *'mobile'* is translated in *Being and Nothingness* as 'motive' and *'motif'* as 'cause', as the translator acknowledges (B&N: 457 n1). The English term 'motive' can be used to indicate either of the things Sartre labels *mobile* and *motif*, as indeed can 'motivation'. The term 'cause', moreover, might be taken to imply that Sartre considers the behaviour to be necessitated by the *motif*, which would contradict his theory of freedom. Arlette Elkaïm-Sartre's revision of this translation adds the French terms in parentheses at a key point (B&N: 467), but this may not be enough to prevent misunderstanding. The problem arises because there is no simple way of preserving the distinction in idiomatic English. So we shall retain the French terms.

Sartre's claim is that for any given action, the agent's motivation can be reported either in terms of mobile or in terms of motif. The two things are, he says, 'correlative' since 'the mobile is nothing other than the apprehension of the motif' (B&N: 471). The mobile is 'consciousness of [the] motif or, if you prefer, the apprehension of the situation as articulated in this or that way' (B&N: 492). My awareness of the room is structured by my desire that it be tidy, which is why it looks untidy to me; my desire that the room be tidy is revealed to me by the room looking untidy. The idea is neither that one sort of explanation of my motivation is incomplete without reference to the other, nor that one sort is true where the other is false, but rather that explanations in terms of motif and those in terms of mobile simply pick out the same explanatory event in different ways. In each kind of explanation, a different aspect of that event is emphasised.

An individual action can therefore be explained in terms of motif or mobile, and both explanations reflect the agent's aims at the time. The senses that our surroundings have for us, the patterns of salience and significance we experience in the world, are a function of the ways in which we are aware of our surroundings, and these in turn result from our aims. Using some of the sartrais discussed in the previous chapter, objects are *constituted* in part by the pursuit of our aims. This does not mean that they are wholly dependent on our aims for their existence, but rather that the mass of mind-independent 'being in-itself' that makes up our material surroundings and our bodies ordinarily appears to us not as brute existence but as a set of entities varying in degrees of salience and kinds of significance in relation to our aims. Things appear to us not just as chunks of matter, but as doors, handles, keys, books, tables, chairs, bicycles, buses, and so on. They can appear as good, bad, useful, useless, broken, mended, frustrating, fortuitous, and so on. The familiar world is not just indifferent stuff: it is articulated in various ways in relation to our aims, and it has that articulation for us because of the aims we have. It is the 'projection of myself toward an original possibility' that 'causes the existence of values, appeals, expectations, and in general a world' (B&N: 63).

32   *The Existentialism of Jean-Paul Sartre*

Our aims are normally reflected in the organisation of objects into means to pursue those aims, and into obstacles and pitfalls impeding that pursuit. This is what Sartre calls, in *Sketch for a Theory of the Emotions*, 'the pragmatic intuition of the determinism of the world' (STE: 39). But our aims are not always reflected in such rational patterns. The essence of emotion, Sartre argues, is the transformation of this instrumental complex into a magical world where we try to live 'as though the relations between things and their potentialities were not governed by deterministic processes but by magic' (STE: 40). Emotion leads us to perform incantatory acts such as fleeing in fear or jumping for joy, and these seek to bypass the normal methods of getting what we want and instead to suppress the existence of the feared object or possess the object of joy by magical means (see STE: part III; also B&N: 318–9).

The details of Sartre's theory of the nature of emotion need not concern us here, nor indeed need its acceptability. What matters is that he considers emotion to be 'a specific manner of apprehending the world' (STE: 35). Whereas we ordinarily see through rational and practical eyes, our emotions endow objects with magical properties. 'I find him hateful *because* I am angry' (STE: 61; see also B&N: 354). These magical properties appear as properties of the objects themselves, just as pragmatic properties such as 'door handle' or 'too heavy' appear as properties of objects. 'It is thus that the man who is angry sees on the face of his opponent the objective quality of asking for a punch on the nose' (B&N: 186). Emotion is not, however, some external interference in our cognitive life. It is rather a motivated response to the difficulty of the instrumental world: when we cannot, or cannot easily, get what we want by practical means, we resort to the ineffective emotional means of magical incantations (STE: 39–40). Sartre does not think, however, that this motivated response is something that we simply decide upon at the time, as we shall soon see.

In both emotional and ordinary experience, therefore, the world that we experience is constituted in accordance with our aims. Sartre uses the term 'world' to denote not the mind-independent stuff that our bodies and surroundings are made of, 'being in-itself', but that stuff as it is organised into the complex of instruments, obstacles, and positively and negatively valued objects and events that we encounter. The key sartrais term 'situation' is intended to capture this idea that the world is the product of the interplay of being in-itself and our own aims. 'Our being is immediately "in situation"; that is, it arises in enterprises', writes Sartre as he introduces this term. 'We discover ourselves then in a world peopled with demands, in the heart of projects', he continues, that 'derive their meaning from an original projection of myself' (B&N: 62–3). His most famous example involves looking through a keyhole: 'there is a spectacle to be seen behind the door only because I am jealous, but my jealousy is nothing except the simple objective fact that *there is* a sight *to be seen* behind the door' (B&N: 283). This notion of a situation as constituted by the agent's own aims, so that one's responses to situations are never simply required by the environment however much they may seem so, is central to Sartre's existentialist outlook as a whole (see also B&N: 48, 162, 219–24, 316, 345–6, 525–30, 637–8). My situation is the motif that explains my action: it is the appearance of my surroundings as organized in a certain way, inviting certain behaviour in order to achieve my aims. This behaviour may be pragmatic or it may be magical. The aims need not be pursued, of course: the invitation can be declined (see B&N: 54–8, 486).

This much does not amount to a theory of character. It details the relation between one's aims and actions in any given situation, but a theory of character is concerned with sustained patterns of actions across a variety of situations. One swallow does not make a spring. Given this account of motivation, a theory of character should explain the patterns in the aims that an individual has in different scenarios, the rhythms running through the ways in which their situations are articulated. When the articulation is pragmatic, it simply reflects the aims that result from the agent's character. But when it is magical, in emotional experience, its relation to character is more complicated. This kind of experience is motivated, as we have seen, by finding the world too difficult, which is obviously relative to the aims one is trying to achieve, which themselves result from character. But character might also be involved in explaining why this person responds emotionally to this difficulty when another person responds calmly to the same difficulty.

One way in which practical behaviour manifests one's character is through the medium of deliberation. Sartre understands this as the weighing up of considerations and argues that the weight ascribed to each consideration is determined by character: a coward is someone with whom personal safety weighs very heavily indeed compared to other concerns, for example, and a hedonist is someone for whom pleasure weighs very heavily. Sartre does not discuss this in much detail. He seems to consider it a less interesting topic than spontaneous behaviour, perhaps because deliberation has been the focus of much philosophical attention in the past at the expense of such spontaneous action.

What he does say is that 'voluntary' behaviour, action manifesting 'the will', is behaviour resulting from deliberation and the idea of 'voluntary deliberation' is 'deception' and 'illusion' (B&N: 472). He does not mean by this simply that deliberation would only be voluntary if we first deliberated about it, and thus prior deliberation could only be voluntary likewise, and so on infinitely. He also means that, since deliberation is not structured this way, it is just measuring against one another considerations whose relative weights, whose degrees of importance, have already been determined by one's own character. Deliberation can only reach a conclusion that is therefore already determined. 'When the will intervenes, the decision is taken, and it has no other value than that of making the announcement' (B&N: 473). Voluntary action is behaviour that flows from one's character via the process of deliberation. In this context, he introduces a phrase that recurs throughout his work: by the time we begin to deliberate, *les jeux sont faits*—the chips are down, the die is cast, the game is up (B&N: 473).

We might demur from this position by pointing out that deliberation might serve to bring to our consideration aspects or potential consequences of the situation not immediately obvious to us, and that even if it is true that the importance these will have for us is already determined in advance it remains that the action resulting from deliberation might be influenced by these new considerations. But this would misunderstand Sartre's point. He is not claiming that deliberation is a charade, that we might as well act spontaneously. The term translated as 'deception' in the passage quoted above is '*truquer*': the claim is that the outcome of the deliberation is rigged, fixed in advance by the relative weights our projects assign to the relevant considerations; this is not the same as the claim that the outcome is a something that would have happened anyway had there been no deliberation (see B&N: 498). We might also disagree with this account of deliberation in other ways, of course, just as we might dispute his accounts of perception and emotion, but this is not important for present purposes.

Two things are important. One is that, contrary to the readings given by those commentators discussed in the last couple of chapters, Sartre's account of human existence certainly does have a place for character traits as functionally defined properties that explain the patterns in the ways their bearers see things, feel about them, and think about them, as well as in the actions motivated in these ways. The other is that we clearly cannot construe Sartre's philosophy in terms of the behaviourist conception of character outlined at the beginning of the last chapter, which defines traits purely in terms of stimulus and behavioural response without reference to mediating states or events, since Sartre understands the production of behaviour in terms of our experience of our environment, our emotional responses to it if there are any, and our deliberation about it if there is any. Our behaviour cannot be understood simply as a response to a chunk of 'being in-itself', on this account, but only to the situation as articulated for us in our thought and experience.

We can also see more clearly now how character can consist in projects. Character traits are defined by their functional roles as dispositions towards certain kinds of views of the world, certain types of feelings and thoughts about it, and certain kinds of behaviour as a result. These things are produced by our aims in any given situation, according to Sartre, and we have these aims as a result of the projects that we pursue: 'it is the ensemble of my projects which turns back in order to confer upon the mobile its structure as a mobile' (B&N: 459). So the patterns in our perceptions, feelings, thoughts, and actions are the result of the projects that we pursue. This is why Sartre describes deliberation as weighing up 'motifs and mobiles on which I myself confer their value before all deliberation and by the very choice which I make of myself' (B&N: 472). One's choice of oneself is, according to Sartre, the set of projects that one has freely chosen to pursue. The emotion of 'fear of dying from starvation', similarly, is to be explained by the larger project of 'the preservation of a life which I apprehend as "in danger"', understandable enough as a project but nonetheless freely pursued (B&N: 459).

It is worth comparing this to McDowell's influential argument, mentioned in the last chapter, in favour of understanding virtue as 'an ability to recognise requirements which situations impose on behaviour', which he also calls 'a reliable sensitivity' to those requirements ('Virtue and Reason', § 2). McDowell is concerned here with virtue, whereas we are concerned with character, but the two cases are parallel: where McDowell takes virtue to consist in seeing situations in the right ways, and indeed thinking and feeling about them in the right ways, Sartre takes character to involve seeing, thinking about, and feeling about one's situations in a particular set of ways. The only difference between these two positions is that one involves the normativity of virtue, where the other is a purely descriptive claim about character. But the Sartrean view goes further, since it identifies the reason why an individual sees, thinks, feels, and acts in a particular way. Sartre, that is to say, argues that this general outlook is grounded in the projects one pursues, where McDowell is content in this passage to leave open the question of precisely what underlies the sensitivity of the virtuous person, whether it is one's habits, one's projects, or something else. McDowell argues for the identification of virtue with this sensitivity by showing that the latter plays the functional role definitive of the former, and we have seen that the same kind of argument links character to projects within Sartre's philosophy.

Through an argument for the unity of the virtues, McDowell reaches the conclusion that we should not think of the virtuous person as really having a set of distinct virtuous character traits, each corresponding to a particular kind of sensitivity, but rather understand that 'we use the concepts of the particular virtues to mark similarities and dissimilarities among the manifestations of a single sensitivity' ('Virtue and Reason', § 2). His point here is that we should not think of the virtuous person as having a range of different capacities, including the correct sensitivity to danger and the correct sensitivity to the feelings of other people, where these capacities could be possessed individually, but should instead see the virtuous person as possessing a single seamless sensitivity to the requirements of situations. The argument for this claim is concerned with situations in which one ought to be honest instead of compassionate, for example, or fair instead of generous, and so cannot be translated out of the normative language of virtue into the purely descriptive language of character. Nevertheless, this idea that the virtuous person possesses the single trait of virtue in general rather than a set of discrete virtues can help to clarify the way that Sartre's theory should be understood.

We need not understand the idea that character consists in projects, that is, to require each trait to itself be a distinct project, as though one could only be jealous or mean if one were aiming to be so. Such a view is clearly implausible. Neither need we understand it to involve the idea of any other kind of one-one mapping between each trait the person possesses and each project they pursue. We need not take the names of particular traits to pick out discrete psychological realities at all. Within the Sartrean account of character, we should rather understand them to mark the similarities and dissimilarities between the many manifestations of the same set of projects over time. We might also add a social dimension to this point and say that trait terms also mark the similarities between the behaviour patterns of different people. Two people can be cowardly, on this view, without having any project in common. Each is simply committed to a set of projects the pursuit of which is often manifested in shrinking from mild dangers and seeing dangers where there are none. Moreover, neither person need have one project in particular that is manifested in this behaviour. Each person's cowardly behaviour might result from different projects in different circumstances.

Sartre's theory of the motivation of action, therefore, ascribes to a person's total set of projects the role of accounting for the patterns in their behaviour that warrant the ascription of certain character traits to them. These projects are neither fixed facts about people, according to Sartre, nor fully deterministic of their actions. We can therefore act to revise our set of projects. Sartre affirms all of this when he writes:

> we find no *given* in human reality in the sense that temperament, character, passions, principles of reason would be acquired or innate *data* existing in the manner of things. The empirical consideration of the human being shows him as an organized unity of conduct patterns. (B&N: 498)

We saw in the last chapter that this theory in *Being and Nothingness*—that character traits consist ultimately in freely chosen projects that can be revised and that only incline us towards certain types of behaviour that they do not determine, his theory that our projects constitute for us an essence but not a nature—replaces his earlier denial of the reality of character in *The Transcendence of the Ego*. We also saw that this shift can be explained by the need to explain the patterns we find in an individual's behaviour over time coupled with the realisation that traits need not be fixed and deterministic. Now that we have investigated the later theory in more detail, however, two further motivations for this change can come to light. The rest of this chapter is concerned with tracing this development.

One motivation concerns the account of emotion that we have already considered. Although emotions are responses to situations that are too difficult, responses that suppress the pragmatic determinism of the world in favour of magical means for achieving our ends, Sartre argues, these emotions are not 'play-acted' but are genuinely felt (STE: 40). To clarify this, he distinguishes between genuine joy at the receipt of a welcome gift and pretended joy at the receipt of a gift one does not want. This pretended joy differs from the enacted joy of the actor on a stage, he claims, because enacted joy is an imaginary and enacted response to an imaginary and enacted situation, whereas pretended joy is a genuine response to a real situation (STE: 49). But unlike genuine joy, pretended joy is entirely under our control. We can begin and end it at will. Genuine emotion, on the other hand, 'fades away of itself, but one cannot put a stop to it' (STE: 49); in the case of fear, for example, 'one can stop oneself from running, but not from trembling' (STE: 50).

What the genuine emotion possesses and both types of false emotion lack, of course, is the physiological dimension that sustains the emotion beyond our control. But there is a further difference between genuine and pretended emotion: behaviour manifesting genuine emotion is sincere in a way that behaviour manifesting pretended emotion is not. Within Sartre's theory, this means that only in the case of genuine emotion does the world appear to one as having a magical structure and objects appear to one as having magical qualities. Genuine emotion commits us to seeing the world magically, pretended emotion does not. In genuine emotion, consciousness '*lives* the new world it has thereby constituted', it 'commits itself to it, and suffers [it]' (STE: 51). 'If we are really to be seized by horror', for example, 'we must be spell-bound and filled to overflowing by our own emotion, the shape and form of our behaviour must be filled with something opaque and weighty that gives it substance' (STE: 49). Sartre claims that this aspect of genuine emotion is also manifested in its physiological dimension: '*to believe* in magical behaviour, one must be physically upset' (STE: 50).

This distinction between genuine and pretended emotion seems perfectly reasonable, but it requires that we accept the reality of character traits. For within the apparatus of *The Transcendence of the Ego*, we could not maintain the distinction between genuine and pretended emotion and explain why people differ in their genuine emotional reactions to situations. We would classify emotions as states, of course, and they would be manifested in actions. But the origin of the state presents a problem. If we claim that it is deliberately adopted as a response to the difficult situation, we need some way of distinguishing genuine from pretended emotion. Were we capable of deliberately bringing about the physiological aspect of genuine emotion, we would surely do so in the case of pretended emotion as well, in order to pretend all the better. So we need to say that in some sense genuine emotions happen to us, whereas pretended emotions are deliberately adopted. To explain why different genuine emotions happen to different people in the same situation, we need to refer to the differing dispositions of those people, because everything else is the same. Sartre does not consider character or projects in *Sketch for a Theory of the Emotions*, though he does consider the pursuit of particular aims in given situations, but it is clear that the theory of emotion he develops there requires the reality of character traits.

This point is sometimes obscured by Sartre's language. Emotion, he tells us, 'is no playful matter': when emotion takes hold, 'we fling ourselves into this new attitude with all the force at our command' (STE: 40). This certainly sounds like the claim that we deliberately adopt a given emotion in a given situation, that the difference between genuine and pretended emotion is a matter of the degree to which we commit ourselves to seeing the world as magical, and this seems to be the way some commentators understand it (e.g., Heter, *Sartre's Ethics of Engagement*, 28–9). Were it the case, genuine emotion could be understood as a spontaneously chosen state like pretended emotion, and the theory would therefore not require the reality of character. But what this reading overlooks is that in pretended emotion we are very well aware of our effort, whereas in genuine emotion, according to Sartre, 'our effort is not conscious of what it is, for then it would be the object of a reflection' (STE: 40). So although we 'fling ourselves into this new attitude', we do not explicitly consider ourselves to be doing it.

Sartre's language here is partly designed to emphasise his central point that although it might seem to us that emotions are reactions to certain kinds of properties in the world, this reverses the true direction of explanation: in fact, things seem lovable, hateful, or fearful to us because we love, hate, or fear them (STE: 61). But his language of choice also seems to show that he had in mind something like the theory of character he develops in subsequent works, although at this stage he need not have formulated it in much detail. This is the theory that our perceptions, thoughts, feelings, and actions manifest our pursuit of relatively long-term projects. Since he also thinks these projects are in some sense chosen, and he often extends the language of choice to anything that results from our choices, he finds it appropriate to describe the emotions that result from our projects as themselves attitudes that in some sense we choose to adopt.

So although he does not discuss character or projects in *Sketch for a Theory of the Emotions*, he does seem to hint at the theory that he subsequently develops. He first makes this theory explicit in *The Imaginary*, published the following year, where he defines 'the me' as 'an harmonious synthesis of enterprises in the external world' (154). The theories developed in this book, moreover, provide further motivation for Sartre's move away from his early denial of the reality of character. The aim of the work is to identify the nature of imagination and its role in our mental life. Sartre is keen to show the falsity of an idea he considers central to almost all previous discussions of both perception and imagination: the idea that the two are the same in kind and differ only in some quality or other. He argues that perception involves one kind of attitude of consciousness, and imagination quite another. The difference between these two attitudes is reflected in the difference between the world of perception and the world of imagination. In perception, we are presented with a world that contains much more than we are aware of, and our attitude is essentially one of gaining information from that world. In imagination, on the other hand, we are presented with a world that contains precisely what we are aware of, because that world is determined by our imagination of it, and our attitude is one of stipulation rather than discovery (IPPI: 5–14, 120–2).

Sartre develops and enriches this theory in many ways, but what matters for our purposes is the contrast he draws between the ways in which we relate to the real and to the imaginary. Whereas the real world appears to present us with demands and difficulties, imaginary objects 'are neither heavy, nor pressing, nor demanding: they are pure passivity, they wait' (IPPI: 125). The perceived world is constituted from being in-itself, which is why it can resist our efforts and fail to fulfil our desires. But the imaginary world is responsive to our every whim. It 'will conform to our desires' in a way that reality will not (IPPI: 145). These are aspects of the difference between the reality that we track in perception and the imagined world we stipulate.

Sartre adds that there is also a difference between the feelings we have towards perceived objects and the feelings we have towards imagined objects. He claims that there are 'two irreducible classes of feeling', which he labels 'genuine feelings and imaginary feelings', though he is quick to clarify the latter term as here labelling real feelings that we genuinely feel but that are directed towards imagined objects rather than feelings that are themselves imagined (IPPI: 145). His claim that these are fundamentally different kinds of feeling is substantiated by his claim that those we have towards somebody in imagination disappear when that person is present, and do so because they are inappropriate. In the absence of the beloved, for example, love 'will be schematized and will congeal' until 'it becomes *love* in general' (IPPI: 144–5). The beloved as imagined loses identity and individuality and is instead constituted by this general feeling of love. When the beloved returns, however, this feeling is replaced by richer and more nuanced feelings appropriate to an individual necessarily more complicated than any schematic imagination of them (IPPI: 145).

The same is true of hatred, he claims. To hate someone in their absence is to form an image of them that is partly constituted by this hatred. The hatred is directed at 'a phantom tailored exactly to its measurements' (IPPI: 146). There is no difficulty in maintaining this feeling of hatred, and it is easy to imagine expressing it in word or in action. But the actual person is more complicated, more independent than their imaginary counterpart. In the presence of the actual person, this kind of feeling is inappropriate because that person is not tailored exactly to its measurements. Sartre's point is not simply that the imagined consequences of my imagined words and actions are entirely under my own control, whereas in reality harsh words or violent actions may very well lead to unplanned and undesirable consequences. It is also that the very same consequences can seem attractive in imagination, but be repulsive in reality. 'If I strike my enemy in image, blood will not flow or will flow just as much as I want', he writes, whereas in reality 'I will expect that real blood will flow, which is enough to stop me' (IPPI: 146). Since the feelings involved in imagination and in perception differ in kind, we can imagine our glee at the blood flowing when in reality we would be sickened by it.

The kinds of feelings we have towards perceived objects are therefore tailored to suit those objects, whereas in imagination feelings have priority and determine the nature of their objects. This theory does not, in itself, commit Sartre to the reality of character. The idea that there are two distinct kinds of feeling, one appropriate to objects present and perceived, the other appropriate to objects as they are imagined, is perfectly compatible with the idea that character traits do not really exist. What commits Sartre to the idea of character is his application of this theory to various aspects of normal and pathological mental life.

One way of obviating the difficulty of the real world, according to Sartre, is to behave as though in an imaginary world, in which one's interlocutor or audience is not unpredictable but is instead exactly as one wants them to be. Hence the behaviour of nervous and somewhat 'stiff and curt' people who sometimes say what they have decided to say to someone without really paying attention to them (IPPI: 146). We might add the nervous public speaker reading or reciting a prepared script without engaging in eye-contact with the audience. Full engagement with interlocutor or audience involves abandoning the imaginative attitude in favour of the perceptual attitude, and the nervous speaker is scared of being unable to go through with their plan once this is done (IPPI: 146).

Sartre goes on to argue that schizophrenia is simply an extreme and pathological form of this kind of behaviour. Finding the real world too difficult for one reason or another, the schizophrenic lives instead in an imaginary world for as much of the time as possible. This preference for the imaginary is not simply a preference for something colourful or exciting over the drab and mundane reality we perceive and live in. It is also a preference for the responsive, malleable, and undemanding nature of the imaginary over the difficult, resistant, and demanding nature of the real. The schizophrenic 'not only flees the content of the real (poverty, disappointed love, business failure, etc.)' but also 'flees the very form of the real, its character of *presence*, the type of reaction that it demands of us, the subordination of our conduct to the object, the inexhaustibility of our perceptions, their independence, the very way our feelings have of developing' (IPPI: 147). Schizophrenia is, according to Sartre, an escape from difficulty.

Whether or not this is a good way of thinking about schizophrenia is not our concern here. Neither need we be concerned with whether Sartre is right about nervous speakers. What matters here is that these accounts of the role of imagination in ordinary and pathological life implicitly require the reality of character. Not all speakers behave as the nervous speaker behaves, for example. So it must be the case that some people do not find difficult what the nervous speaker finds difficult. Since there need be no difference in the situations these people find themselves in, the difference must lie in the people themselves: nervous speakers are different from confident speakers. This must be a difference, moreover, in relatively long-term dispositions, since nervous speakers habitually and characteristically behave in a certain way and do so in response to perceived difficulties that they would rather not face. It is not a matter of choosing to find this difficult on this occasion but of generally facing this difficulty and adopting a strategy to deal with it.

The same point can be made about schizophrenia as Sartre understands it. The schizophrenic flees the very nature of the world habitually, not just occasionally, and most people do not live this way. So schizophrenics must be disposed to find the real world unbearable, on Sartre's picture, because otherwise they would be perfectly capable of simply deciding to find it bearable. Similarly, in order to explain why the sight of real blood flowing as a result of my actions would be repulsive to me, where it is not repulsive for everyone, we need to postulate a dispositional difference between myself and those people who would react differently. Sartre's account of why people imagine enjoying things that they would not really enjoy, that is, requires that there is some reason why people's real emotional reactions are not under their control in the same way as their imagined reactions, and this requires that people have dispositions to respond in certain ways, to find certain things attractive or repulsive, even if they do not want to respond in that way on a given occasion.

Sartre's account of the differing roles of emotion in perceptual and imaginative experience requires the reality of character, therefore, just as his distinction between genuine and pretended emotion requires it: character is required to explain why certain reactions to the world are not under direct voluntary control. This is perfectly compatible with Sartre's insistence on describing these responses to the world as in some sense chosen, however, since Sartre understands the dispositions they manifest to consist ultimately in freely chosen projects. Some critics of Sartre's philosophy have failed to understand his language of freedom and choice in this way, as we will see in the next two chapters, and their criticisms of his position are thereby mistaken.

In his two works of 'phenomenological psychology' published shortly after *The Transcendence of the Ego*, therefore, Sartre develops various theories that commit him to affirming the reality of character and rejecting his earlier claim that 'qualities' form no real part of the transcendent ego. The language of *Sketch for a Theory of the Emotions* hints at an understanding of character traits as in some way chosen, but goes no further. At one point in *The Imaginary*, Sartre explicitly describes the theory that he is to develop in *Being and Nothingness*. He is concerned in this passage to understand the hallucinations involved in some forms of obsessive–compulsive disorder (which he calls by the name it had at the time, 'psychaesthenia'). He argues that these hallucinations do not involve mistaking the imaginary for the real or even mistaking thoughts that are the patient's own for images or sounds from elsewhere. The problem is rather that the 'opposition between me and not-me, so noticeable for a normal person, is attenuated' (IPPI: 154). Here he defines 'the me' as 'an harmonious synthesis of enterprises in the external world' (IPPI: 154): these kinds of hallucinations occur when one no longer recognises one's own actions as part of one's set of projects, which Sartre calls here 'the me' (*le moi*).

This is his first explicit articulation of the theory that one's character consists in the projects one pursues: in shrinking from danger, the coward is manifesting some project or other that is also manifested in other behaviour. One's traits, according to this view, incline us towards actions that they do not determine and consist in projects that have been chosen and can at any point be rejected. This is only the bare outline of a theory, however. To understand it better, we need to clarify the notion of a project involved and the relation between projects and actions, which we will investigate in the next chapter. Sartre embraced this theory as a replacement for his earlier theory that there is not in fact any such thing as character at all. We have seen in this chapter some of the pressures that led to this change of view, and we saw in the last chapter that it may well have been facilitated by certain realisations about the inadequacy of the earlier view and the possibility of non-deterministic character traits.

The same years saw another development in his thought, one that has been well traced by Andrew Leak in the first three chapters of his book, *Jean-Paul Sartre*. Sartre's writings of the 1930s had predominantly literary and philosophical concerns, and he had deliberately eschewed any involvement in political events as unbecoming of the intellectual who, he thought, should remain aloof in the ivory tower in order to maintain a clear and undistorted vision. But his capture and imprisonment during the first year of the Second World War and his subsequent experience of the occupation of Paris changed all that, and in the 1940s he was clearly committed to social change through political activity and especially through writing. He soon became a proponent of the idea that the intellectual is always and necessarily socially and politically engaged in some way or other, so each thinker and writer must recognise this and affirm it through careful consideration of the social and political implications of their work.

That Sartre's approach to life underwent this change is undeniable: his diaries from the time attest to it, as do writings and interviews later in life, as Leak points out. Sartre provides a transmuted, fictionalised version of this change in his series of novels, 'The Roads to Freedom': *The Age of Reason*, *The Reprieve*, and *Iron in the Soul*. The central character, Mathieu, is a philosopher who has always seen himself as unable to do anything that he has not carefully decided upon for good reasons and therefore wanted to avoid simply falling into line with his society. Across the three novels, he comes to see that this image of an isolated and self-sufficient rational self is mistaken and begins to understand himself instead in terms of the enterprises he undertakes within his socially determined circumstances (e.g., TR: 274–5, 298). This conversion is liberating. He finds that he can now commit himself to life-changing actions when previously he could only engage in trivial demonstrations of his supposed independence while failing to carry out any of his more significant plans (e.g., IS: 225). Crucial to this conversion is the recognition that his aloof inaction has not been preserving him intact despite the vicissitudes of his surroundings, but has rather been defining him as someone who tries to seal himself off from his surroundings rather than someone who aims to transform them.

It might be tempting to argue that the evolution of Sartre's approach to character was part of the evolution of this bigger picture of the relation between the individual and their social context. His realisation that the individual is essentially social rather than a self-contained unit, that is, might be seen as driving his acceptance of the notion of character. For the anthropology of *The Transcendence of the Ego* seems to preclude the idea that one's social and historical setting is part of one's essence: if there are only actions and states, material surroundings and the past, and the freedom to behave in any way whatsoever, then it seems that society can be at best part of the story of one's past actions and material surroundings, and the free agent remains hermetically sealed in the way that Mathieu comes to realise that he is not. If, on the other hand, the individual does have qualities that incline them towards certain patterns of behaviour, then these character traits could be understood to have some relation to the individual's social context as part of their structure.

We have seen, however, that Sartre developed his theory that character consists in the projects one pursues in the 1930s, before his experience of imprisonment and then occupation, and that this development occurred under theoretical pressures resulting from his accounts of emotional and imaginative experience rather than as a necessary condition for a theory of the relation between individual and society that he had come to find attractive on the basis of his wartime experience. At best we can say, then, that although his change of attitude towards the relation between individual and society was the result of his experience of solidarity in prison and under occupation, his new attitude was facilitated and circumscribed by a theory of character that he had arrived at quite independently of that experience. This is the theory that one's character consists in projects that one has freely chosen to pursue and freely continues to maintain, projects that respond to the human condition in general and one's own circumstances in particular, where both condition and circumstances have social as well as material dimensions.

4 Freely Chosen Projects

In a phrase just as unhelpful as it is memorable, Sartre summarises his account of our existence by saying that each of us is 'a being which is what it is not and which is not what it is' (B&N: 81). This he intends to contrast with the stuff that surrounds us, which simply is what it is (B&N: 21). The air of paradox is generated by equivocation: there is nothing contradictory about saying that what something *is* in one sense it *is not* in another. Although commentators never fail to recognise this wordplay, they disagree over what exactly Sartre is trying to say with it. They disagree, that is, over just what senses of 'is' are in play. This disagreement arises because Sartre uses this phrase in different contexts, with reference to different aspects of human existence as he sees it, and it is not entirely clear how these different uses are intended to fit together. Thus, some commentators emphasise the role of this phrase in explaining the temporality of our lives, while others emphasise its place in depicting the relation between consciousness and its objects. But we will see that interpretations of this slogan purely based on its use in these contexts are mistaken and that Sartre rather intends it to capture the idea that character consists in freely chosen projects.

Temporality is clearly important in understanding the slogan, which first occurs in a discussion of various ways in which we can relate to our past and our future in bad faith (B&N: 81), is prefigured earlier in a discussion of the relation between consciousness and its own past and future (B&N: 58), and later occurs in a discussion of the notion of time itself (B&N: 157). This has led a number of commentators to read it wholly or partly in terms of our temporality. David Cooper, for example, writes that the slogan is claiming that individuals are not identical with their sets of past actions, on the basis of which other people form opinions of them (*Existentialism*, 118–19), since people are intelligible only in relation to the future self that they are becoming through the pursuit of their projects (75). Ronald Santoni concurs, reading Sartre to be claiming that a human being is 'never just its past, for it is also "what it is not" but could be; that is, its possibilities, its future' (*Bad Faith*, 14). This emphasis on temporality seems supported by the fact that the slogan is borrowed from Alexandre Kojève's lectures on Hegel delivered in Paris in the 1930s. Kojève intended the phrase to capture Hegel's notion of becoming: no longer being what one has been in order to be what one will be (see Schrift, *Twentieth–Century French Philosophy*, 24–5).

Catalano presents a slightly expanded version of this reading in his *Commentary*. He agrees that the first part, that we are what we are not, claims that we are a set of possibilities that are themselves to be understood in terms of goals that are not yet actualised. But he adds that this part of the formula also claims that we are identical with our possibilities plus our consciousness, which is something that 'we are not' since it cannot be ascribed a definite nature (84). He understands the second part of the slogan, that we are not what we are, to claim that we are not merely identical with our facticity, and describes facticity as including our bodies and our environments as well as our pasts, but does not mention characters that incline us towards particular kinds of action (84; see also McCulloch, *Using Sartre*, 59). Arthur Danto more or less follows suit in reading of the second half of the slogan as claiming that we are never identical with the roles that we play or with other predicates that can be applied to us, including those that describe our bodies and our past actions (*Sartre*, 60). His reading of the first half, however, follows Catalano's addition to the usual reading while discarding the rest. He takes it to claim that we are at least partly a consciousness that cannot be defined without reference to its objects, which are mostly things other than ourselves (59).

Kathleen Wider draws a more sophisticated connection between the slogan, consciousness, and temporality in her book *The Bodily Nature of Consciousness*. She takes the idea that my past cannot determine my present actions and these in turn cannot determine my future self to explain why Sartre employs this slogan (49). But she goes on to argue that the slogan is not intended to express the temporality of human existence but rather to capture a deeper fact about human existence that explains why our temporality is this way (57). This deeper fact is the structure of consciousness and its inclusion of self-consciousness (50): we must be distinct from the consciousness that we in some sense are, on this reading, not only because that consciousness cannot be defined without reference to its object, but also because we are always to some extent aware of that consciousness (53).

Sartre certainly does relate his slogan to both the structures of consciousness and the temporality of human existence, and Wider is right to distinguish between things that Sartre uses the slogan to illuminate, which may have influenced the choice of phrase, and what he intends the slogan to express. But what he intends it to express, as we will see, is neither the structure of consciousness nor our temporality, but something else, an aspect of our existence that is underpinned by the structure of consciousness and that underpins our temporality. We can approach this aspect of our existence through the connection that Sartre draws between the slogan and his denial of psychological determinism.

Sartre draws this connection when he claims that bad faith would not be possible were psychological determinism true: 'any project of bad faith would be impossible for me', he writes, if 'I were not courageous in the way in which this inkwell is not a table', or to put it another way, 'if I were isolated in my cowardice, stuck to it', or 'if it were not on principle impossible for me to coincide with my not-being-courageous as well as with my being-courageous' (B&N: 90). Bad faith, he concludes, requires 'human reality, in its most intimate being' to 'be what it is not and not be what it is' (B&N: 90). The condition of bad faith that Sartre is here summarising in the controversial slogan is that human individuals possess character traits such as courage or cowardice but these are not fixed and deterministic like the properties of such mere things as inkwells. In some of the sartrais that should by now be familiar, Sartre intends his slogan to capture the thought that we have essences that are not natures.

Bad faith is related to psychological determinism in a second way, according to Sartre. For bad faith is, as we will see in more detail in chapters 6 and 8, essentially the affirmation of psychological determinism. It is faith in our actually having fixed natures after all. So there is some irony in the thought that our actually having such natures would render bad faith impossible. That the controversial slogan is intended to express the thought that we have revisable characters, essences that are not natures, is also clear from its use at the very end of the book. Here Sartre describes the attitude of authenticity, which we will see in chapter 8 to be the acceptance of the true structure of our characters, as accepting that we are what we are not and are not what we are (B&N: 647). The famous slogan is clearly intended, therefore, to state or at least to entail that we have essences that are not natures, characters that are not fixed, and that psychological determinism, as Sartre understands it, is therefore false.

The claim that we are on a trajectory from a past that we are no longer towards a future that we are not yet does not capture this denial of psychological determinism, since it is perfectly compatible with our having natures that determine the trajectory that we follow. Were we to have deterministic character traits that evolve in response to experience and in accordance with fixed laws, for example, then our past actions would neither determine our present or future actions nor alone provide a sound basis on which to predict them, and it would remain the case that we were on the way to becoming something different from our present and past selves. Since the slogan is intended to either state or entail the falsity of psychological determinism, and this account of temporality does not do so, we should not take the slogan to express Sartre's picture of the temporality of human existence. We should rather take it to express some deeper fact that accounts for the precise way in which we are heading for our future selves.

The claims that consciousness can never be fully described without reference to objects distinct from itself and that consciousness is always accompanied by self-consciousness also seem, on the face of them, perfectly compatible with the psychological determinism that Sartre rejects. If we agree with both of these claims about consciousness, that is, we are still left with the further question of whether or not our experience and self-awareness progress through time according to deterministic laws. Sartre's answer to this question involves his metaphysics of being and nothingness: these aspects of consciousness both entail, he claims, that consciousness is not a being at all but rather a nothingness; since deterministic laws can only relate beings to one another, there can be no deterministic laws governing consciousness (see B&N: 46–9).

Whether or not this metaphysical outlook is indeed required for consciousness to be directed on an object and include self-awareness, as Sartre seems to think, need not concern us here. For we cannot understand the controversial slogan that a person is 'a being which is what it is not and is not what it is' as an attempt to express this idea that consciousness is a nothingness (whatever that means) and so does not fall under deterministic laws. Sartre understands the slogan, as we have seen, to state or entail that character traits are real but neither fixed nor deterministic, that there is indeed a sense in which someone can be courageous or cowardly but that this is not the same as the sense in which an object has a certain height or weight. The claim that consciousness is outside of the deterministic network does not, in itself, explain how it is that some people are courageous where others are cowardly. It does not explain, that is, either the constitution or the aetiology of character traits. It might be compatible with such explanations, as Sartre seems to think it is, although we will see in the next chapter that this is at least controversial, but it certainly does not itself provide them.

Understanding the slogan in a way that does capture its relation to the denial of psychological determinism requires us to bear in mind that Sartre considers character to consist in the set of projects the individual pursues, has in some sense chosen, and can revise. The slogan should be interpreted as expressing precisely this claim. When Sartre claims that a human being 'is not what it is', in the second part of the famous slogan, he is indeed claiming that we are not identical with our facticity. Many commentators have been right about this, but have been mistaken in assuming that the aspect of facticity in question is our past. Once we see that it is in fact our character, it becomes clear that this is a statement about the future: although your character explains the patterns in your behaviour, it does not determine that those patterns will continue, so you cannot be identical with that aspect of your facticity.

The first part of the slogan, the claim that we are what we are not, has often been read as the claim that our behaviour has to be understood in terms of our projects, as we have seen. But here commentators have gone wrong in assuming that it therefore involves a reference to the future. They have assumed, that is, that if we understand someone in terms of their projects then we must understand that person in terms of the kind of person that they are on the way to becoming or the state of affairs they intend to bring about in the future. Mary Warnock's influential article 'Freedom in the Early Philosophy of J.-P. Sartre', for example, is partly premised on the idea that Sartre understands action as necessarily rooted in projects aimed at bringing about things that are not already the case (see esp. 5–6). But it is a mistake to assume that a project must have some definite future objective that is not yet already the case. One very clear counterexample is Sartre's discussion of someone who accepts a low paid job out of fear of dying from starvation, a fear that Sartre claims can be understood only within the context of the project of staying alive (B&N: 459). This project aims at maintaining an actual state of affairs, not at bringing about some specific event or state of affairs that is not yet the case. We will see later in the chapter that this is far from an isolated example.

Negation does not enter into the first part of the slogan through the structure of the project, but rather through the relation between an individual and their projects. The negation expresses the claim that one cannot be identified with one's projects since one can always revise these projects and remain the same person. To say that I am what I am not is therefore to make a statement about my past: I need not have chosen the projects that I have chosen and whose pursuit has brought me to where I am now; I am not identical with those projects. The slogan overall, then, expresses the thought that my self or character consists in a set of projects that it need not consist in (is what it is not) and that these projects do not determine my future actions (is not what it is). The first part denies that character is fixed, the second denies that it is deterministic.

The slogan first appears at the end of a paragraph describing two forms of bad faith as 'affirming that I am what I have been' and affirming 'that I am not what I have been' (B&N: 81). To affirm that I am what I have been is to understand my past actions as flowing from a fixed character, and hence is the attitude that my future actions will also flow from this character. This is why Sartre describes someone who has this attitude as someone 'who deliberately *arrests* himself at one period in his life' (B&N: 81). The correct attitude is to affirm that I am not what I am, that I am not identical with my character, that my character is not a fixed determinant of my actions. To claim that I am not what I have been, on the other hand, is to deny that my past behaviour manifested my character, my set of chosen projects. In this attitude, someone 'dissociates himself from his past' (B&N: 80). The correct attitude is to affirm that my past behaviour did manifest my projects and my current character does consist in my projects, even though those projects need not continue into the future.

Wider is right to draw a connection between Sartre's slogan and his account of the structure of consciousness, even though she is wrong to conclude that the slogan is designed to express the structure of consciousness. The slogan rather expresses the relation between projects, character traits, and actions in Sartre's philosophy. But what it expresses about that relation is that character traits are neither fixed nor deterministic, a denial of determinism that Sartre argues for by arguing for the nothingness of consciousness. The connection between the slogan and the nothingness of consciousness is clearest when the slogan is contrasted with what Sartre says of ordinary objects in the world. Mere being in-itself, he says, 'is what it is' (e.g., B&N: 21): it has properties that it cannot change and that determine its behaviour. The reason that we do not have such properties is precisely that we have a different kind of being, one that involves the nothingness of consciousness, which he calls 'being for-itself'. The theory of the structure of consciousness is therefore part of Sartre's justification for his claim that the slogan applies, but it is not itself the meaning of that slogan.

The general metaphysics, or ontology, that underpins Sartre's theory of the nature of character is not our concern in this book. To understand his theory of character, we do not need to look in the first instance at this ontology, since it might well turn out that the theory of character does not require it and would be compatible with any of a variety of alternatives. What we do need to investigate is the very notion of project at work in Sartre's account, the relations between the projects a person pursues, and the relations between projects and actions. Once these are clarified, we can return to Sartre's idea of 'radical freedom', which is grounded in his metaphysics of being and nothingness. We will see in the next chapter that his philosophy of character does not require it and is probably better off without it.

There has been very little exegetical work concerned with Sartre's notion of a project. It seems that commentators have generally assumed that Sartre uses the term in its ordinary sense. While this term is mostly used in ordinary language to denote undertakings with the objective of bringing about something that is not yet actual, in the way that a research project aims to produce new information in published form, we can also use the word of undertakings that have no intended terminus and thus can describe marriage and parenthood as projects. Sartre certainly intends to use the term in this extended sense, at one point referring to the project of staying alive, as we have seen, so it is mistaken to assume that he thinks of projects as necessarily related to things that are not yet the case.

Sartre provides another good example of a project with no intended terminus in his analysis of anti-Semitism, written the year after the publication of *Being and Nothingness* (see A&J: 71n). There he argues that genuine anti-Semitism, by which he means the kind that makes people feel viscerally disgusted by the presence of Jewish people, is the result of a particular project that underlies all forms of racial hatred. This is the project of denying the three cardinal structures of the human condition: that we must earn our keep and our place in the world, that we must choose what to value as good and bad, and that we are responsible for our own actions. Anti-Semites, according to Sartre, see the first of these as resulting from being dispossessed of their birthright by a Jewish conspiracy rather than as a fact about being human, consider the birthright an objective good and the dispossession an objective evil, and consider this attitude to have been forced upon them by the intolerable circumstances in which they find themselves. The project that underlies genuinely anti-Semitic feelings and attitudes, as opposed to mere words and deeds that may or may not express such feelings and attitudes, therefore, is not the project of altering the ethnic landscape. Neither is it the project of changing the human condition, as if that were possible. It is simply the project of *continually denying* the human condition. Where the project of staying alive aims to make something really the case, this project aims only to colour the way the agent experiences and thinks about the world, and perhaps also to influence others to do likewise (see A&J: part I, esp. 50–4).

This example highlights an important difference between the ordinary sense of the term 'project' and the Sartrean sense. In order for this project of racial hatred to be successful, as Sartre understands it, the person pursuing it must not acknowledge that they are doing so. For one cannot succeed in persuading oneself of a Jewish conspiracy, or whatever, while acknowledging that one wants to believe this in order to deny the truth about the human condition. So although projects are in some sense chosen, this does not mean that undertaking them involves clear-eyed awareness of having made this choice or of continuing to affirm it. Projects need not be the result of explicit decisions. Sartre does not for a moment deny that the anti-Semites he describes really believe that there is a Jewish conspiracy. He even emphasises that they are genuinely viscerally disgusted by the presence of Jewish people. He is rather claiming that these attitudes and responses are rooted in a general outlook that the person is motivated to adopt, even though that person does not acknowledge this.

This lack of self-awareness might seem surprising, given Sartre's insistence that consciousness is always accompanied by 'non-thetic' or 'non-positional' awareness of it, an awareness that makes our thoughts and experiences available to us for reflective consideration (B&N: 8–10, 176). But there is no contradiction between this reflective availability and the projects in which our character traits consist not being immediately or easily accessible to us, or perhaps not even being accessible at all. In order to see this, consider the way in which Sartre understands projects to exert their influence on our behaviour: as we saw in chapter 3, they are responsible for the particular aims we have at any given time, and are hence responsible for the way the world seems to us, our emotional reactions to the world, and the weights we attach to each consideration when we deliberate about how to behave. There is no obvious incoherence in the idea that we can be aware of the structures of our experiences, our emotions, and our thoughts without being aware of the deeper reasons why we have precisely these experiences and emotional reactions or why we consider certain things more important than others. This is what Sartre means when he claims that what reflection reveals is 'not the pure project of the for-itself' but 'the concrete behaviour' or 'the specific dated desire' that manifests it (B&N: 591).

Sartre dramatises this point in his celebrated play *Huis Clos*, published the year after *Being and Nothingness*. Garcin is troubled by his inability to understand exactly why he deserted the army at the outbreak of war and tried to flee to safety. He knows that he intended to make a stand against the war by launching a pacifist newspaper. He knows that he had considered very carefully whether or not to desert, that he had very good reasons for acting as he did, and that he had planned out how to make his stand. What he cannot work out is whether this reflects his real motive, so that he can consider himself a hero who failed, or whether his deliberations were directed by an underlying motive of cowardice (HC: 214–15). His being in Hell cannot be considered evidence of a cowardice for which he is being punished, since he treated his wife abominably and so would have ended up there anyway (HC: 201–2).

Garcin, therefore, cannot tell whether he is cowardly or not. He says that he has spent his life aiming at being 'a real man', 'a tough', and has 'deliberately courted danger at every turn' (HC: 220). But he is aware that the truth could be either of two things. He might, on the one hand, be a coward who is prevented from seeing this by his project of seeing himself as 'a tough'. Inez might be right, that is, to say that this project colours the way he experiences and thinks about his own actions and decisions (HC: 220). Or he might, on the other hand, not be a coward at all but 'a tough' who is so worried by other people considering him a coward that he wonders whether they are right. So he simply cannot tell which character traits he possesses, which projects underlie his thoughts, feelings, and actions. This is partly because one's projects colour one's perceptions of one's own past deliberations, emotions, and actions just as much as they colour one's perception of one's current situation (see B&N: 519–21). We will see in chapters 7 and 9 just how important this thought is in Sartre's philosophy.

This example also provides a good illustration of Sartre's understanding of the relation between projects and actions. Garcin's action of deserting the army and heading for the border could have manifested either a project of cowardice or a project of heroic pacifism. Garcin is right to complain that his friends should not judge him a coward on the basis of a single action (HC: 216, 220). This much is a philosophical commonplace: the same action can be motivated in a number of different ways. But notice that deserting the army and heading for the border can also be understood as a project, since it is a sustained series of smaller actions that are motivated by, and to be understood in terms of, a specific aim. The same activity can be described as an action manifesting a project, therefore, and as a smaller project manifested in a series of smaller actions. This smaller project could be divided further into yet smaller projects, such as escaping from the barracks or getting together a disguise. Projects can therefore be ways in which other, larger projects are pursued. Such a project can, in turn, be pursued by means of pursuing further, smaller projects.

Projects can be related to one another, that is, as determinables and their determinations. Just as colour is a determinable of which red is one among many possible determinations, and red is in turn a determinable of which scarlet is one among many determinations, so particular projects are determinables whose determinations can be either actions or other projects. In order to pursue the project of desertion, for example, Garcin escaped from the barracks. Escaping is itself a project, in this case one pursued as a way of pursuing the larger project of desertion. Other ways of deserting are possible, however, such as fleeing when out on manoeuvres. So both fleeing from manoeuvres and escaping from the barracks are possible determinations of the same determinable. But this determinable is itself a determination of another project: deserting the army was something that Garcin was doing as a way of pursuing a larger project. His difficulties in understanding himself come from his inability to identify this deeper determinable project. His desertion could have been a determination of a project of heroic pacifism, as he would prefer to think it was, or it could have been a determination of the project of seeking his own safety at whatever cost, a form of cowardice.

Through relating to one another as determinables and their determinations, therefore, the projects a person pursues form an integrated hierarchy. One project can be a way of pursuing another which in turn is a way of pursuing yet another, for example, or two projects can be related as two ways in which one pursues the same deeper project. Sartre gives the name 'possibles' to our projects, as they are things we can undertake but need not. We can understand each person, then, as a 'hierarchy of possibles' (B&N: 486). An individual is not just a mosaic or constellation of distinct character traits, therefore, since the set of projects in which their character consists is not simply a set of independent pursuits. Each person is, as Sartre puts it, a 'totality' (B&N: 584). But this is not to say that a person cannot pursue contradictory aims, as we will soon see, only that the relations between their projects are intelligible within the framework of determinables and determinations.

Such a hierarchy is not open-ended. For one thing, there are some actions that cannot be understood as projects made up of smaller actions. Sartre's discussion of yielding to fatigue while out hiking with friends provides a good example. Simply stopping and sitting down cannot be understood as a project. It must be understood as a basic action, one that is a determination of some determinable project, but which is not itself a determinable. There are different ways of doing it, of course, such as resignedly, melodramatically, comically, and so on. But the differences between these ways of stopping and sitting down should be understood as ways of pursuing different projects rather than as different ways of pursuing the project of sitting down. The same action can manifest a number of traits at the same time, so that laziness and wit could both be manifested by comically giving up, for example. In Sartre's schema, this would involve the same basic action being a determination of more than one determinable project. When my companion, who is as tired as I am, refuses to stop, this could manifest both the 'project of a trusting abandon to nature' and 'at the same time the project of sweet mastery and appropriation' (B&N: 477).

This language of determinations and determinables should not be confused with the idea of determinism, despite the similarity between these words. One need not hold that one's projects or actions are causally determined or necessitated in order to consider them to stand in the hierarchical relations outlined above. Indeed, Sartre is clear that he does not consider our actions to be determined by the projects of which they are determinations. 'To relieve my fatigue, it is indifferent whether I sit down by the side of the road or whether I take a hundred steps more in order to stop at the inn which I see from a distance'; the projects I pursue are not sufficient conditions for my actions (B&N: 492). We should understand projects as determining only how the world appears to the agent and how the agent thinks and feels about it. They thereby set limits to the range of actions that the agent is likely to perform, the range of actions that would manifest those projects, that would determine those determinables, but this is not the same as necessitating or determining a particular action.

The point Sartre makes about actions in this example can be extended to the relation between projects. The point is that the determinable does not determine which particular possible determination of it will be actualised. If there is more than one way of pursuing a given project, that project does not determine which way it will be pursued. If Garcin is indeed a coward, this cowardice is not sufficient to determine that he will engage himself in the project of deserting the army at the outbreak of war. There are many other ways in which this cowardice could have been manifested. Sartre understands this to show that the determination of a given determinable involves the 'spontaneous invention' of the motivation to perform a specific action or pursue a more specific project within the parameters set by the larger project (B&N: 492). But the mere fact that a given project does not determine precisely how that project is to be pursued does not have this consequence. It remains possible that the way in which one pursues a given project is wholly determined by that project in concert with one's other projects, or with some set of them. The way in which I manifest my laziness, for example, could be determined by that laziness along with my other traits.

We will return to the issue of freedom and determinism in the next chapter. For the rest of this chapter, we will be concerned with the implications for Sartre's theory of character of seeing projects in terms of determinables and determinations. One implication concerns the idea that we might not necessarily be aware of the projects we are pursuing and provides a clear way of understanding the metaphor that a project might be a *deep* part of our character. We might be well aware that we are pursuing certain projects, but unaware that the range of projects from which they were chosen was circumscribed by an underlying project of which they are possible determinations, and therefore also unaware that the way in which we are pursuing them manifests this underlying project. This also explains what it might mean for a project, or part of one's character, to be not only deep but *buried*: since some projects require that the person pursuing them does not acknowledge that they are doing so, such a project might be hidden by those projects that are in fact determinations of it.

We have already seen how Sartre's understanding of anti-Semitism requires that anti-Semites do not acknowledge their underlying project to themselves. Another good illustration is provided by Sartre's analysis of someone whose 'initial project' aims at being 'inferior in the midst of others (what is called the inferiority complex)' (B&N: 493). This project delimits my choices of other projects: 'I can persist in manifesting myself in a certain kind of employment *because* I am inferior in it, whereas in some other field I could without difficulty show myself equal to the average' (B&N: 494). The project of inferiority must also colour the way in which other projects are pursued, since even unplanned success would undermine the project of presenting oneself to oneself as inferior. The other projects chosen and pursued with the aim of proving one's own inferiority must not, of course, be explicitly acknowledged as such. One must seem to oneself to have chosen projects for wholly other reasons and to have pursued them wholeheartedly.

To prove oneself inferior by becoming a failed artist, for example, requires that one explicitly '*wish* to be a great artist' and postulate false motivations such as 'the love of glory' and 'the love of the beautiful' in order to mask the true motivation (B&N: 495). The necessity of self-deception in this project is particularly acute, since not only will awareness of one's true motive undermine one's credence in any evidence of inability, but also if one were to engineer some spectacular evidence of inability this would itself show that one was quite capable at least of doing this (B&N: 495). The projects that manifest the inferiority project, that are determinations of it, must not be understood by the person pursuing them to be determinations of it, therefore, and can even include projects aimed at denying that one is pursuing the inferiority project. Pursuing the inferiority project requires burying it.

The second area of Sartre's thought that is illuminated by the analysis of projects and actions in terms of determinables and their determinations is his notion of a 'fundamental project'. McInerney describes the question of the relation between the fundamental project and other projects as 'one of the most grievous unclarities of *Being and Nothingness*' ('Self-Determination and The Project', 667). He takes Sartre to be claiming that the fundamental project is the project of becoming a certain kind of person, a reading also endorsed by McCulloch in *Using Sartre* (66), Morris in *Sartre's Concept of a Person* (see 58), and many others. McInerney then rightly complains that 'there is no nonarbitrary way to draw the line' between projects aimed at changing the world and this purported project of becoming a certain kind of person, since being a gracious person, for example, involves putting people at their ease, and putting people at their ease makes one (to some extent) a gracious person ('Self-Determination and The Project', 668).

This is not, however, what Sartre means by describing a project as 'fundamental' (*fondamental*). We have already seen that for Sartre projects need not be aimed at bringing about any specific change, in the world or in the agent. Were Sartre to be claiming that an individual pursues a single fundamental project of becoming a certain kind of person, moreover, and that this explains the rest of their projects and actions, then his position would be subject to two related criticisms. The first is that this seems unmotivated: he does not provide any philosophical account of why it need be the case. The second is that it seems implausible and would be immediately vulnerable to empirical refutation: to find an example of just one person who does not seem to be pursuing such a unifying project would jeopardise the theory, leaving any defender of it in the precarious position of continually having to explain away such apparent counterexamples.

Given the conceptual apparatus of determinables and their determinations, a project is fundamental simply by not being a determination of some deeper project: it would be the point at which the question 'why is that person pursuing that project?' cannot be answered with reference to a further, distinct project. This reading is confirmed by Sartre's description of existential psychoanalysis as aiming to 'disengage the meanings implied by an act—by every act—and to proceed from there to richer and more profound meanings until we encounter the meaning which does not imply any other meaning and which refers only to itself' (B&N: 479). The aim is to uncover an agent's fundamental project by understanding their actions in terms of their projects, and these in turn in terms of the deeper projects they manifest, and so on until we find a project that is not a determination of some other project, that cannot be made intelligible in terms of some deeper project. (This is a second reason why the hierarchy of projects is not open-ended.)

In order to clarify this, we need to distinguish between Sartre's terms 'initial project' and 'fundamental project'. When he describes the inferiority project as 'initial' (*initial*), this term is relative to the further projects he goes on to discuss, such as aiming to be a great artist (B&N: 493). In order to understand anti-Semitism, we need to understand that it occurs within the context of an initial project of denying the human condition. The question remains open whether this initial project is itself fundamental or whether it can be made intelligible with reference to another project. Sartre complicates this by going on to describe the inferiority project both as fundamental (B&N: 495, 497) and as chosen 'as the best means of attaining being' (B&N: 494), the latter of which appears to indicate the pursuit of a more fundamental project of attaining being. This apparent contradiction cannot be fully resolved until we have investigated what Sartre means by 'attaining being' in this context, which we will consider in chapters 6 and 8. We will find that the inferiority project cannot be adequately specified without reference to the project of 'attaining being', so this latter project is not distinct from and deeper than it.

Our analysis of the idea of a fundamental project also allows us to see that Morris is right to argue that Sartre does not make the implausible claim that each and every person is (at any given time) pursuing one and only one project. She is right to say that the fundamental project is not the pursuit of a single, dominating, exclusive end but is rather 'a top-priority end which sets the stage for working out other purposes' (*Sartre's Concept of a Person*, 119; see also McInerney, 'Self-Determination and the Project', 667; Jopling, 'Sartre's Moral Psychology', 113–16). But we can be more specific. The fundamental project limits the range of other projects that can be pursued and the ways in which we can pursue them. Morris gives the example of Sartre himself pursuing the project of being a writer. We should not agree that this is an example of a fundamental project, as we will see in chapter 8, but Morris is right to say that the pursuit of this project did not prevent Sartre from pursuing other projects, but rather that it was 'as a writer, rather than an elected politician' that he was engaged in politics and as a writer 'that he has travelled, made friends, gone to peace conferences' (*Sartre's Concept of a Person*, 199). The project of being a writer was a determinable with these among many other determinations, even if it was not the most fundamental determinable among his projects.

A second aspect of Sartre's account that might seem implausible is his claim that we can understand 'the meanings implied by an act—by every act' in terms of the projects manifested by that act, and ultimately in terms of the fundamental project (B&N: 479). This is no mere slip: Sartre insists that 'every action, no matter how trivial' manifests our projects (B&N: 481) and that 'every human reaction is a priori comprehensible' (B&N: 482). Existential psychoanalysis is based on this idea that an individual 'expresses himself as a whole even in his most insignificant and his most superficial behaviour', that 'there is not a taste, a mannerism, or a human act that is not *revealing*' (B&N: 589). We have seen that Sartre accepts that any given action might manifest any of a number of distinct projects that make it intelligible, which is why Garcin has such trouble understanding his desertion. So Sartre is not simply claiming that we can understand a person's character or projects simply on the basis of a single action, taste, mannerism, or whatever. But he does claim, nonetheless, that all of these things manifest the agent's projects and that a sufficient study of them will reveal the patterns that make clear what those projects are.

One reason why this might seem implausible, one that Sartre anticipates in the passages just quoted, is that some actions might seem trivial. Does someone really manifest their fundamental project in brushing their teeth? Or in brushing their teeth in this way rather than that? These kinds of actions make up a substantial amount of our lives and yet might appear not to have any bearing on our projects, as Morris points out (*Sartre's Concept of a Person*, 125). To see that Sartre's view is not so implausible as it might at first seem, consider the transitivity of the relation between determinables and their determinations. Since scarlet is a determination of redness, and redness is a determination of colour, scarlet is a determination of colour (or, to put it another way, one way of being coloured is being scarlet). If seven is a prime number, and prime numbers are odd numbers, and odd numbers are integers, then seven is an integer. If my action of brushing my teeth hurriedly this morning is part of getting to the job interview on time, and this is part of getting a specific job, which is part of projecting a certain kind of image to others, which is a way of pursuing some deeper fundamental project, then it is true to say that my brushing my teeth hurriedly this morning manifested my fundamental project. It is not true to say, of course, that my fundamental project can simply be read off this action, or even that the more immediate project within which it should be understood can be read off this action, but it is true to say that the action is ultimately part of the way in which I pursue my fundamental project.

Morris adds a different kind of objection to the idea that all of one's behaviour manifests one's projects, where these are unified by the fundamental project. She claims that this idea 'seems to contradict Sartre's point that there can be uncharacteristic actions' and points out that this idea is central to Sartre's theory of freedom from psychological determinism (125). This need not be understood solely as an internal criticism of Sartre's philosophy, of course, since the idea that people sometimes act out of character seems plausible on the basis of our own experience. But as an internal criticism, the point seems to misunderstand what Sartre means by uncharacteristic actions. Sartre does not understand such actions as simple anomalies in the otherwise consistent pursuit of a project, but rather as bringing about the alteration of the projects one is pursuing, as 'an abrupt metamorphosis' of one's projects (B&N: 486), as we will see in more detail in the next chapter.

The objection of implausibility can be met by considering again the relation between determinables and their determinations. Since a deep, perhaps fundamental, project is a determinable, there seems no reason why an agent should not pursue simultaneously two or more determinations of this project, and since these determinations might differ in various ways there seems no reason why they should not make conflicting demands in some specific situation. This is an important aspect of Sartre's understanding of projects, and one that is highlighted by the example of the inferiority project: it is possible to pursue one project by pursuing aims that appear to contradict that project, such as aiming to be a great artist as a way of proving one's inferiority, and it is equally possible to pursue two or more contradictory projects as ways of pursuing the same deeper project. The idea that character consists in projects, even ultimately in a single fundamental project, is therefore perfectly consistent with an individual having inconsistent aims and displaying incoherent behaviour patterns.

Nothing that we have seen so far about the nature of projects, however, provides positive support for Sartre's view that the whole of an individual's behaviour can ultimately be understood as manifesting a single fundamental project. There seems no obvious reason why one might not pursue two or more projects, none of which are determinations of other projects or require the context of other projects for their intelligibility. Everything said in this chapter remains compatible with the pursuit of more than one project that meets our definition of a 'fundamental project'. So why does Sartre insist that there is always, necessarily only one? We will return to this question in chapter 8, since the answer depends on Sartre's related theories of freedom and bad faith.

5 Radical Freedom

Sartre is often quoted as saying that humans are 'condemned to be free' (B&N: 462; EH: 29; see also TR: 308). We are condemned to the kind of existence we have because we did not choose it and we cannot escape it, except by ceasing to exist altogether. This kind of existence includes freedom because the ways in which the world seems to us, the ways in which we think and feel about it, and the ways in which we behave in response to it are all ultimately manifestations of projects that we have chosen to pursue, that we need not have chosen, and that each of us can yet choose to change. Our characters are not simply given to us, on this view, but are things that we have freedom over. My essence is not my nature: 'I am condemned to exist forever beyond my essence' and 'beyond the motifs and mobiles of my act' (B&N: 461–2).

This philosophy of character, which we have considered over the last few chapters, grounds Sartre's comments on responsibility. Since my situation has the meaning that it has for me 'only in and through my project', or again 'on the ground of the engagement which I am', he writes, it is 'senseless to think of complaining since nothing foreign has decided what we feel, what we live, or what we are' (B&N: 574). Sartre even goes so far as to say that 'in a certain sense I choose being born' (B&N: 576). He does not mean that I chose to be born, of course, but rather that the fact of my birth has a certain kind of meaning for me, and this meaning is dependent on the projects I have chosen. This is true, he claims, for all aspects of my situation, including the very fact that I have been born. The articulation of my situation as having this sense or that is my responsibility. If I find myself involved in a war, then 'this war is my war; it is in my image and I deserve it' (B&N: 574; see also IS: 88).

We might criticise Sartre here for seeming to draw too simple a connection between causal responsibility and moral responsibility. We might also criticise his apparent assumption that my responsibility for the ways in which things are constituted brings with it a responsibility for the things that are so constituted. If the meaning an event has for me is dependent on my projects, it does not follow that the event itself is dependent on my projects, and even if it is it does not follow that I can rightly be said to deserve it. We will not be concerned with these issues in this chapter, however. We will rather be concerned with clarifying Sartre's idea of freedom, to which he often attaches the epithet 'radical', and considering the ways in which this idea has been criticised. We will find that this idea is not required by the theory that character consists in projects that we have chosen to pursue, and indeed that the theory of character may well be better off without it.

Sartre's account of freedom involves the denial of all forms of determinism. Our actions cannot be given a complete and deterministic causal explanation, according to Sartre, and our freedom requires that this is so. His theory therefore seems vulnerable to David Hume's influential objection that indeterminist freedom 'is the very same thing with chance' (*Treatise*, book 2 part 3 § 1). If actions are not causally determined, the objection runs, then it is always a matter of chance whether or not any given action occurs. Since people's actions manifest their characters, and hence exhibit patterns that are not simply random or chance, we know from experience that we simply do not have this kind of freedom. If our actions were subject to chance in this way, moreover, then we would not have the control over our actions that we like to think we have. If this is right, then we should be very glad that we do not have the freedom Sartre describes, irrespective of whether we agree with him about the responsibility it would bring with it.

Sartre explicitly resists this application of Hume's criticism of indeterminist freedom to his theory, however, and closer inspection shows that he is, to some extent, right to do so. Hume is concerned to show that there can be no such thing as what he terms 'the liberty of indifference', which would be the absence of any causal necessitation between a motive and the ensuing action. Against this liberty of indifference, he argues that we know from experience that 'actions have a constant union and connexion with the situation and temper of the agent' (*Treatise*, book 2 part 3 § 1). Motives are followed by corresponding actions, he writes, with the same regularity as any causal connections we may observe, so we must conclude that motives cause actions and if causes necessitate their effects then we must agree that motives necessitate actions. This point underlies the classic debate over whether we have any 'free will': libertarians argue that we do have free will because our actions are not necessitated by prior states, whereas Hume and his followers argue that human freedom just consists in the ability to act on our motives without external restraint.

Sartre argues that this debate misplaces the central locus of freedom, and is therefore irrelevant to his own theory, which recognises that locus. The crucial question is not how we get from motives to actions, according to Sartre, but rather how our motives are constituted in the first place. Because our motives manifest our freely chosen projects, those motives are already themselves freely chosen, he thinks. Sartre understands explanations of actions to refer to the same explanatory event either as a motif or as a mobile, as we saw in chapter 3. My action of tidying the room might be explained by the motif of the room looking untidy to me or by the mobile of my desire that it be tidier, where this motif is nothing but the way this mobile is manifested to me. Motif and mobile are therefore two ways of referring to the same motive for the action, and this motive reflects my longer-term projects, which I can choose to revise.

Libertarians have traditionally denied that motives necessitate actions, Sartre points out, by claiming that a motive to do a certain kind of action might be followed by that action, but might be followed by an entirely different action that does not itself manifest an appropriate motive. Sartre is keen to distance himself from this theory, which he rightly refers to as a theory of *la liberté d'indifférence,* the liberty of indifference, misleadingly translated in *Being and Nothingness* as 'free will'. According to this theory, an action can occur with no motive at all, simply following on from a motive to do something quite different, something that then remains undone. Freedom is then supposed to consist in the gap between motive and action: we are free to act on any given motive or instead to do something entirely different. Sartre argues against this theory by arguing that an action that does not manifest a motive 'would lack the intentional structure of every act' and would be 'absurd' (B&N: 459). In calling such an unmotivated action absurd, Sartre echoes Hume's point that it would be simply a matter of chance and hence entirely unjustified, but Sartre also adds here that such events should not really be considered actions at all (see also B&N: 455).

Yet he holds nonetheless that the opponents of this theory of the liberty of indifference, Hume and those who agree with him, are wrong to conclude that freedom is nothing but the ability to act on one's motives without external restraint. They have overlooked, he thinks, the crucial question of the nature and origins of motives. Freedom, for Sartre, consists in the fact that we have control over the motives that we find ourselves with, because we have control over the character that those motives manifest, because we have control over the projects our character consists in. Freedom is to be found in the nature and origin of motives, not in the relation between those motives and the actions that manifest them.

But Sartre is wrong to imply that the Humean criticism of the denial of determinism is therefore irrelevant to his own theory of freedom. He is right to say that his theory does not require unmotivated actions, as we will see, but wrong to think that it thereby evades the objection. For his theory does require that the motives for an action do not necessitate that action. He is aware of this and distinguishes two ways in which it is true. One is that there is a narrowly circumscribed arena of the liberty of indifference since my motives do not determine precisely how they are to be acted upon. 'To relieve my fatigue, it is indifferent whether I sit down on the side of the road or whether I take a hundred steps more in order to stop at the inn which I see from a distance' (B&N: 492). We could disagree with this and argue instead that my projects together, as what Sartre calls a 'totality', do indeed determine precisely how I act on my motives. My action of giving up on the hike might manifest one project, and the way I do it manifest one or more further projects. If we took this option, we could nonetheless retain the Sartrean idea that motives manifest the projects we pursue and even the further idea that these projects are within our control, as we will see shortly. So this element of indifference is not at the heart of Sartre's theory of freedom and we need not dwell on it.

The other way in which actions are not necessitated by their motives is central to Sartre's account. Motives can fail to result in the relevant actions, not by being followed by an entirely unmotivated action, but rather by being replaced with new motives that issue in a different action. It is possible to overthrow the projects that any given motive manifests and thereby remove that motive altogether. In the ordinary course of things, any given motive is either acted upon or defeated by stronger motives for competing actions present alongside it. But the strongest motives need not issue in action, according to Sartre's account. They necessitate only that *either* they will result in the relevant actions *or* they will be replaced by new motives reflecting new projects, at least for the time being. Although 'it is impossible in fact to find an act without a mobile', Sartre writes, 'this does not mean that we must conclude that the mobile causes the act; the mobile is an integral part of the act' (B&N: 460). My wanting the room to look tidier does not simply cause my tidying the room. It is rather that my tidying the room is an action only because it continuously affirms and sustains my wanting the room to be tidier, where I could instead have adopted a new project that would not be manifested in my wanting the room to be tidier. The Humean objection to indeterminism can be raised again at this point, as we will see, but first we need to clarify Sartre's theory.

On this account, as Sartre points out, it is true to say of any action of mine that 'I could have done otherwise', but he insists that in order to understand the way in which this is true we must ask the further question: 'at what price?' (B&N: 476). The cost of doing otherwise, he maintains, is 'a radical conversion of my being-in-the-world', 'an abrupt metamorphosis of my initial project', 'another choice of myself and my ends' (B&N: 486). I cannot do otherwise while continuing to pursue the same projects, except perhaps in the trivial sense in which there is more than one way to act on any given motive, but nonetheless I can always modify my projects, my character, and so act on new motives. This is what Sartre means by describing freedom as 'radical'. The term is not meant to emphasise the range of our freedom but rather its depth; it is not meant to indicate that all of our actions are free, although Sartre does think that is true, but rather that our actions are free because they are ultimately rooted in our projects, which are themselves freely chosen and maintained. He uses the term in the sense indicated by its etymology: freedom is a matter of the roots of our actions.

Combining this point with the understanding of projects as the hierarchy of determinables and determinations outlined in the last chapter allows us to see why certain criticisms of Sartre's theory of freedom are misplaced.

McCulloch argues, for example, that some of our most basic projects are not necessarily things we choose but can just as easily be things we find ourselves doing. 'Someone might just have drifted into a career without reflection', he points out, and such a person cannot be said to have chosen their career (*Using Sartre*, 66). It is certainly true that someone might drift into a career, but Sartre's theory holds only that this very drifting will itself reflect deeper projects that the agent is pursuing, and their continuing in that career will reflect deeper projects. That this person is not bothered about the nature of their career might reflect their emphasis on projects that can be pursued only outside the world of paid work or might reflect a negative attitude to work in general, and this may manifest some deeper project of maintaining some attitude or other towards the human condition. Each of these projects is, according to Sartre, chosen, and so the career is also chosen if we follow Sartre in extending this term to every determination of a chosen determinable. Whether or not Sartre is right to extend the language of choice in this way is not our concern here. All that matters is that McCulloch's example presents no significant problem for Sartre's theory of freedom.

Dagfinn Føllesdal criticises the connection Sartre draws between projects and the constitution of motives, but he is mistaken about exactly what that connection is. Føllesdal argues that Sartre is wrong to think of the way the world seems to us as in any way chosen. We have control over whether we see a duck-rabbit picture as a picture of a duck or as a picture of a rabbit, he points out, but cases like this are notable precisely because we do not normally have this kind of freedom over the way things seem to us. He concedes that 'it is possible that with some training we might be able to do this in many more cases', but that Sartre has not shown that this is the case ('Sartre on Freedom', 401–2). But the theory of freedom in *Being and Nothingness* does not require that this is the case. It only involves the more restricted claim that the pressures that our environment seems to exert on our behaviour, the values it contains and the tools and obstacles that it presents, are themselves ultimately a function of our projects. Sartre need not show that this is also true of the way objects are individuated and differentiated in order to defend his account of freedom. Neither need he show, moreover, that we can vary these evaluative aspects of our perceived environment at will, nor that we can directly manipulate the ways in which we think or feel about the things and people that surround us.

Sartre provides a good illustration of this in chapter 7 of his novel, *The Age of Reason*, published two years after *Being and Nothingness*. Daniel has decided to take the three cats he keeps in his apartment, which he adores and which take up a lot of his time, and drown them in the river Seine. He wants to prove to himself that he is really a hard and forbidding character and not the soft and sentimental person that he would seem from his caring for these cats (AR: 85). He also wants to destroy what he loves most in the world, in order to prove his freedom from being determined by his attachments to the people and things surrounding him, and to prove that other people's images of him as having some specific character are wrong (AR: 89–90). But in the end, at the water's edge, he finds that he simply cannot drown his cats, the very idea sickens him, and he turns around and takes them back home. His desires or intentions to drown them were, in Sartre's apt metaphor, merely cheques without the funds to meet them (see AR: 86–7). Daniel has failed to displace his motives towards looking after his cats, even though he thought that he wanted to be rid of them. He has failed to constitute the world differently, to overthrow the positive value his cats have for him, and so is an example of precisely the point that Føllesdal thinks stands against Sartre: that we do not have direct control over the way the world seems to us.

Exactly why Daniel has failed in this regard is something to which we will return in this chapter. But it is worth noting that the general reason is that he has failed to correctly identify and abandon the project that his love of the cats manifests. For this reason, he has failed to displace the motives rooted in that project, failed to change the way the world seems to him, and so failed to carry out the smaller project of drowning the cats. Had he succeeded in drowning the cats, this action would not simply have been the uncharacteristic anomaly that he thinks it would be, a proof that his actions do not fit the patterns other people see in them. Neither would it have been unmotivated or gratuitous. It would rather have been the abandonment of the project in which his love of the cats is rooted and the inauguration of a new project in its place. It would have had its own motives, created in the moment along with the new project that they manifest and that displaces the project abandoned.

In *Being and Nothingness*, Sartre gives two literary examples of this kind of abandonment of one project in favour of another: 'the instant at which . . . Philoctetes casts off his hate' in André Gide's play *Philoctetes* and 'the instant when Raskolnikov decides to give himself up' in Fyodor Dostoyevsky's novel *Crime and Punishment* (B&N: 497). He describes such 'conversions' as 'extraordinary and marvellous instants when the prior project collapses into the past in the light of a new project which rises on its ruins and which as yet exists only in outline'. Such moments, he continues, have 'often appeared to furnish the clearest and most moving image of our freedom' but are in fact 'only one among others of its manifestations' (B&N: 497–8). These examples must not be mistaken, that is, for brief moments of freedom. It is not simply that we are free when we abruptly change our projects in this way. It is rather that our actions are always free because they manifest projects that do not bind us: we could, at any time, abruptly abandon them in this way, so our continual pursuit of them is our continual affirmation of them.

The central problem for this account, however, is that it seems to be subject to a revised version of Hume's criticism of indeterminist theories of freedom. Sartre does not eliminate the element of chance to which Hume objects, but simply moves it to a different part of theory of action and thereby alters its ambit. It is not, according to Sartre, a matter of chance whether or not any given action reflects the agent's motives, for an action must issue from motives, but it does remain a matter of chance whether any given set of motives will be acted on. For if we can reject our motives at any time in favour of new ones, by rejecting our projects in favour of new ones, and if this rejection is not dependent on having other motives for it rooted in other projects, then it seems a matter of sheer chance whether we will do this or not at any given time. It seems, that is to say, that it would be a matter of sheer chance whether the project is acted on or abandoned, and that if it is abandoned it would be a matter of sheer chance what it is replaced with.

Chance would seem to be involved in the Sartrean picture of action in other places, too. If it is genuinely indifferent whether I relieve my fatigue by sitting down at the side of the road or by walking to the next inn, then it would seem to be a matter of chance which of these I do. This point can also be made about the choice of projects as determinations of larger projects. If Daniel's project of denying the view that others have of him does not determine that he will pursue it one way rather than another, and if the way in which he does pursue it is genuinely undetermined, then it is to some extent a matter of chance that he will set out to drown his cats. It is difficult to see why Sartre should insist that projects do not determine how they are to be pursued. This element of chance hardly seems to secure freedom, rather than randomness and lack of control.

We could easily deny this aspect of his theory, however, and insist that the totality of projects collectively determines the way in which any given project is pursued, or at least sets strict parameters that leave room for only trivial variation. That is, as mentioned before, the basic Sartrean idea that character consists in projects that are freely chosen and can be revised requires only that at any time we can abandon any motive and the project or projects it reflects instead of simply acting on it. It does not require that we can do this without any motivation. This is where the central problem for Sartre's idea of radical freedom lies: it is not only that my earliest projects must have been chosen without any motivations so that it is a matter of chance that I pursue these projects and not others that I might have plumped for, but also and more importantly that at any given moment it is a matter of chance whether my motives are acted upon or whether they are overthrown.

This objection can be taken in a number of different ways. It could be argued, following Hume, that were the choice of projects to be genuinely a matter of chance in this way and the rest of Sartre's theory to be correct, then we should expect to find no intelligible patterns in people's behaviour as they would be abruptly changing projects at random moments. Since we do find intelligible patterns in people's behaviour, since people do seem to pursue sustained projects, the argument would run, Sartre must be wrong about the element of chance involved in the constitution of motives. The objection could also be taken to point out that this element of chance simply is not what we mean by freedom, but is rather a lack of self-control that we clearly do not suffer. Understood in this way, the objection has been developed into at least three different arguments against Sartre.

The simplest is McInerney's claim that Sartre's theory is incoherent: the sustained pursuit of a project is incompatible with this element of chance in the constitution of motives ('Self-Determination and the Project', 675–6). More complicated arguments based on the same objection are cast in terms of the nature of choice. The randomness that Sartre seems to be committed to is not compatible with his claim that we choose our projects, one argument runs, so were he right to say that the adoption of projects is entirely unmotivated he would be wrong to say that it is a matter of choice. Sartre agrees that an action must be motivated, as we have seen, but since he does not extend this point to choosing a project, as Føllesdal points out, he thereby departs significantly from our usual understanding of choice ('Sartre on Freedom', 402). McCulloch makes a similar point, though he approaches it from a different angle, when he argues that once my projects have become deeply entrenched, once I have become deeply committed to them and to the motives with which they provide me, I am unlikely to be able to see my way clear to abandoning them in favour of new ones. It might be logically possible for me to do so, he concedes, but it is psychologically extremely unlikely or perhaps even impossible, given that the projects themselves provide motivation for retaining them (*Using Sartre*, 64–6).

The strange thing is, however, that Sartre's theory of our freedom over our character can be retained even while his indeterminist conception of freedom is denied, so these arguments cannot rule out theories of character that are Sartrean in all respects except this one. This is strange because Sartre is adamant that indeterminism is correct, which gives the impression that it is crucial to his overall picture. To see that this impression is mistaken, we will first consider his examples of the experience of our freedom to change our projects. Walking along a clifftop path, I might be filled with horror at the prospect of falling, or perhaps even of jumping, over the edge. While this horror 'calls for prudent conduct', any conduct on my part appears to me 'as only possible', which leaves open the possibility that I will behave imprudently. I become aware that 'nothing compels me to save my life, nothing prevents me from precipitating myself into the abyss' (B&N: 55–6). Sartre takes this to be an awareness of the fact that my present motives do not determine my future conduct, an awareness that he here calls 'anguish in the face of the future', and which he had earlier called 'the vertigo of possibility' (TE: 47). Sartre immediately follows this example with one of what he calls 'anguish in the face of the past'. A compulsive gambler has resolved to quit, and 'when he approaches the gaming table sees all his resolutions melt away' (B&N: 56), just as Daniel's resolution to drown his cats melts away at the water's edge. Our resolutions cannot bind us. 'What the gambler apprehends at this instant is again the permanent rupture in determinism' (B&N: 57).

Sartre is clear that he does not intend these examples 'as a *proof* of human freedom', but rather as illustrations of our awareness of our freedom (B&N: 57). Had he meant them as proof, they would have been vulnerable to obvious objections. The anguish on the clifftop path could be taken purely as an awareness that nothing is stopping me from throwing myself over the cliff should I want to do so, that it is perfectly possible to want to do so, and that had things been different it could have transpired that I wanted to do so now, none of which requires my motives to be rooted in my projects, still less that neither the initial choice of these projects nor their subsequent revision requires any motivation. The example of the gambler would fare even worse, since it is not obvious why he should understand his temptation as evidence that his new project does not determine his action rather than as evidence that he has not fully abandoned his old project.

Towards the end of *Being and Nothingness*, Sartre develops a theory of the relation between negative feelings such as anguish and the projects we pursue, which we will consider in detail in chapter 8. This theory explains the feeling of anguish in these examples as motivated by the recognition of our freedom over our characters and over the way the world seems to us, a freedom that he thinks we aim to deny. We become aware that we could arrange things so that we prefer to throw ourselves off the cliff or to return to the gaming table, and this awareness is unpleasant. This theory does not require that we can change ourselves without having any motivation for doing so, however, so does not require indeterminism. Sartre does write that it 'would be in vain to object that the sole condition of this anguish is ignorance of the underlying determinism', but this is an argument against the idea that my actions have motives of which I am ignorant (B&N: 57–8). Sartre is implacably opposed to such an idea, but as we saw in the last chapter this opposition is compatible with the ultimate reasons why I have these motives not being easily accessible to me.

Sartre's discussion of anguish is therefore compatible with determinism, and he does not intend it to be otherwise. His argument that we are free in the incompatibilist sense, that our motivations and hence our actions are exempt from the determinism that rules the rest of the world, is based on his ontology of being and nothingness. The very structure of projects involves nothingness, according to Sartre, or more precisely every project involves some 'nonbeings' or 'négatités': a project always involves something that does not have being. Since causal determination is only a way in which beings can affect and be affected by one another, he claims, the presence of nothingness in the structure of our projects means that projects cannot be causally determined (B&N: 46–9). Although this ontological aspect of Sartre's philosophy is not our concern in this book, it is important for our understanding of his theory of character and freedom to get clear on exactly what 'nonbeings' or 'négatités' are. They are 'those little pools of nonbeing' that we encounter in the world (B&N: 43). They are 'realities' that 'are experienced, opposed, feared, etc., by the human being and which in their inner structure are inhabited by negation' (B&N: 45). They are aspects of the world as we experience it that do not have being in-itself but are rather ontologically dependent on our experiencing of them, like the noticeable absence of Pierre from the café in which I expected to find him (B&N: 33–6).

Commentators often assume that the négatités involved in projects are the ends, purposes, or goals of those projects, or at least are dependent on them. McInerney, for example, distinguishes three ways in which the goals of projects involve nothingness: 'the end does not now exist', he writes, and so 'with reference to the end, what now exists is deficient', and because the present is deficient, it lacks completeness or perfection ('Self-Determination and the Project', 669; see also Warnock, 'Freedom in the Early Philosophy of J.-P. Sartre', 6). This assumes that every project has as its aim bringing about some specifiable objective, some state of affairs that is not presently the case. But this simply does not adequately capture Sartre's notion of a project, as we saw in the last chapter, since among the projects Sartre discusses are those that aim at staying alive, at convincing oneself of one's inferiority, and at denying the human condition. Projects can aim at continuing what is now the case: they are not necessarily concerned with change.

What has misled commentators here is that Sartre does write that a 'motive is understood only by the end; that is, by the non-existent' and follows this by saying that the end 'is therefore in itself a négatité' (B&N: 459). But he does not mean that the goal is something that is not the case. He goes on to explain that if I am motivated by a fear of dying, the goal is the preservation of my life, which can be understood 'only in relation to the value which I implicitly give to this life', which is to say that 'it is referred to that hierarchical system of ideal objects which are values' (B&N: 459). The nothingness lying at the heart of the structure of the project, and hence implied by any motive, is not the nothingness of the goal itself, but the nothingness of the value involved in that goal. The brute mass of being in-itself does not contain positive or negative values of any kind, according to Sartre. Value is bestowed by the agent. Its lack of being means that any goal involving a value cannot be in-itself, and so is itself a nothingness, a nonbeing, a négatité. This is not the claim that we can value only things that do not exist, as Heter claims it is (*Sartre's Ethics of Engagement*, 147). It is the claim that nothing that we value possesses any value in and of itself.

There are two ways in which values are related to projects. One is that the aim or goal of a project is something that is thereby valued. The other is that a value can be generated as instrumental to the fulfilment of a project. If I want to be a great concert pianist, for example, and this is my overarching aim in life, then I will take care to preserve my life for long enough to achieve this aim, so my staying alive will have a certain value for me precisely because of this project. Staying alive will thereby become a project

Radical Freedom 69

too, of course, but one that should be understood within the larger project that gives my life its value for me. The value my life has for me is in this case a by-product of my project of becoming a great concert pianist, not its aim or purpose. With respect to that project, it is merely instrumental. But with respect to preserving my life, it is bound up with the goal of that project more intimately. That project aims at preserving something that has positive value for me.

Sartre's analysis of the inferiority project shows that one's projects can have conflicting values. The project of inferiority requires that the agent pursue certain other projects and fail in them, but the agent must value the ends of those other projects otherwise the failure will not provide evidence of inability. If my inferiority project is pursued through my project of being a great artist, then I must value the end of being a great artist and the production of great artworks, even though this project is really part of the pursuit of failure (B&N: 494–5). Daniel's project of drowning his cats is motivated by his deeper project of humiliating himself in his own eyes and in the eyes of those around him, of showing himself to be contemptible. Had he drowned his cats, he might have earned the contempt of others. But his failure to drown the cats provides better prospects of success in this deeper project: it humiliates him in his own eyes, makes him despise his own cowardice and feel 'too ashamed to talk in his own presence' (AR: 90–1). In order to have this effect, he had to value the aim of drowning the cats, even though that project was just a determination of a deeper project of self-abasement that required him to fail to drown his cats.

The role that values play in the structure of projects allows Sartre to describe projects as involving nothingness and is therefore a crucial part of his argument against determinism, as we have seen. But we are not concerned with the metaphysical underpinnings of Sartre's theory of character in this book, only with that theory itself. We have seen, moreover, that Sartre's opposition to all forms of determinism renders his theory of character vulnerable to various objections which can all be understood as varieties of the Humean objection that behaviour free from determinism is merely chance or random behaviour, which does not reflect what we mean by the notions of freedom or choice and which does not seem to be the way behaviour actually is. For the rest of this chapter, we will see how Sartre's account of the relation between values and projects, along with some suggestive comments he makes elsewhere, allows us to formulate an account of character that is Sartrean in all respects except that it is compatible with determinism. We will see, that is, that Sartre's theory of character does not require his theory of radical freedom.

Consider again the passage discussed at the beginning of this chapter. Sartre claims there that it is 'senseless to think of complaining since nothing foreign has decided what we feel, what we live, or what we are' (B&N: 574). If my life were just the pursuit of a set of projects with a consistent set of aims and values, then why should I ever think of complaining about anything? That the world or other people might frustrate my efforts, of course, could give me reason to complain, but this is not the kind of complaint that Sartre is objecting to here. His point is rather that I cannot complain about the demands the world is making of me, because the world only makes those demands because of the projects that I am pursuing. These demands reflect my own aims. So if my pursuit of projects were to lead to consistent sets of values reflected in the articulation of the world for me, why would I ever want to complain?

We can ask the same question in relation to Sartre's idea of existential psychoanalysis: why would anyone ever be motivated to seek out analysis if their motives always reflected a consistent set of projects? Patients are presumably generally unhappy about some aspect of their lives, but where does this unhappiness come from if their values simply reflect what they are doing? Again, that they might be unhappy about external frustrations is not to the point, because nobody seeks psychoanalysis to help with that kind of problem: they must be unhappy with themselves, which requires a felt dissonance between at least some of their character traits and at least some of their values. To put it another way, if what I want is determined by what I do, then how could I be unhappy about what I do?

The answer, of course, is that there is no reason to suppose that one's set of projects ground a consistent set of values. The character of Daniel is a case in point. Were he unaware of the deep reason why he is unable to drown his cats, were he to face similar problems regularly, then he might indeed complain that he is always unable to go through with his plans and perhaps seek to find out why. Since the values of some projects conflict with the values of deeper ones, Daniel might abandon the deeper project in favour of leading a life in which his aims are more often achieved. Sartre might seem to argue against this idea when he writes that my rejection of my project of inferiority 'could in no way find its motifs and mobiles in' any project pursued as a way of proving myself inferior, 'not even in the suffering and shame which I experience, for the latter are designed expressly to realize my project of inferiority' (B&N: 497). Such suffering and shame cannot themselves motivate me to root out their cause, that is, because they are precisely what my inferiority project aims at: they are therefore suffering and shame that, deep down, I welcome and do not want to be rid of. This thought is perfectly compatible, however, with the further claim that the continuing suffering and shame brought about by the successive failure of my projects might conflict with some other project of mine, such as one of being happy, and together with this other project provide me with genuine motivation for rooting out the cause of my suffering and shame.

Sartre does not consider this further idea, because in this passage he is considering the inferiority project as the fundamental project the individual pursues. It therefore sets the parameters within which all of that individual's projects are pursued, as we saw in chapter 4, so the individual cannot be pursuing any project, such as a project of being happy, that will conflict with it. People pursuing this fundamental project might go through the motions of aiming to be happy, of course, but this would just be another move in the inferiority game. They might complain about their problem, perhaps even visit a psychoanalyst, but this would be a charade since they cannot really have any aims that are not encompassed within the inferiority project. Motivation for abandoning one project can be found in other projects, that is to say, when the outcomes of that project conflict with the values of those other projects, but this simply cannot arise when the one project in question is fundamental and hence all of the agent's other projects are determinations of it.

The only way out of the inferiority project that Sartre discusses in this passage is by a radical conversion: since 'at each moment I apprehend this initial choice as contingent and unjustifiable', he writes, I am always 'well placed' (*á pied d'oeuvre*) to 'surpass it and make-it-past' (*le dépasser et le passéifier*) by simply embarking on a new project in its place (B&N: 497). We can reject a project at any time without any motivation for doing so, that is, because we are always to some extent aware that it is merely a contingent fact about ourselves. We have already seen in this chapter a number of reasons not to accept the idea of unmotivated revisions to our projects. We can add a criticism specific to this claim about rejecting the inferiority project. It is central to Sartre's account of this project that it is not just deep, or even fundamental, but that it is buried: one could not pursue such a project while explicitly admitting so to oneself; one's strategies for pursuing it must involve occluding it from one's view. In which case, one simply is not well placed to see that it is merely a contingent aspect of oneself, since one cannot see that it is an aspect of oneself at all.

Unmotivated radical conversion is not, however, the only available way of revising one's fundamental project, according to Sartre. The inferiority project is an unrepresentative example, since someone pursuing it does not really value achieving their other goals, but rather values failing to achieve them. Sartre considers bad faith, on the other hand, to be a fundamental project whose rejection can be motivated by values rooted in projects pursued within its parameters. Our social and interpersonal lives are constrained by bad faith to involve only projects from a given range, he argues. But these projects will always be experienced as inadequate for achieving the goal of bad faith. Experiencing this inadequacy motivates replacing one such project with another. It is the project 'itself which furnishes us with the motifs for getting out of it' (B&N: 403). Sartre aims to show us that all such projects are inadequate, as we will see in chapter 10, because he thinks that realising this will motivate us to abandon the deeper project that drives them, the project of bad faith.

Sartre's argument here builds on details of his philosophy that we will consider during the next few chapters. One complication is that the contrast just drawn between the inferiority project and bad faith as two possible fundamental projects is a little misleading: Sartre in fact holds the inferiority project to be a form of bad faith, as we will see in chapter 8, but this does not substantially alter his point that our frustrations in achieving the goal of bad faith can lead us to abandon that goal even if it is our most fundamental one. It is important, therefore, not to generalise the comments about abandoning the inferiority project. He does not mean them to illustrate the lack of any possible motivation for abandoning any fundamental project. Neither does he mean that values rooted in the determinations of a given project cannot motivate abandoning that deeper, determinable project. His point rests on the peculiarity of the inferiority project, that it specifically aims at frustrating one's other projects.

We can accept Sartre's picture of the hierarchy of projects, the relation of values to projects, and our ability to change any of these projects however deep it is, therefore, without also accepting his view that we can alter our projects without any motivation for doing so. Any uncharacteristic actions that inaugurate new deep projects in place of old, that is, need not be understood as unmotivated or random. We could rather agree with Hume that when we cannot account for someone's behaviour in terms of what we know of their character, we ought to assume that 'contrariety proceeds from the operation of contrary and concealed causes' (*Treatise*, book 2 part 3 § 1). We could agree, that is, that the 'most irregular and unexpected resolutions of men may frequently be accounted for by those who know every particular circumstance of their character and situation' (Hume, *Enquiry*, § 8 part 1).

We could combine this, moreover, with the idea that although the way a project is pursued is not determined by that project itself, it is determined by the total set of one's projects, or at least is so in all but trivial respects. Doing so would allow us to retain the claim that it is senseless to complain about the demands the world makes of us, since those demands reflect our projects and there is no project that cannot be abandoned, and the description of anguish as awareness of this relation between the world's demands and our projects. These alterations would therefore seem to leave Sartrean existentialism largely untouched while overcoming the Humean objections to the indeterminism involved in Sartre's own formulations of it. It would also provide, as we will see in chapter 8, a framework for understanding why each individual pursues the particular projects they pursue. The ontology of being and nothingness that underlies his existentialism would need to be altered or even abandoned, of course, but a different ontology could be provided.

Perhaps it was recognising these points that led Sartre to revise his theory of the roots of action in his later writings. As his career progressed after *Being and Nothingness*, he became increasingly interested in the influence of upbringing and social position on the projects people pursue. As he filled in this historical aspect of the individual, he seemed to close the gaps in which chance resides in his early philosophy: the gap between a project and the way that project is pursued and the gap where projects are adopted or rejected without any motivation. His later claims that he has never abandoned existentialism could be read as indicating a continuing commitment to the theory that character consists in projects, even though he had famously abandoned the emphasis on radical freedom. To show that this is the correct reading of the progression of Sartre's thought, however, would be a large task outside the scope of this book.

6 Anguish, Bad Faith, and Sincerity

One of the most famous claims of *Being and Nothingness* is that we are aware to some extent of our freedom and the responsibility that comes with it, but we try to hide this from ourselves. We are aware, claims Sartre, that the pressures and demands that the world presents to us are the result of the ways in which we see and engage with things, and that this in turn is the result of our changeable characters rather than any fixed natures. But explicitly thinking about this induces in us a feeling of anguish (*angoisse*). In order to avoid this, we try to deny this responsibility for the way we are and the ways in which we behave. This is what Sartre calls 'bad faith' (*mauvaise foi*). To be more precise, he uses this term in more than one way. In its most general sense, it labels the attempt to deny the basic structure of human being, that the way an individual sees the world is determined by that individual's character, which in turn can be changed by that individual. We deny this by pretending our characters are fixed and unchangeable.

Sartre also uses the term in a more restricted sense, to label one of the two principal kinds of bad faith in the more general sense. The denial of the structure of human existence, that is, can take either of two forms, according to the theory of *Being and Nothingness*, one of which Sartre labels 'sincerity' (*sincérité*) or occasionally 'candour' (*franchise*), the other of which he labels 'bad faith' (*mauvaise foi*). This double use of the same phrase, its having both a general and a more specific sense, has understandably caused some confusion among commentators over just what Sartre thinks bad faith is all about.

Bad faith in the general sense is the affirmation of what Sartre calls 'psychological determinism', which he describes as 'a reflective defence against anguish' that 'provides us with a *nature* productive of our acts' (B&N: 64; see also B&N: 67–8). To deny our responsibility for the ways in which the world is articulated for us and the ways in which we behave in response to that articulation, we tend to think of ourselves as having fixed and unchangeable characters that determine these things. The difference between the two species of this attitude concerns the relation between our actual characters and the fixed natures that we ascribe to ourselves: sincerity is taking one's

Anguish, Bad Faith, and Sincerity 75

actual character to be fixed, whereas bad faith in the narrow sense is ascribing to oneself a fixed nature that is different from one's actual character.

Although Sartre considers this attitude of excuse to be a motivated denial of the radical freedom of which we are in some sense aware, his descriptions of this attitude do not require that kind of freedom. His account of bad faith in general, that is, does not require that we do indeed have the ability to alter or overthrow our projects without any motivation whatsoever for doing so. It is perfectly compatible with the revised Sartrean account of freedom recommended in the last chapter. So long as our character traits consist in projects that we have chosen, so long as each of these projects can be revised and replaced, and so long as we have some awareness that the demands the world seems to make and the ways in which we respond to those demands result from these character traits, then we might seek to deny all of this by adopting the attitude that our characters are fixed and determine our actions.

Many commentators, however, have taken sincerity to be the only kind of bad faith to involve ascribing to oneself a fixed character of any sort, and have taken the other kind of bad faith to involve the denial that one has any character or essence at all. In this chapter, we will see why commentators have been led to various forms of this interpretation, but also why this interpretation is mistaken. Both kinds of bad faith in the general sense involve the affirmation of psychological determinism, which is why Sartre describes this as 'the basis of all attitudes of excuse' (B&N: 64).

The usual misreading is not only due to Sartre's confusing use of the term 'bad faith' in both a general and a restricted sense. It is also due to his failure to mark clearly the distinction between extensional and intensional varieties of statements ascribing conscious states. Somebody can be aware *of* something without registering *that* it is the case: if Lois Lane is unaware that Clark Kent is Superman, then when she sees Superman standing before her she does nonetheless *see Clark Kent* standing before her even though she does not *see that Clark Kent is* standing before her; the sentence 'Lois Lane sees Clark Kent standing before her' is, in this case, true in its extensional but not its intensional sense. The statement 'Lois Lane sees Superman standing before her', on the other hand, is true in both senses. When Sartre gives examples of bad faith, he sometimes describes the agent as being aware *of* their freedom without clarifying whether he also thinks that they are aware *that* they are free to change their character. He sometimes means such sentences in their extensional senses without clarifying whether he thinks they are also true in their intensional senses. We will see that understanding that Sartre fails to mark this distinction is crucial to interpreting his discussion of bad faith, and we will see in chapter 9 that it is also crucial to understanding his account of interpersonal relations.

Sartre describes bad faith in the general sense as an attitude towards the relation between the two cardinal structures of human existence, facticity and transcendence. In this attitude, we 'affirm facticity as *being* transcendence and transcendence as *being* facticity' so that in thinking about either one of these I find myself 'abruptly faced with the other' (B&N: 79). We have already seen in chapter 2 the ways in which commentators often misunderstand these terms. They typically take one's facticity to include only one's past and the material facts about one's body and environment, and typically understand transcendence to be the same as freedom. We should rather understand facticity to include one's character as well as one's past and material body and surroundings, where this character consists in the set of projects that one is pursuing and that one can alter, and we should understand transcendence as the ability to move beyond one's current situation into a new one, an ability that Sartre considers to involve freedom but which would still be a form of transcendence if it did not. We can summarise Sartre's position, using some of the sartrais defined in chapter 2, by saying that one's facticity includes one's essence and it is because this essence is not a nature that one can transcend one's facticity freely.

By describing bad faith in the general sense as the attempt to identify facticity with transcendence, therefore, Sartre is claiming that in bad faith we attempt to think of our ability to go beyond the current situation as itself identical with our character, past, and material body and surroundings. This involves taking one's character to be fixed in the same way as the other aspects of one's facticity are fixed. Were this set of facts entirely unchangeable, then it would indeed determine the way one behaves, just as the nature of an acorn or an axe determines what it does in any given situation. The claim that transcendence involves freedom, on the other hand, requires that at least some aspect of facticity is changeable, and this can only be character. So long as we understand the meaning of Sartre's terms 'facticity' and 'transcendence' correctly, therefore, we can see that his claim that bad faith in the general sense is the attempt to identify the two rules out the possibility of a kind of bad faith that denies that one has any character at all.

Sartre's well-known description of the behaviour of a café waiter provides an excellent illustration of this. 'His movement is quick and forward, a little too precise, a little too rapid' as he is 'trying to imitate in his walk the inflexible stiffness of some kind of automaton while carrying his tray with the recklessness of a tightrope walker' precisely because 'he is playing *at being* a waiter in a café' (B&N: 82). Sartre italicises here to emphasise that what the waiter is playing at is being a waiter in the sense in which 'this inkwell is an inkwell, or the glass is a glass' (B&N: 83). In one sense, he does not need to play at being a waiter because that is precisely what he is, rather than a journalist or a diplomat. But in another sense, of course, he is not just a waiter, because he does not have fixed waiterly properties that determine what he does in the way in which the properties of a coffee machine determine what it does. Nobody is really a waiter in this sense, the set of fixed waiterly properties is simply an ideal to which waiters are to aspire. This waiter is acting as though he has this nature, when in fact he does not. He is attempting to 'realise' the 'being in-itself of the café waiter' and is doing so in order to pretend that it is not within his power to resist the demands of his job and do something else instead (B&N: 83).

To be more precise, the waiter exemplifies one kind of bad faith in the general sense. His behaviour manifests properties that he really does have, including dispositions to treat the customers well and to keep the café clean, but these are not fixed in the way that he pretends that they are. His behaviour therefore manifests sincerity. Of course, Sartre also uses the term 'bad faith' in a restricted sense to mean the kind of bad faith that involves denying some aspect of one's character. In this sense, then, Anthony Manser is right to claim that the waiter is not an intended as an example of bad faith ('A New Look at Bad Faith', 66). Manser means that the waiter is an example of sincerity, but his point is obscured by two terminological difficulties. One is that he does not distinguish the general sense of 'bad faith' from the restricted sense so although he uses the term in its restricted sense it is not immediately clear that he does. The other is that he uses the term 'good faith' to label what we have been calling sincerity. We will see in the next chapter that this use is mistaken, although there are close connections between what Sartre means by 'good faith' and his notion of sincerity.

Two other commentators have recently denied that the waiter is in bad faith in the general sense, however, and understanding why they are mistaken to do so will provide us with further insight into the nature of bad faith in general. These commentators draw attention to two aspects of the example that are often overlooked: that the waiter's exaggerated gestures caricature the ideal of a waiter and thereby betray his awareness that he is merely playing at being a waiter, and that this behaviour is a response to the social pressure exerted by his customers (Cox, *Sartre*, 101–4; Bernasconi, *How To Read Sartre*, ch. 4).

This interpretation fails to grasp the importance of Sartre's insistence that bad faith in the general sense is not an honest mistake or a conceptual confusion, but rather a form of self-deception motivated by awareness of the freedom whose full acknowledgement induces anguish. This requires that the waiter be aware that his behaviour has this purpose. Sartre takes the exaggerated gestures of the waiter to betray this awareness, to betray the fact that he does not wholly believe that he has a fixed waiterly nature. It is this aspect of bad faith in general that raises the puzzle of self-deception: how can people persuade themselves of something that they are aware is not the case? Sartre's response to this question will be explained across this chapter and the next, and is central to the account of his theory of interpersonal relations presented in chapters 8 and 9. What is important here is simply that Sartre claims that the waiter behaves in this exaggerated fashion in order 'to attempt to realize . . . a being-in-itself of a café waiter, as if it were not in [his] power to confer value and urgency on [his] duties and the rights of [his] position, as if it were not [his] free choice to get up each morning at five o'clock or to remain in bed, even though it meant getting fired' (B&N: 83).

The commentators who deny that the waiter is in bad faith, however, also deny that his behaviour is aimed at pretending to himself that he has no freedom over his actions, no choice but to behave in certain ways. They argue that this impersonation of waiterhood is rather motivated by the demands of the customers. To an extent, they are right to draw attention to this social dimension of bad faith since it is often overlooked. In the middle of his discussion of the waiter, Sartre explicitly turns his attention to the expectations that accompany social roles and describes them as 'precautions to imprison a man in what he is' that seem to be motivated by 'fear that he might escape from it, that he might break away and suddenly elude his condition' (B&N: 83). The customers demand that the waiter present himself as nothing but a waiter, as having the fixed nature of a waiter, and do so presumably because they prefer to believe that people in general, and hence they themselves, have fixed natures. This is why 'a grocer who dreams is offensive to the buyer, because such a grocer is not wholly a grocer' (B&N: 82). Earlier in *Being and Nothingness*, Sartre draws attention to the social dimension of bad faith when he describes 'alarm clocks, signboards, tax forms, policemen' as 'guard rails against anguish' (B&N: 63). Our strategies for refusing to acknowledge the true nature of our existence help to shape the world around us. We will see the importance of this aspect of bad faith in more detail in the next three chapters.

Although the example of the waiter is partly designed to highlight this social dimension of bad faith, it is mistaken to claim that the waiter himself is not in bad faith and only his customers are. We have already seen that Sartre also emphasises the waiter's motivation of refusing to acknowledge that he has any real choice in his lifestyle and the patterns of behaviour imposed by his job. What is more, Sartre immediately follows the example of the waiter by telling us that 'we are dealing with more than mere social positions; I am never any one of my attitudes, any one of my actions' (B&N: 83). He is here emphasising that the social motivation for the waiter's behaviour is not the only one.

This point is submerged by his following it with two further examples that do involve social roles: the attentive pupil and the public speaker. The first of these concentrates on acting as though he had the nature of an attentive pupil and thereby fails to pay attention to the teacher, but the second is a successfully fluent public speaker precisely because he takes the ability to speak in public to be part of his nature (B&N: 83–4). (This second example is somewhat obscured by the translation of *'beau parleur'* as 'glib speaker', which would be appropriate if 'glib' meant only fluent and well-prepared, but is inappropriate due to its connotation of being shallow and facile.) Despite the social expectations concerning pupils and public speakers, these are examples of people identifying with a set of properties as though these determine their behaviour and are intended to underscore this aspect of the waiter's behaviour.

We should therefore read the example of the waiter as illustrating the motivated strategy of refusing to acknowledge one's responsibility for the demands that the world seems to make and one's behaviour in response to those demands by behaving in ways designed to persuade oneself that these are accounted for by one's nature, which is fixed and beyond one's control, though we should also bear in mind that such strategies have social aspects including the expectation that other people behave in ways that seem to manifest their fixed natures. The qualities that actually explain the waiter's continuing in the job are in fact rooted in the waiter's projects, which can be revised and replaced. Notice that this does not require Sartre's view that such revision or replacement can be entirely unmotivated, so this account of bad faith can be retained if the theory of radical freedom is rejected, as recommended in the last chapter.

Notice also that, as mentioned earlier, the waiter is thereby taking as fixed some qualities that he does genuinely possess, rather than falsifying his qualities themselves. His bad faith is therefore of the kind that Sartre calls 'sincerity': this kind 'does not assign to me a mode of being or a particular quality, but in relation to that quality it aims at making me pass from one mode of being to another' (B&N: 89). The very fact that we are often asked to aspire to sincerity or candour, argues Sartre, shows that we do not actually have the fixed properties that we are thereby being asked to own up to. Were character genuinely fixed, were we to possess natures rather than revisable essences, our words and deeds could only manifest our true natures, so sincerity or candour would not be an ideal to aspire to but would rather be the permanent state of our existence (B&N: 82). The demand that people be sincere about their own characters, therefore, seems to be something that Sartre considers another social manifestation of bad faith: our own beliefs in our own fixed natures will be reinforced by such avowals from others.

The other kind of bad faith in general, bad faith in the restricted sense in which Sartre uses that term, involves falsifying one's character: the fixed nature that one ascribes to oneself does not adequately reflect one's actual qualities. Sartre describes two different varieties of bad faith in this restricted sense. One involves denying one's actual character by ascribing to oneself a nature comprised of qualities that are opposed to one's actual character, such as considering oneself brave when one is in fact cowardly. The other is more subtle, and involves identifying with some aspects of one's character to the exclusion of others, thereby effectively denying those other qualities. This variety of bad faith might be employed to deny one's own cowardice by considering the relevant actions to flow from prudence and a sense of responsibility, where in fact one does possess these qualities alongside one's cowardice.

Before considering in detail Sartre's discussion of these two varieties of bad faith in the restricted sense, however, we need to see why an influential alternative interpretation of these passages is mistaken. This is the reading that holds bad faith in the restricted sense to be the outright denial of facticity altogether, and the identification of oneself with one's transcendence. The most detailed presentation of this interpretation is Manser's paper, 'A New Look at Bad Faith'. This takes Sartre's term 'transcendence' to mean not the ability to surpass one's current situation toward a new situation, the ability to move beyond the current facts about one's self and surroundings, but rather 'the ability to take up different attitudes to these facts and to attempt to change some of them' (59).

Most of the time, we are absorbed in what we are doing and as a result see the world as a situation that we are in and that makes demands of us. But we can take up a different perspective and reflect instead on ourselves and our relation to our situations. Manser understands this to involve the kind of external perspective that we can have on someone else's behaviour, and indeed others can have on ours. Taking up this perspective, we find that the demands the world appears to make of us are simply the function of our values and commitments. We transcend our situations, on Manser's reading of Sartre, not by simply moving beyond them, but by taking up this kind of perspective on them. This perspective is necessary for the exercise of freedom over our motivations: changing our characters requires understanding the roots of our behaviour patterns, and this requires reflection on the structure of our usual, absorbed, unreflective behaviour. Manser is not alone in this understanding of 'transcendence'. It appears in Catalano's *A Commentary on Jean-Paul Sartre's Being and Nothingness* (82–3), which perhaps influenced Manser, and it seems to underlie McCulloch's equation of transcendence with freedom and his emphasis in this connection on our ability to reflect on our motivations and change them (*Using Sartre*, 36–44, 56–62). It also seems to underlie the reading favoured by Cox and Reisman, according to whom one kind of bad faith involves identifying oneself with one's transcendence as something self-contained in isolation from one's facticity (*Sartre*, 98, 115; *Sartre's Phenomenology*, 118–19).

This reading is partly motivated by Sartre's example of the unhappy homosexual and his friend, the 'champion of sincerity': the unhappy homosexual feels guilty about his past sexual behaviour and wants to deny that he is genuinely homosexual, but his friend wants him to accept that he is by nature homosexual and to consider his past sexual behaviour as determined by this fixed nature; Sartre tells us that both of these characters are in bad faith (B&N: 87). This passage does seem to involve a commitment to the idea that sexuality is an aspect of character and under our control, which might well seem questionable. We will return to this issue in chapter 11, but for the purposes of understanding Sartre's account of bad faith we should read this example as though we agree with him on this point. Sartre wants this example to illustrate the two main kinds of bad faith in the general sense, and it seems clear that the champion of sincerity does indeed illustrate the form that Sartre calls 'sincerity': he wants his friend to accept certain of his qualities and understand them as a fixed nature.

It is less clear exactly what the unhappy homosexual himself is doing, however. It is clear that Sartre takes him to be denying qualities that he does in fact possess. Catalano, Manser, McCulloch, Cox, and Reisman take him to be denying that his facticity is any real part of him. Since they take facticity to include only one's past, material body, and material surroundings, they take him to be denying that these are real aspects of him and identifying himself with just his ability to take a disengaged perspective on these things and to behave differently in future. Heter presents a slightly different reading, according to which the unhappy homosexual is simply refusing to accept the term 'homosexual' as the correct way of summarising the patterns in his past behaviour (*Sartre's Ethics of Engagement*, 64–6, 70; see also Morris, *Sartre's Concept of a Person*, 149). If we allow that facticity also includes qualities of character, as we saw in chapter 2 that we should, then this reading takes the unhappy homosexual to be denying that he has any genuine qualities as well.

This reading of the example might appear to be supported by Sartre's claim that the goal of this kind of bad faith, bad faith in the restricted sense, can be expressed as 'to be what I am, in the mode of "not being what one is", or not to be what I am in the mode of "being what one is"' (B&N: 89). This rather obscure sentence might be read as claiming that in this kind of bad faith, one identifies oneself with that aspect of oneself that prevents one from being merely identical with one's facticity. The two parts of this sentence would be alternative formulations of this same idea: the first talking of identifying myself with the aspect of me that prevents me from being identical with the predicates that correctly describe me, the second talking of refusing to allow that those predicates correctly describe me at all.

The problem with this reading of this sentence and the example in general, however, is that the account of bad faith in the restricted sense of the term that they support is inconsistent with some of the things that Sartre says about bad faith in the general sense of the term. As we have already seen, Sartre describes bad faith in general as understanding 'facticity as *being* transcendence and transcendence as *being* facticity' (B&N: 79). But this seems a wholly inappropriate description of someone who identifies with their transcendence and denies their facticity. It also seems an inappropriate description of sincerity if we are to agree with Catalano, Manser, McCulloch, and Cox that Sartre intends the term 'transcendence' in this context to indicate the freedom we have over our characters and the demands the world appears to make of us. For sincerity is precisely the denial of this freedom, the pretence that one's facticity is all that there is to one.

Moreover, Sartre describes belief in 'psychological determinism' as 'the basis of all attitudes of excuse' (B&N: 64), as we saw at the beginning of this chapter. The psychological determinism he has in mind is the idea that we have fixed natures that explain our thoughts, feelings, and actions. If that is genuinely the basis of all attitudes of excuse, then it cannot be that we sometimes make excuses for ourselves by denying that we have any qualities or any facticity at all and instead identifying ourselves with our ability to freely transcend our situations. Sartre also argues that these excuses are motivated by the anguish induced by the recognition that the demands the world appears to make of us and the invitations it appears to offer us are the result of our own changeable aims and projects. Why is the unhappy homosexual not put off identifying himself with his freedom by the anguish involved in the recognition of freedom? This account of bad faith in the narrow sense seems to remove the motivation for sincerity: if this man can happily accept his freedom, what is stopping the waiter and the champion of sincerity from doing the same? The answer to this cannot simply be that the unhappy homosexual has a particular motivation that these other characters lack and so is content to endure the anguish in order to deny his facticity, since there is another strategy open to him that would avoid the anguish altogether: to identify himself with a fixed nature that explains his actions in a way consistent with his not actually being homosexual.

This is in fact the strategy that Sartre ascribes to the unhappy homosexual when he writes that this man affirms that he is not homosexual 'in the sense in which this table is *not* an inkwell' (B&N: 87): the table does not simply lack the fixed nature of an inkwell, it also possesses the fixed nature of a table. This man ascribes to himself the fixed properties of inquisitiveness, adventurousness, and restlessness in order to explain his past conduct in a way consistent with his having the fixed property of heterosexuality. Sartre goes on to say of bad faith in the restricted sense that it 'is not restricted to denying the qualities which I possess, to not seeing the being which I am' but rather 'attempts also to constitute myself as being what I am not', giving the example that I might thus consider myself 'positively as courageous when I am not so' (B&N: 90).

What has misled commentators here is in part Sartre's failure to distinguish clearly between extensional and intensional senses of psychological vocabulary. Sartre writes that the unhappy homosexual 'has an obscure but strong feeling that an homosexual is not an homosexual as this table is this table or a red-haired man is red-haired' (B&N: 87). The man is aware that he does not have the property of homosexuality in the way that tables have properties like height and weight that determine their behaviour in given situations. But this does not mean that he has correctly identified his freedom over his character in any explicit way: he is aware *of* this freedom, but not necessarily aware *that* he has it, which is why Sartre describes this awareness as an 'obscure' feeling. Instead of reflecting on this feeling in a way that might make its content explicit, that might bring him to be aware *that* he has a certain freedom over his character, the unhappy homosexual 'slides surreptitiously toward a different connotation of the word "being"' and concludes that homosexuality is not part of the nature he does possess

(B&N: 87). His attitude does include 'an undeniable comprehension of the truth', which explains his 'refusal to be considered as a thing' in the way that the champion of sincerity wants to consider him, but this should not be taken as an indication of his insistence on his own freedom (B&N: 87). This comprehension should be understood in an extensional rather than an intensional way: his refusal of the champion of sincerity's proposal does not involve the explicit acknowledgement of freedom.

This idea of an obscure feeling, a comprehension of the truth, should be understood in terms of the concept of 'non-positional', 'non-thetic', 'pre-judicative' awareness that Sartre develops across *Being and Nothingness*. Sartre intends such awareness to play a role in motivating certain kinds of attitudes while not being so explicit that we can report it or form beliefs on the basis of it. We have this kind of awareness of our freedom, which allows us to adopt motivated strategies for refusing to explicitly acknowledge or believe in that freedom. The nature and possibility of such awareness need not concern us here. All that matters is that we bear in mind that Sartre does not always clearly signal his use of psychological vocabulary with reference to this vague, inexplicit, undetailed kind of awareness, despite his stated intention to do so (B&N: 10). As a result, he does not clearly mark the distinction between his extensional and his intensional uses of psychological vocabulary.

We can see this at work in Sartre's description of the champion of sincerity as motivated by his awareness of freedom. Sartre tells us that he must be aware of this since he tells his friend that if he acknowledges his true homosexual nature then he need no longer be bound by it. He is aware, therefore, that we do not praise and blame people for things that flow from their fixed properties, which is why 'such a confession will win indulgence for him' (B&N: 87). The champion of sincerity, Sartre tells us, is therefore partly motivated by his awareness that if his friend's homosexuality is part of his nature then he need not feel guilty about it, which implies that he need feel guilty only about things that are within the ambit of his freedom. But this awareness of freedom is not an explicit acknowledgement of it: the champion of sincerity is motivated not only by the desire to help his friend, but also by his desire to suppress his awareness of his own freedom. He is 'in bad faith to the degree that he wants to reassure himself, while pretending to judge': classifying someone else in this way is 'reassuring' because it 'removes a disturbing freedom from a trait' (B&N: 88). Like the waiter's clientele, the champion of sincerity makes demands of other people in order to bolster his pretence that people have fixed natures that determine their behaviour, in order to avoid the anguish induced by his awareness of his own freedom.

The example of the unhappy homosexual is therefore consistent with the idea that bad faith in the general sense is the attempt to persuade oneself that one has a fixed nature in order to avoid acknowledging one's responsibility for the way the world seems to one and the way one behaves in response to it. As the example of the waiter makes clear, this is not a merely mental exercise. Rather than a simple attempt to directly manipulate one's beliefs by telling oneself a lie, this involves publicly observable behaviour that one can understand as emanating from one's fixed nature and that can help to persuade others that one has such a nature so that they then treat one accordingly and thereby further support one's belief in this nature. The demand that others behave as though they have fixed natures is motivated in the same way: such behaviour from them will strengthen the impression that people generally have fixed natures, which will help to support the idea that one has such a nature oneself.

Sartre divides such strategies into two kinds, as we have seen, according to the relation between the fixed nature that the agent wishes to manifest and the qualities that agent actually possesses: sincerity involves taking one's actual qualities to be fixed, and bad faith in the restricted sense involves denying one's qualities. Bad faith in this restricted sense is motivated by the dim awareness that we do not possess our qualities in the way that mere objects possess their properties, so it occurs only because we are aware of not having fixed natures. Bad faith in the restricted sense, moreover, comes in two varieties and so far we have only considered an example of one of them. The unhappy homosexual denies qualities he actually possesses by considering himself to have a fixed heterosexual nature. The other variety is exemplified in Sartre's description of a particular woman out to dinner for the first time with a man whose sexual advances she is well aware of but would prefer not to acknowledge.

Sartre tells us that she is flattered by his attentions but does not want to be simply the object of bodily desire, but neither does she want to be the object of a purely personal attraction with no physical aspect to it. What she wants is for his desire to 'address itself to her body as object' but at the same time to be 'a recognition of her freedom' (B&N: 78). Sartre means this in an extensional rather than an intensional sense, which allows him to say that this is what she wants even though 'she does not quite know what she wants' (B&N: 78). She finds uncomfortable the thought that his desire might be wholly concerned with her body rather than her as an embodied person, and Sartre considers this discomfort to manifest an awareness of her freedom. But this awareness is not an explicit acknowledgement of that freedom, for if it were she would know what it is that she wants.

Her first tactic is to think of the man she is with as himself having a fixed nature that accounts for his words and actions in order to understand these as being directed towards her in the way that she finds acceptable. Sartre tells us that when 'he says to her "I find you so attractive", she disarms this phrase of its sexual background' by taking it quite literally, as a report of the way in which something with the nature he has responds as a matter of course to her: 'she attaches to the conversation and to the behaviour of the speaker the immediate meanings, which she imagines as objective qualities' (B&N: 78). She takes him to be attracted to her as iron is attracted to a magnet or a sunflower to sunlight. He 'appears to her as sincere and respectful as the table is round or square', as having these qualities 'fixed in a permanence like that of things' (B&N: 78). His nature is quite incompatible with his simply using these words as part of a seduction technique.

Her second tactic is in response to his taking her hand: she 'draws her companion up to the most lofty regions of sentimental speculation; she speaks of Life, of her life, she shows herself in her essential aspect—a personality, a consciousness', and through this tactic 'the divorce of the body from the soul is accomplished' (B&N: 79). It is this part of the story that has been interpreted as claiming that the woman is simply denying her facticity and identifying herself with her freedom or transcendence. Manser reads the example this way, understanding the divorce of the soul from the body to indicate her identifying herself with her ability to take a disengaged perspective on her past, her body, and her current situation, and thereby denying that these things are genuinely part of her. He considers her and the unhappy homosexual to be alike in this respect: she is acting as though 'one is one's transcendence in the way that a thing is a thing' ('A New Look at Bad Faith', 59). Cox agrees and explains further that this involves treating transcendence as though it were self-contained, deliberately ignoring that it can only be the transcendence of a particular body in a particular situation (*Sartre*, 98).

It is difficult to see how this can be understood as a tactic for avoiding the anguish induced by recognising one's freedom over one's character and the demands the world appears to make, and how any excuses she makes on the basis of this attitude could be rooted in what Sartre calls 'psychological determinism'. Cox writes that the woman is treating the facts of her situation as though they are 'a transcendent power over her' (*Sartre*, 98), but this does not seem compatible with her considering herself to be her freedom or transcendence. Identifying herself with this free transcendence would require seeing the situation as something over which she has control. It is also difficult to see how this interpretation can explain the relevance of the first tactic that Sartre describes her as employing, that of ascribing a fixed nature to her companion. This part of the story seems wholly irrelevant if we understand the example in this way. What is more, it seems that her first tactic would undermine her employment of the second: if I consider myself to be nothing but a free transcendence, how can I consider someone else not to be such without being acutely aware of the inconsistency?

We can make better sense of this example if we understand this woman to be identifying herself with the intellectual and sentimental aspects of her character, taking these to make up her fixed nature. It is her discomfort at being seen as just a body that inclines her towards emphasising these aspects of herself, but as we have seen this discomfort does not need to involve an explicit acknowledgement of freedom in order to be based on some awareness of it. The reason that this emphasis on the intellectual and sentimental aspects of her character involves identifying herself with a fixed character comprising only these things is that she already has the attitude that people have fixed natures. Bad faith is this underlying attitude. Although she is aware of her freedom, she would rather not acknowledge it. She wants to understand this situation as the interaction of two fixed natures according to the laws that govern them.

Like the unhappy homosexual, this woman is denying certain aspects of her character. Indeed, like him, she is denying her sexuality, but in her case it is not by considering herself to have a different sexuality but rather by considering herself to be wholly sentimental and intellectual, thereby excluding sexuality from herself altogether. Sartre classifies this as a form of bad faith in the restricted sense, because it involves the denial of some of her actual qualities. But this classification is somewhat arbitrary. We could just as well classify the woman on a date together with the waiter and the champion of sincerity, since she is identifying with qualities that she genuinely does possess. She differs from those, of course, in that she is doing so partly in order to deny some other qualities that she possesses. But she also differs from the unhappy homosexual. The arbitrariness of where to classify this case arises from Sartre's division of bad faith in the general sense into two categories that he considers to be exclusive and exhaustive but which are not defined one as the negation of the other. This leaves room for a third kind, exemplified by this woman, that involves both.

This is, nevertheless, Sartre's classification. The two kinds he distinguishes do not differ in the way that Catalano, Manser, McCulloch, Morris, Cox, and Heter take them to, where one is the emphasis of facticity at the expense of transcendence and the other the emphasis of transcendence at the expense of facticity. It is rather that 'the goal of sincerity and the goal of bad faith are not so different' (B&N: 90), where 'bad faith' is here used in the restricted sense. The goal of sincerity is to 'bring me to confess to myself' that I am 'in the mode of the in-itself, what I am in the mode of "not being what I am"' (B&N: 89). It aims to bring me to think of myself as being identical with my qualities, where these are properties that can be correctly ascribed to me but which are not fixed.

The goal of bad faith in the restricted sense, on the other hand, can be expressed in either of these two ways: 'to be what I am, in the mode of "not being what one is", or not to be what I am in the mode of "being what one is"' (B&N: 89). We have already seen how this obscure phrase could be read as stating in two different ways the same strategy of identifying oneself with one's transcendence or freedom, but if the argument of this chapter is right that is the wrong way to read it. We should rather read the two parts of it as expressing the two varieties of bad faith in the restricted sense. The first expresses the bad faith exemplified by the woman on a date, which explains the similarity between it and the phrase Sartre uses to summarise the goal of sincerity: the goal is to identify oneself with some of the properties that one has but with which one is not, in fact, identical. The second expresses the bad faith exemplified by the unhappy homosexual:

it aims to deny some of the properties that one has, by identifying oneself with properties incompatible with them.

None of this requires, of course, that we have the radical freedom that Sartre describes and that we saw in the last chapter to be problematic. This account of the varieties of bad faith rests solely on the idea that the qualities that we have, that explain the way the world seems to us and the way we behave in response, are things that we can change. It does not require that we can do this without any motivation to do so. It does not require, that is, that we can decide to work at changing some aspect of our character without having reasons whose importance to us is itself a result of some other aspect or aspects of our characters. The revised account of freedom recommended in the last chapter, that retains the idea that we can alter our character but insists that can only do so on the basis of some motivation that itself expresses some part of our character, is perfectly compatible with Sartre's account of the ways in which we try to hide from ourselves this freedom over our own characters. The rejection of radical freedom leaves Sartre's account of strategies of bad faith untouched.

Not only that, but what has been said in this chapter does not seem, on the face of it, to require the Sartrean account of character as consisting in projects. It requires only that we can revise our characters if we want to do so, that we are in some sense aware of this, and that we prefer not to acknowledge it. The underlying structure of character that accounts for our freedom over it seems to be, so far as the theory of the content of bad faith is concerned, another matter entirely, so long as that structure does account for this freedom.

But Sartre's discussion of bad faith is not limited to his account of its motivations and strategies. He is well aware that the very idea of deceiving oneself about this freedom seems paradoxical, since it would not be deception unless it involved awareness of both the truth to be denied and the intention to deceive, and awareness of either of these things would seem to prevent one from being deceived. Sartre wants to dispel this appearance of paradox to insist that bad faith is not an attitude occasionally taken up when it suits and is not a purely internal cognitive achievement, but is rather a project that colours the way the world appears to one and flavours the way one behaves in response to the world. This is a project that he considers to be pervasive in our culture. What is more, he considers it to be a fundamental project, one at the very root of an individual's integrated hierarchy of projects, which can and should be replaced by the acceptance and indeed affirmation of the true structure of our existence, a project he calls 'authenticity'. We will consider these claims in detail over the next four chapters.

7 The Project of Bad Faith

Although our characters consist in projects that we freely pursue and can revise, according to Sartre, we generally prefer to consider them to be fixed natures over which we have no control. We would rather not acknowledge our responsibility for the way we are, the way things seem to us, and the way we respond to them. This is the basic aim of bad faith, as we saw in the last chapter, and it is not an honest mistake. Sartre frequently describes it as a project and, as we will see, this project is not merely a cognitive exercise but involves the way we relate to the world around us. The behaviour of the café waiter provides a good example: his gestures are not just those we would expect from someone with fixed waiterly characteristics, they do not merely manifest a belief that the waiter has about himself, but are exaggerations that together present a caricature of such a person, conscientiously enacted to persuade himself and his customers that he is nothing but a waiter. Since bad faith is the project of hiding our freedom from ourselves, the very idea of it raises the difficult and intricate question of how it is even possible for people to hide things from themselves.

This is not just a question for Sartre's philosophy, of course, since it is generally agreed that people do deceive themselves about various things in life. The puzzle arises because it seems that deceiving oneself, like deceiving other people, is a purposive activity that requires the deceiver to know the falsity of the belief to be inculcated and to know their own intention to deceive. We cannot deceive other people without keeping these things from them, it seems, since if they know the falsity of what we want them to believe or if they know that we intend to deceive them, they will simply not fall for it. So self-deception seems to require one and the same person to both know and not know the falsity of the belief they are is trying to inculcate and to both know and not know of their intention to deceive. How is it possible to both know and not know the same things? This is a puzzle rather than an argument against the possibility of self-deception since it is generally agreed that self-deception is possible, even quite common. The point of the puzzle is that solving it should tell us something about the ways in which our minds work.

It might be thought that we do not need to consider this puzzle in order to assess the plausibility of Sartre's theory of the nature and knowledge of character. Since we all agree that self-deception is possible, the argument might run, this is no more a problem for accepting Sartre's philosophy than it is a problem in general. This is not an acceptable response, however. Bad faith involves a specific kind of self-deception, on Sartre's view, in which one is continuously presented with evidence that we do not have fixed natures, in the form of an awareness that we ourselves need not behave in the ways in which we do behave. It therefore requires that self-deception is possible not in cases where one chooses to forget evidence once it is out of sight or in cases in which one chooses not to go looking for any evidence on the matter, but in the face of the continuing presence of evidence to the contrary of the cherished belief.

If we are to accept Sartre's diagnosis of bad faith as a strategy for denying our freedom over our character, moreover, then we also need to know that self-deception is not simply a matter of being deceived by some unconscious part of the mind whose operations cannot really be said to be strategies that the agent pursues. Sartre devotes some pages at the beginning of his discussion of bad faith to dismissing this picture of self-deception, which he ascribes to Sigmund Freud. This picture presents self-deception as an activity aimed at keeping in the unconscious something that one would rather not consciously acknowledge. Sartre's argument here is somewhat obscured by his conflation of terms from different phases of the development of Freud's thought and by his focus on the notion of resistance, which is the purported phenomenon of a psychoanalytic patient engaging in a variety of strategies to prevent the analyst from getting to the truth. We can pare down Sartre's argument, however, into a form that makes it independent of the acceptability of any particular set of Freudian terminology and even of the veracity of reports of resistance.

The central point is that the purported activity of censorship must involve recognising evidence for the truth that the agent is denying, whether this evidence is in the form of the analyst's probing or any other form, and burying that evidence by outright denial or more evasive strategies such as changing the subject of discussion or simply thinking about something else. The activity of censorship, that is, involves awareness of facts about oneself or one's environment that might constitute evidence, awareness of the nature of the truth to be hidden, awareness that that truth is to remain hidden, awareness of the conflict between the potential evidence and the aim of keeping the truth hidden, and deployment of mental and behavioural strategies in response to this conflict. Far from being mechanical and unthinking, this censorship seems much like any sophisticated conscious activity. Rather than an activity of the nonrational drives and impulses of the unconscious, this seems to involve a process of reasoning.

If this is right, then the Freudian picture of self-deception either collapses or requires an implausible view of the agent, depending on the relation between this conscious activity of censorship and the conscious beliefs the agent possesses. If one thinks that the agent is simply self-deceived about the activity of censorship, engaging in it but somehow hiding this fact, then we are back where we started: the possibility of this self-deception needs to be explained. It appears that the only other option is to consider the activity of censorship to be the work of a second, distinct, autonomous, rational, conscious mind that is capable of directing my thought and my behaviour in response to information from my own senses. This takes us a long way from Freud's intended functional division of our mental activities between the rational ones we are aware of and the nonrational ones we are unaware of.

We do not need to assess the impact of this argument on Freudian psychoanalysis, since our concern in this chapter is with Sartre's alternative account of self-deception. This reconstruction of the argument does, however, tell us three things about Sartre's account. The first, and most obvious, is that he wants to explain bad faith without the kind of unconscious activity that is central to the Freudian understanding of the mind. The second is that he has not here attempted a general critique of the Freudian idea of the unconscious, since his argument has nothing to say about the possibility of drives and appetites that are unconscious but not actively censored. Sartre does present such a general critique in *Sketch for a Theory of the Emotions*. His argument there is essentially that since experiences and actions manifest the aims and projects that rationalise and explain them, there is simply no causal-explanatory role available for purportedly unconscious drives and appetites that cannot be manifested in or rationalise the experiences and actions that they cause (STE: 28–34). We will return to this argument at the end of the chapter, when we consider in more detail just what Sartre's opposition to the Freudian unconscious involves.

The third is that he takes this critique to show that we should not model self-deception on lying to someone else. It is not simply an internal mental procedure in which I quietly tell myself something that I know not to be true and then somehow end up believing it. We can think of bad faith as lying to oneself, Sartre writes, but only 'on condition that we distinguish the lie to oneself from lying in general' (B&N: 71; see also B&N: 90–1). It is to argue for this distinction that Sartre raises the notion of the Freudian unconscious in the first place, which he presents as the only candidate solution to the puzzle of self-deception available if we continue to think of self-deception on the model of lying to someone else. His argument is that on closer inspection this presents no solution at all.

Rather than a reflexive form of lying, Sartre argues, bad faith is more like a reflexive form of distraction (B&N: 77). One does not tell oneself something untrue, but tries to steer one's mind away from the truth and perhaps towards things that suggest some contrary idea. Such distraction is not some purely internal exercise of which behaviour can be only an effect, but rather involves behaviour as part of the strategy. This does not, on its own, solve the puzzle of self-deception that Sartre is faced with, however. In order to distract you from the nearby cliff-edge that fills you with fear, I need to be aware that the cliff-edge is there and fills you with fear and I need to be aware that I am distracting you from it. You can be successfully distracted even if you are aware that this is what I am doing, but only by being absorbed by my behaviour to the exclusion of thinking about the cliff edge or my reasons for behaving in this way now. It is not clear how one could do this to oneself, since one's motivation for continually doing so involves an awareness of precisely what one would be trying to exclude from one's awareness.

Understanding bad faith as self-distraction rather than self-deception is, nevertheless, integral to Sartre's account of bad faith. Before unpacking that account, we need to be aware of two ways in which Sartre's theory of bad faith is more complicated than the discussion in the last chapter implies. Where that chapter describes Sartre as using the term 'bad faith' in two senses, one general and the other more restricted, this is not quite true. It is true that he uses it in both of those senses. It is also true that he uses it in a general sense to indicate the aim of seeing oneself as having a fixed nature and in a restricted sense to indicate the aim of seeing oneself as having a fixed nature that does not include certain traits that one does in fact possess. But it is also true that Sartre sometimes uses the term in another sense, one in which it has already been used in this chapter. This sense does not refer to the content of the strategies of self-deception that he discusses, but rather to the structure or form of those strategies. He uses the term in this sense interchangeably with 'self-deception', and bad faith in this sense is what this chapter is all about. What is more, as we will see, Sartre also uses the term 'bad faith' to refer to a certain attitude towards evidence that is involved in this self-deception or self-distraction. All of this has generated some confusion.

The second complication is that, in addition to the two forms of bad faith in the general sense discussed in the last chapter, sincerity and the restricted sense of bad faith, Sartre talks about an aspect of bad faith that he calls *'l'esprit de sérieux'*, usually translated as 'the spirit of seriousness' but which might be better rendered 'serious-mindedness' or just 'seriousness' (B&N: 601). This is the attitude that takes the demands the world appears to make to be genuinely independent of one's own projects, genuinely objective values in the world that are there to be recognised by anyone and that make the same demands of all of us. This should not be understood as another form of bad faith, one that is concerned with the structure of the world rather than with one's own character, however. It is rather a strategy that one can pursue as part of the project of seeing people as having fixed natures, as we will see later in this chapter.

At the heart of Sartre's account of the structure of bad faith, of the self-deception or self-distraction involved in seeing ourselves as having fixed natures, is his insistence on understanding it not simply as an action or an event or a process, but as the ongoing pursuit of a goal—in short, as a *project*. The exaggerated behaviour of the waiter is part of this project, since he engages in it in order to provide himself with evidence of his fixed waiterly nature. So too is the attitude of his customers, since this manifests their requirement that the waiter provides for them evidence that people have fixed natures, or at least does not provide evidence to the contrary. Sartre does not mean his descriptions of characters in bad faith to simply show symptoms of this condition: the behaviour is not caused by an inner mental condition of bad faith, but is itself part and parcel of the project of bad faith.

This is not to say that Sartre thinks that bad faith always and necessarily involves such excessive behaviour as displayed by his example of the waiter, however. Were it his view that we can only attempt to display a fixed nature by caricaturing it, then his apparent view that bad faith is very common, even socially pervasive, would seem to be at best a diagnosis of a certain kind of requirement made by the society around him at the time, at worst plainly false. After all, in Paris these days, it is only in the cafés near the busy crossroads now named Place Sartre-Beauvoir—the Flore and the Deux Magots that Sartre and his colleagues famously frequented—that the waiters behave in the extravagant yet mechanical way Sartre describes while their customers carry the accoutrements and strike the poses of archetypal post-war French intellectuals without the merest hint of irony.

Most people in bad faith engage in rather more subtle behaviour: Sartre's other examples, of the woman on a date, the unhappy homosexual, and his friend the champion of sincerity, do not involve the kind of self-conscious caricaturing that the waiter engages in. Pursuing a project, moreover, does not require that the behaviour aimed at pursuing it is explicitly thought of in this way by the person engaging in it, and part of the point of understanding bad faith as a project is that this will help us understand how this self-deception is possible. I need not constantly think about the goal of getting to my office or about the procedure of walking in order to be walking to my office. All that is required for the pursuit of a project is that an ongoing pattern of behaviour is unified by a single goal. It does not require ongoing explicit thought about that goal or about the actions involved in pursuing it.

Walking to the office does require awareness of the environment and of one's goal, of course, but this awareness need not be precisely and explicitly articulated. In order to navigate the environment successfully to achieve this goal, one must engage in intelligent and responsive behaviour, but this need not involve conceptual thought. In terms of some of the sartrais discussed in the last chapter, it requires only non-thetic awareness of one's environment and goal, not thetic awareness of them; one need only be aware of these things in the extensional sense of 'awareness'.

The pursuit of a project does, however, structure one's experience. The articulation of one's surroundings as having this sense or that, the constitution of one's situations, the mobiles and motifs that explain one's behaviour, result from the projects one is pursuing, according to Sartre, as we saw in chapter 3. Since bad faith is a project, therefore, the person in bad faith lives in a world constituted at least in part by this bad faith. This is why Sartre describes bad faith as involving a 'weltanschauung'—a worldview, or outlook (B&N: 91). For the behaviour of the waiter to provide him with evidence of his fixed nature, for it to form part of the project of distraction from his awareness that he need not behave in the ways in which he does, he needs to *see* that behaviour *as* manifesting a fixed waiterly nature rather than see it as a comedy routine, as evidence of bad faith, or in some other way. This is not only true of the waiter himself, of course: his customers must see his behaviour in this way in order for it to reinforce their view of people as having fixed natures. Bad faith must be a project that, like other projects, constitutes the world a certain way.

It is part of the very motivation for bad faith, however, that we are dimly aware of the dependency of the articulation of the world, it having the meanings it has for us, on the projects that we are pursuing. So it is already built into Sartre's account that the constitution of the behaviour of others as manifesting their fixed natures will never be wholly convincing. The person in bad faith will always be aware of the contingency of seeing this behaviour in this way and of their preference for seeing it this way. The waiter's customers are therefore nervous that the waiter will do something that will disrupt their comforting worldview. This is why they positively require him to restrict himself to waiterly behaviour. The champion of sincerity, similarly, sees the behaviour of his friend as manifesting a fixed homosexual nature, but at the same time he wants his friend to confirm this. Such a confirmation is 'reassuring', Sartre tells us, because it 'removes a disturbing freedom from a trait' (B&N: 88). The freedom is disturbing because it shows the comforting worldview to be the pretence that it really is.

This requires, however, that there is more to the constitution of the world in bad faith than just seeing people's behaviour as manifesting their fixed natures. Our awareness of our own lack of a fixed nature and of our project of pretending that people do have fixed natures, albeit an inexplicit and non-thetic awareness, threatens to undermine our confidently seeing the world as providing evidence for the idea that people have fixed natures. For this reason, bad faith in general needs to involve a certain kind of attitude towards evidence itself, one that will protect the confident belief in fixed natures from this threat. Such an attitude towards evidence is also required by the form of bad faith that involves considering one's own fixed nature to exclude certain traits that one does in fact possess, which we called in the last chapter 'bad faith in the restricted sense'. In this form of bad faith, one needs somehow to play down the weight of evidence against one's preferred understanding of one's character. The unhappy homosexual needs to focus on his awareness that he is not homosexual in the way in which the red-haired man is red-haired in order to conclude that he is not homosexual at all, despite the evidence presented by his behaviour.

For both of these reasons, therefore, Sartre describes 'the world of bad faith' as including a 'peculiar type of evidence' that he calls 'non-persuasive evidence' (B&N: 91). The worldview of bad faith, that is to say, is not restricted to understanding behaviour in certain ways and to shunning the correct interpretation of it. It has built into it a specific kind of epistemic attitude, without which the project of bad faith would be unsuccessful. Sartre generates further confusion over the exact nature of his theory of bad faith by using the term 'bad faith' to label this particular epistemic attitude, as well as to label self-deception, the belief in fixed natures, and the belief that one's own fixed nature does not include certain traits that one does in fact possess. It is in explaining this epistemic attitude, moreover, that Sartre uses the contrasting term 'good faith' (*bonne foi*). There is some disagreement among commentators over what this contrast is.

According to Catalano, Sartrean bad faith exploits the inevitable underdetermination of belief by evidence. Since there is always more than one possible conclusion to draw from a given set of evidence, on this reading of Sartre, to believe something in good faith is to believe it with a degree of confidence proportionate to the strength of the evidence in its favour and to be ready to revise that belief in the light of future evidence. Bad faith, on the other hand, is belief based on poor evidence and held with a certitude that protects it from future contrary evidence. What is more, the person in bad faith justifies this epistemic attitude by construing good faith to be nothing more than simply belief that is not strictly required by the evidence, and thereby taking any belief that is not strictly required by the evidence to be equally acceptable. Catalano sums this up by saying that 'bad faith has a bad faith view of good faith' ('Successfully Lying to Oneself', 684; see also 685, 687).

Sartre does indeed describe bad faith as involving belief held with certitude on the basis of poor evidence. But on Catalano's reading, his theory draws a false dichotomy by contrasting bad faith and good faith with respect to *both* the degree of confidence with which the belief is held *and* the strength of the evidence for the belief. This account rules out, that is, the possibility of a belief based on good evidence of its truth but held with certitude not warranted by the evidence and insensitive to future evidence. We need a taxonomy of epistemic attitudes here that keeps separate the issues of whether the belief itself is warranted and whether the certitude with which it is held can be warranted for beliefs in that domain. Sartre's account does, in fact, keep these issues separate.

What good faith and bad faith have in common, as Manser points out in 'A New Look at Bad Faith' (63–5), is that they are both forms of *faith*, which is to say that they both involve accepting something with absolute conviction and ruling out the possibility of anything counting as evidence against it. While such certitude might be appropriate in the case of logical or mathematical beliefs, the arena of faith excludes such beliefs and includes only beliefs whose evidence cannot warrant certitude. Both forms of faith, good faith and bad faith, that is to say, are epistemically irresponsible because

The Project of Bad Faith 95

both involve unwarranted certitude and disregard for future evidence. Sartre contrasts this faith with the attitude that 'escapes it in favour of evidence' (*s'évade vers l'evidence*), an attitude that he calls 'science' (B&N: 93).

The difference between good faith and bad faith is that they involve different attitudes towards the evidence on which they are based. Good faith is holding with unwarranted certitude a belief that is nonetheless warranted by the evidence. Bad faith, on the other hand, is holding with certitude a belief that is not warranted by the overall evidence. Catalano is right to point out that bad faith therefore involves the attitude that the meagre evidence in favour of the preferred belief is as good as any evidence for any belief since evidence is never wholly conclusive. This is what Sartre means by saying that bad faith 'does not hold the norms and criteria of truth as they are accepted' by the critical thought of good faith' (B&N: 91): good faith does at least base the content of the belief on the preponderance of evidence, whereas bad faith takes *any* evidence to be sufficient warrant for belief.

The champion of sincerity is therefore in good faith when he considers his friend to be homosexual, and his friend is in bad faith when he denies this, since the evidence does point towards the trait of homosexuality. But this is not to say that 'sincerity' and 'good faith' are synonymous in sartrais, as Manser seems to take them to be (64–6). There is more to sincerity than just drawing conclusions in good faith about a person's character on the basis of behavioural evidence. Sincerity also involves, as we saw in the last chapter, understanding those character traits as part of a fixed nature. This further belief is not based on strong evidence, according to Sartre, since the only evidence we have concerning whether or not our character traits are fixed is our awareness of the dependency of the way the world seems to us, and of our behaviour patterns in response to it, on the projects that we are pursuing and which we can revise.

Sincerity is not only a form of good faith in that it ascribes the character traits that the evidence indeed suggests, therefore, but is also a form of bad faith in two closely related senses: it is a form of the belief that we have fixed natures, and it is the acceptance of this on the basis of non-persuasive evidence. The unhappy homosexual is in bad faith in the following senses: he understands his character as fixed; this understanding is based on non-persuasive evidence; he denies possession of certain traits he does in fact possess; the character he ascribes himself is not that suggested by the preponderance of evidence; and this ascription is based on non-persuasive evidence. The diagram overleaf is intended to clarify the relations between the different senses in which Sartre uses the term 'bad faith' in *Being and Nothingness*.

The project of bad faith, of maintaining that one's behaviour flows from a fixed nature despite the evidence to the contrary, therefore, involves constituting the world in a particular kind of way. It runs deeper than just constituting observed behaviour as expressive of fixed character traits. The world must be seen to present evidence for this view that is at least as good

96 The Existentialism of Jean-Paul Sartre

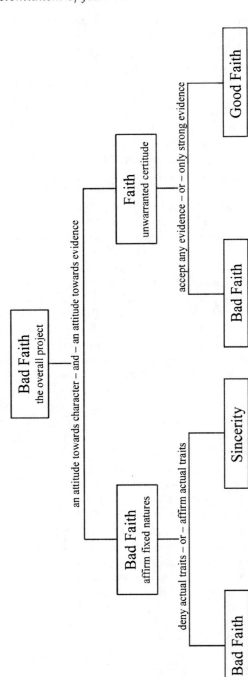

The various ways in which Sartre uses the term 'bad faith' in *Being and Nothingness*.

as any evidence it could present for or against it, which requires the attitude that since the evidence cannot be wholly conclusive it does not matter whether the evidence one has is wholly conclusive. Without this epistemic attitude, the constitution of observed behaviour as flowing from fixed character traits, rather than simply from character traits, would seem to be threatened by one's awareness that the patterns in one's own behaviour reflect the projects one pursues.

Bad faith in the general sense outlined in the previous chapter, therefore, requires a project of bad faith in the sense of basing one's beliefs on non-persuasive evidence. This acceptance of non-persuasive evidence, moreover, can reinforce itself. If one is aware that the evidence is far from conclusive and that one is using it to support a comforting belief, then this awareness might threaten one's acceptance of the evidence as convincing. This problem is a version of the paradoxes of self-deception that we started with: how can one genuinely believe something on the basis of evidence that one does not take to be persuasive?

The thought that accepting non-persuasive evidence does not require realising that it is not persuasive will not help here. Since we are aware that our actions do not really flow from fixed natures, on Sartre's account, we will find any evidence that people have fixed natures less than persuasive. The form of bad faith that involves denying some aspects of one's actual character, moreover, such as the unhappy homosexual's claim to be an adventurous heterosexual, can be based only on evidence that is clearly far from persuasive. Sartrean bad faith must be possible, therefore, even when the evidence for one's cherished belief does not strike one as persuasive. For this to be possible, one must take the evidence to be at least as good as any evidence for any contrary belief. One must take one's conclusion as warranted, that is, on the grounds that no contrary claim is more warranted.

Within the attitude of accepting non-persuasive evidence, moreover, one can provide evidential reasoning for the idea that no contrary belief has better evidence. One can point to the fact that good faith also goes beyond the evidence in its favour and affirm that it is therefore necessary to believe something that is not conclusively proven by the evidence. Such reasoning, of course, is unsound: it exploits the gap between strong evidence and wholly conclusive evidence to license certitude on the basis of even weak evidence, when this gap should rather be taken to show that certitude is out of place whenever evidence is not wholly conclusive. This evidential reasoning in favour of accepting non-persuasive evidence is itself not persuasive, therefore. But this need not undermine its utility in reinforcing the attitude that non-persuasive evidence can rightly be accepted: since the person reasoning in this way already accepts non-persuasive evidence, the non-persuasive nature of this reasoning will not prevent them from accepting it. From within the attitude of accepting non-persuasive evidence, that acceptance can seem reasonable. This is why 'the project of bad faith must itself be in bad faith' (B&N: 91). The evident circularity here means that such reasoning is logically unacceptable; it does not mean that it cannot, psychologically, be accepted.

This is not to say, however, that the project of bad faith requires that one never takes the epistemically responsible attitude of proportioning strength of conviction to strength of evidence and remaining open-minded about whether this belief will need to be revised in the light of future evidence. It does not require, that is to say, that someone who does take this epistemically responsible attitude in some areas of life, such as a professional enquiry into some subject or other, cannot also be in bad faith about the nature of character. Psychologically, one need not apply a consistent epistemic standard across the range of topics that one holds beliefs about. One could treat the epistemic attitude that Sartre calls 'science' as appropriate in some domains but inappropriate in others, perhaps reserving it for specialist theoretical enquiry and considering the everyday understanding of ourselves and one another to be simply not amenable to it. Whether or not one had persuasive evidence for this lack of amenability, of course, need not be a problem.

In addition to this epistemic attitude and to the constitution of observed behaviour as manifesting fixed natures, there is a third way in which Sartre considers bad faith to be manifested in the structure of experience. Seen through the lens of the project of bad faith, the values that the world presents to one cannot be acknowledged to be what they really are, contingent appeals rooted in the projects that one is pursuing but can revise. There are therefore two ways in which one can understand values. One is to recognise their dependence on the way one sees the world but take this to reflect one's fixed nature. This is to take values as independent of one's own contingent choices, but not to take them as the same for everyone since people may differ in their fixed natures. The other is to deny the dependence of values on the way one sees the world, but rather to reverse this direction of explanation by taking the values to be objective facts about the world and one's awareness of values to be recognition of such objective facts.

It is this latter option that Sartre calls 'seriousness'. Although bad faith requires that we do not recognise that values are dependent on our freely chosen projects, therefore, it does not require that we employ the strategy of seriousness in order to achieve this. Seriousness is one strategy of bad faith. People who are serious in this sense consider their actions to flow from a fixed nature that simply reacts to the values and demands that the world objectively contains. Sartre considers both 'revolutionaries' and 'possessors' to exhibit this attitude of seriousness, the former in finding the world to have a structure that is objectively wrong and that therefore must be replaced with an objectively right structure, and the latter who find the current structure of the world to be objectively right (B&N: 601; compare A&J: part 1). By taking the values of the world to be objective in this way, 'the serious man', Sartre tells us, is 'hiding from himself the consciousness of his freedom' (B&N: 601; see also B&N: 646).

There is more to this aspect of bad faith than simply taking values to be objective, however, since Sartre also seems to understand it to involve fabricating evidence for the objectivity of values in the form of cultural objects that make demands of us. Hence 'there exist concretely alarm clocks, signboards, tax forms, policemen, so many guard rails against anguish', guard rails that 'collapse' when I affirm the dependence of such values on my freely chosen projects (B&N: 63). The social dimension of bad faith, as mentioned in the last chapter, is not restricted to attitudes towards others, but includes physical constructions in the world. Although this seriousness is available as a social dimension to the project of seeing people as having fixed natures, regardless of whether one is sincere about one's own character traits, it is not actually required for such bad faith, as already mentioned, since one could alternatively take values to depend on one's fixed nature. Sartre does not seem to consider this possibility in *Being and Nothingness*.

By understanding bad faith as a project, Sartre understands it as something that one can do without explicitly thinking about it and as something that structures the ways the world appears to one. We have seen how this second aspect of bad faith as a project explains how one is able to view one's own behaviour and the behaviour of other people as manifestations of fixed characters, thereby seeming to provide some evidence for the view that people have fixed characters. We have seen how this project can be manifested in taking the values one finds in the world to be fixed, objective facts to which one simply responds, and that this can also be taken as evidence for a worldview that does not allow values to depend on one's freely chosen projects. We have also seen how the project of bad faith can involve expectations that people will behave in ways that conform to the view that they have fixed natures, expectations that can be enforced through social pressure, and how it can involve the construction of physical objects that seem to present objective values.

But none of this quite explains how it is possible to pursue the project of bad faith without one's awareness of one's pursuit of that project undermining the success of the project. That bad faith involves accepting something with absolute conviction on the basis of non-persuasive evidence helps to explain how one can ignore or overlook any awareness that one need not behave in the way that one is behaving, since one's belief in fixed natures is a matter of faith and therefore not responsive to further evidence. Nevertheless, this complicated strategy of distracting oneself from one's true condition by fabricating evidence that we all have fixed natures would still seem to be undermined if one could easily become aware that one is pursuing this project as a way of denying one's responsibility for one's own character and actions.

While it is true that a project can be pursued without explicit awareness of the purpose of that project, in most cases one can easily become aware of this purpose. Walking to the office is not something I need to think about in order to do, but neither is it something that I cannot easily acknowledge that I am doing. My non-thetic awareness of my purpose and activity can easily become thetic awareness. It might seem, therefore, that the account given so far needs to be supplemented in a way that explains why people pursuing the project of bad faith cannot easily acknowledge that they are doing so. The explanation of this, however, can be drawn from the details of the account of bad faith already given. Part of the explanation is that bad faith itself provides a strong motivation against reflecting on this project in any way that would reveal that one is pursuing it. Bad faith, that is to say, 'dare not speak its name' (B&N: 646).

Another part of the explanation, a deeper one, involves the relation between projects and experiences. It is not just awareness of the world that is structured by the projects one pursues: it is awareness of anything. This includes, therefore, my awareness of myself—my experiences, my actions, and my projects. The project of bad faith, therefore, will structure my reflective awareness such that my own experiences, actions, and projects will all seem to manifest a fixed nature of mine no less than the actions of other people seem to express their fixed natures. This is not to say, however, that my experiences, actions, and projects will seem to emanate from this or that particular fixed nature. The problem Garcin faces in *Huis Clos*, as we saw in chapter 4, is that he does not know whether or not his past should be seen as that of a coward. It is just to say that our projects determine the way we seem to ourselves, just as they determine the way everything else seems to us (see B&N: 519–21).

The project of bad faith therefore conceals itself in a way that most projects do not. While my project of walking to the office structures my experience so that aspects of my environment appear as useful or as obstacles, when I reflect on what I am doing or think about myself more generally, my project of walking to the office is not necessarily relevant to what I am thinking about. I might appear to myself to be lazy for not having started the journey earlier in the day, for example, but the project of walking to the office does not itself influence my view of myself. The project of bad faith, on the other hand, requires my thoughts, decisions, emotions, and actions to seem to me to manifest a fixed character. This includes the very fact that they seem to me in this way: my very experience of these things as flowing from my nature must itself seem to flow from my nature. It will seem to me fixed and inevitable that my thoughts, decisions, emotions, and actions seem to me to express my unchangeable character: the relation between these seeming this way and my project of bad faith will thereby be obscured. Bad faith, as Sartre puts it, 'has obscured all its goals' (B&N: 646). In the metaphor explained in chapter 4, bad faith is a *buried* project.

It is not impossible to reflect on oneself in a way that presents one's thoughts, experiences, and actions exactly as they are, according to Sartre, but such 'pure' reflection is unusual and can be brought about only by 'a sort of katharsis' (B&N: 177–8, 182). The more common form of reflection is 'impure': this 'is given first in daily life' (B&N: 182). Sartre also describes this reflection as *complice*, translated as 'accessory' but perhaps better rendered 'complicit' (B&N: 178). What it is complicit in is the project of seeing oneself as having a fixed nature: 'this reflection is in bad faith' (B&N: 184). Quite how one achieves the ability to reflect purely rather than impurely is not something that Sartre tells us. 'This is not the place to describe the motivation and structure of this katharsis', he says (B&N: 182).

The project of bad faith, like any project, then, influences the ways everything seems to us. It is in this regard that bad faith is like dreaming and that it 'is as difficult to get out of it as to wake oneself up' (B&N: 91–2). Sartre develops a theory of dreaming in *The Imaginary* as part of his overarching theory of all forms of imaginative consciousness. There he argues that dreaming involves awareness of real things, be they parts of the world or events occurring within the body, but in a way that transforms them to have some meaning within the narrative of the dream (IPPI: 159–75). The sound of a real alarm clock, for example, cannot be apprehended within the dream as the sound of that alarm clock, since the real world is no part of the dream, so it will appear as the sound of drums or a fountain or even an alarm clock in the dream world. Within the project of bad faith, similarly, everything that one is aware of appears within the framework of the denial of our freedom over our characters.

This is why 'bad faith is a type of being in the world, like waking or dreaming, which by itself tends to perpetuate itself' (B&N: 92). Nothing in the dream can motivate the dreamer to wake up, since nothing in the dream can present any aspect of the real world for what it is. 'The dream is a consciousness that cannot leave the imaging attitude', since everything of which the dreamer might be aware will be experienced as part of the dream (IPPI: 164). The ending of the dream requires some cause external to the dream itself, such as waking up or falling into a deeper sleep for reasons external to the dream itself. Analogously, all of one's experiences in bad faith will tend to confirm that people really do have fixed natures, even one's reflection on the experiences, thoughts, and behaviour that are in fact ways in which one is pursuing the project of bad faith.

Sartre goes on to describe the structure of bad faith as 'metastable' (B&N: 92). Although this term has often been taken to be a neologism, it is in fact a term that Sartre has borrowed from the physical sciences, as Robert Solomon has pointed out ('True To Oneself', 152). The appropriation is apt: a metastable state is one that is relatively stable and enduring despite requiring more energy than some more stable state since it is unable to pass into the more stable state without some external interference. Bad faith requires all the complications of self-deception explained so far in this chapter, but since one can live in bad faith, continuing to see evidence everywhere that people do indeed have fixed natures and accepting that evidence even if it is poor evidence, giving up the project would require some reason other than one's experience of oneself, the world, and the behaviour of others. We will consider the kinds of reasons there might be for this escape from bad faith in chapter 10.

The metastable nature of the project of bad faith explains how it is that we can engage in this self-deceptive project without either our goal or our motivation for pursuing that goal being unconscious. Since we can be aware of these things in the purely extensional sense of 'awareness', bad faith can be a project intelligently undertaken rather than an interference from an inaccessible region of the mind, while at the same time the structure of this project can prevent us from easily becoming explicitly, thetically, conceptually aware that we are pursuing this project and are doing so for this reason. Because projects constrain the ways things seem to us, pursuing the project of bad faith itself makes it genuinely difficult to acknowledge that we are pursuing it.

This also helps to clarify exactly what it is about the Freudian unconscious that Sartre is opposed to. It is clearly not that the explanations of one's behaviour might not be easily accessible to one, since this can be true of projects like bad faith. Sartre agrees that the root causes of our behaviour are best uncovered not by simple reflection but by psychoanalysis (B&N: 591). It is rather that the ways that we see the world and the ways in which we behave can be fully explained, according to Sartre, as ways of pursuing the projects that we have adopted. The project that explains the experience or behaviour, therefore, *rationalises* what it explains: the goal of persuading oneself that people have fixed natures rationalises the waiter's role-play, which is simply a way of pursuing that goal; stuttering is a way of proving oneself inferior (B&N: 493).

If we accept the Freudian picture, on the other hand, we can see only a symbolic relation between the experience or action and the unconscious drive that explains it. The activities of a kleptomaniac might express symbolically the Oedipus complex, for example, by breaking a social taboo and enacting an illicit possession. But the theft does not itself aim at fulfilling the desires of the Oedipus complex. It is not a way of pursuing that project: on this picture, 'the desire is not involved in its symbolic realisation' (STE: 30). The underlying cause is not manifested in and cannot rationalise what it explains. Sartre's theory of character, however, leaves no room for causally explanatory aspects of the mind that are not manifested in and do not rationalise the experiences and behaviour they explain. If experience and action can be fully explained, as Sartre thinks they can, in terms of the projects that they manifest, then there is nothing left to be explained by unconscious drives whose actual goals are not pursued in the actions they purportedly cause.

The pursuit of a project, as we have seen, does not require explicit awareness that one is pursuing that project or why one is doing so, but it does require at least non-thetic awareness of the goal and the motivation. The aim of existential psychoanalysis, therefore, is not to uncover something of which the patient is entirely unconscious but rather to articulate conceptually and bring the patient to acknowledge something of which they are already non-thetically aware. The analyst is dealing with 'a mystery in broad daylight' rather than 'an unsolved riddle' (B&N: 591). Sartre here returns to the theme of his critique of the Freudian solution to the paradoxes of self-deception: the idea that the correct diagnosis of the patient is not a revelation of something previously unknown but is rather recognised by the patient as correct (B&N: 496, 594).

Precisely what this recognised project might be is the subject of the next chapter, but it is worth noting that the Sartrean analyst cannot be satisfied with an explanation in terms of brute and unanalysable drives, tastes, appetites, or inclinations. Where traditional psychoanalysis aims to explain behaviour in terms of certain kinds of sexual desire or the ambition to dominate, Sartre argues, these cannot be understood as qualities the individual possesses in the way that mere objects possess properties, but must rather be seen as manifestations of the projects the individual is pursuing. What is more, they must be understood as integrated rather than mutually independent: a person is 'a totality and not a collection' of such qualities (B&N: 589; see also B&N: 623). This returns us to two related issues that we raised at the end of chapter 4: what exactly is the ultimate level of behavioural explanation that cannot be analysed any further, according to Sartre, and why must we accept that all of an individual's experiences and behaviour are unified in this way? We are now in a position to address these issues.

8 God and the Useless Passion

In the course of expounding his theory of imagination, three years before *Being and Nothingness*, Sartre makes a comment that might seem somewhat surprising. 'It is not determinism', he tells us, 'but fatalism that is the inverse of freedom' (IPPI: 47). He might seem to be denying here that there is any opposition between determinism and freedom, thereby endorsing a compatibilist approach to freedom rather than the incompatibilist account we considered in chapter 5. He might seem to be saying, that is, that freedom would be threatened only by fatalism, by the inevitability of some future outcome regardless of our current thoughts, decisions, and behaviour. This would be the claim that although Oedipus was not free to avoid killing his father and marrying his mother, our futures are indeed contingent on the decisions we make, so we have a freedom that was denied to Oedipus regardless of whether determinism is true or not.

This is not what Sartre means to be saying here, however. In saying that fatalism is the 'inverse' (*envers*) of freedom, he does not mean that it is the opposite of freedom but rather that fatalism and freedom are as two sides of the same coin: fatalism is the *flipside* of freedom. He has in mind Hume's claim, which we considered in chapter 5, that if there were no determinism, our actions would be random or chance and therefore not free. Hume considers determinism to be the flipside of freedom. In saying in this passage that determinism, 'which could in no way apply to the facts of consciousness' (IPPI: 47), is not the inverse of freedom, Sartre is denying that freedom requires determinism, claiming instead that it requires fatalism, which 'posits that such event must happen and that it is that future event that determines the series that will lead up to it' (IPPI: 47). He understands freedom as the flipside of the teleological nature of consciousness and behaviour, of the fact that our experiences and actions are motivated and structured by their role in our pursuit of projects.

Sartre holds that freedom over our projects requires that we can adopt or alter them without being motivated to do so by our existing projects, and since he holds that all motivation is rooted in projects, this requires that we can do so without any motivation whatsoever. We have seen in chapter 5 that we can reject this claim while retaining the rest of Sartre's existentialist moral psychology. The link he draws in this passage in *The Imaginary* between fatalism and the falsity of determinism appears to involve the idea that genuine goal-directedness is incompatible with determinism, the idea that goals we pursue as a result of deterministic laws are not genuinely goals we have selected at all. The deterministic version of Sartrean existentialism recommended in chapter 5 must reject this idea.

The point Sartre makes in this passage, however, actually provides us with grounds for rejecting it. We saw in chapter 5 that Sartre's view that we can abruptly revise or replace any given project without having any motivation for doing so renders his position vulnerable to various forms of the Humean criticism that unmotivated actions are not free but random or chance. But we can also see that such actions would not be goal-directed, since they would have no motivation at all. So if Sartre is right to say that freedom requires teleology, then he is wrong to say that the revision or replacement of a project can be both free and unmotivated. If freedom requires fatalism, then it seems that we must accept that it is compatible with determinism. The teleological aspect of Sartre's conception of freedom therefore requires the compatibilist version of his moral psychology recommended in chapter 5.

Highlighting the centrality of teleology to Sartre's theory of freedom, moreover, allows us to be more precise about his theory of anguish. This is the recognition not of the absence of determinism but of the teleological structure of experience and action. Anguish is the recognition that the way the world seems and the ways in which we respond result not from fixed facts about it or us, but ultimately from the goals that we are pursuing and need not pursue. It is the recognition of the truth of Sartre's theory of character rather than the recognition of the falsity of determinism.

Sartre does say that 'psychological determinism' is 'the basis of all attitudes of excuse', of course, but he also explains that what he means by 'psychological determinism' is the response to anguish that 'asserts there are within us antagonistic forces whose type of existence is comparable to that of things' and thereby 'provides us with a *nature* productive of our acts' (B&N: 64). This is why his account of bad faith is compatible with the deterministic version of his moral psychology recommended in chapter 5: bad faith requires only that we do not have fixed natures productive of our acts. We should be careful, therefore, not to gloss bad faith as an affirmation of determinism rather than the affirmation of a specific kind of determinism.

This affirmation of fixed natures is, as we have seen in the last chapter, a complicated affair involving a specific attitude towards evidence. It can succeed, insofar as it does succeed, only as a project that, like all projects, colours our experience of the world, of other people, and of ourselves. Specific activities in bad faith that Sartre highlights, such as the waiter's mechanistic behaviour, should not be read as distinct moments or pockets of bad faith that punctuate our lives, but rather as the more obvious manifestations of the ongoing project of bad faith that structures the lives of those who pursue it. Given that bad faith has a social dimension, given that the waiter's behaviour is at least partly a response to the demands made by his customers in order that their bad faith is not disrupted, moreover, we should not take Sartre to be describing just the outlook and behaviour of some individuals: he means to be describing an integrated and pervasive social phenomenon. Chapters 6 and 7 of this book, that is, have shown that Sartre considers the belief in fixed natures to be part of the structure of our culture.

Although Sartre denies that *Being and Nothingness* contains any ethical philosophy, claiming that it is purely a descriptive work (B&N: 645), it is clear from the liberationist tenor of much of the text, and indeed from the very label 'bad faith', that he considers bad faith to be a bad thing. This raises some important issues. One is whether he is indeed right that it is a bad thing. Perhaps we are better off not facing the truth about some things, and perhaps the true nature of our existence is in this category. What is more, even if we would do better to face the truth it is difficult to see how we could be motivated to do so if bad faith genuinely structures our outlook and motivations in the way that Sartre's theory claims that it does. In addition to these issues surrounding how we could and whether we should be motivated to abandon bad faith, there are further issues concerning the way life would be were we to embrace the truth (or perhaps just Sartre's theory) about the nature of human existence. These issues are addressed in the next couple of chapters.

Before turning to them, however, we need to make sense of a puzzling passage towards the end of *Being and Nothingness* that might seem to proclaim that bad faith is a necessary and inevitable part of human existence. This passage is puzzling because the whole point of the book is to detail the structure of human existence, which would seem to be at best pointless if it turned out that we could not help but think of it in some specific and erroneous way. Sartre does seem to want us to recognise the truth (as he sees it) of the human condition, that is, but the section entitled 'Existential Psychoanalysis' might be taken as arguing that we are, as a matter of the very structure of our being, incapable of doing so. The relevant passage is where Sartre argues that 'man fundamentally is the desire to be God' (B&N: 587).

Sartre uses the term 'God' here to denote a being that is a conscious and self-aware *personal* being, rather than a mere impersonal object like a chair or a rock, but at the same time has a fixed nature. Sartre considers this to be contradictory: there simply cannot be such a being, which he calls a being-in-itself-for-itself, since consciousness and self-awareness, which are required for personal being, are essentially dynamic and therefore cannot be part of an unchanging being. The use of the name 'God' to refer to such an impossible being alludes to the traditional idea of philosophical theism that God, while personal and conscious, is perfect and timeless and hence immutable or unchangeable. Implicit in this characterisation of human

God and the Useless Passion 107

existence, therefore, is an argument against the existence of God. There are various similar attacks on the ontology of traditional theism in *Being and Nothingness*, but these are not our concern here. What matters here is that when he claims that we desire to be God, he does not mean that we want to be the all-knowing and all-powerful creator of everything, but simply that we want to possess the solidity of a fixed nature while also being conscious.

Sartre continues the religious analogy when he summarises this point at the end of the chapter. In the Christian story of the Passion, God becomes human in the person of Christ and then allows Christ to be sacrificed on the cross so that humanity can be freed from the clutches of sin and be reborn as the humanity that God had intended. Sartre writes that 'the passion of man is the reverse of that of Christ' in that we aim to sacrifice our very humanity, our existence as nothing but the pursuit of projects, in order that we may become God, that God may exist. Sartre sums this up in the slogan 'man is a useless passion' (B&N: 636). This famous phrase translates Sartre's *'inutile'* as 'useless', where it might be more accurately rendered 'futile' or 'in vain': man is a futile passion because the aim of this passion, being in-itself-for-itself, is contradictory and hence cannot be achieved.

It is quite unclear just how Sartre intends this discussion to sit with his theory of bad faith, and hence just what it is he intends to say here. Some commentators have read this passage to be claiming that we want be God in the sense of having both freedom to choose how to behave and a fixed nature to justify our choices (see, e.g., Barnes, *Sartre*, 45). The idea that we want to affirm our freedom to choose does not seem to be consistent with Sartre's claim that our awareness of this freedom is anguish and that we strive to pretend to ourselves that we have fixed natures in order to avoid this anguish (B&N: 64; see chapter 6). What is more, Sartre does not claim in the relevant passage that we want to affirm our freedom, but rather that it 'is as consciousness that [we] wish to have the impermeability and infinite density of the in-itself' (B&N: 587). Bad faith and the desire to be God are consistent with one another in their aims, indeed they seem to have the same aim, and herein lies the problem.

Sartre describes the desire to be God as 'the fundamental project of human reality' (B&N: 587). As we saw in chapter 4, an individual's fundamental project is the project that all of that individual's other projects are ultimately ways of pursuing and that itself is not a way of pursuing some other project. Sartre describes such a fundamental project as a 'self-evident irreducible', by which he means that we cannot find a way of understanding this project in terms of some deeper project (B&N: 586; see also B&N: 581, 584–5). Each individual pursues a fundamental project that can be described as aiming to have a fixed nature and be a conscious person, but people pursue this project in different ways since they pursue different fixed natures (B&N: 585–6). In his discussion of the 'inferiority project', which we considered in chapter 4, Sartre describes it as a 'fundamental project'

(B&N: 495). There is no contradiction between this and the claim that the desire to be God is the fundamental project we all pursue, because we could understand the inferiority project as aiming to possess the fixed nature of an inferior person—or perhaps better, an inferior fixed nature—while still being a conscious person.

Difficulty only arises because Sartre seems to describe the desire to be God as a necessary or inevitable aspect of the kind of existence we have, being-for-itself. This kind of existence, he tells us, is 'the being which is to itself its own lack of being'. What is more, the 'being which the for-itself lacks is the in-itself'. From this he derives the claim that 'the end and goal of the nihilation which I am is the in-itself' and thus that 'human reality is the desire for being-in-itself' (B&N: 586). He goes on to qualify this by saying that we do not want to stop being conscious people, and hence what we desire is the impossible combination of consciousness and being in-itself that he calls 'God'. This passage does seem to imply that the desire to be God is part of the ontology of human existence, that the project of overcoming our lack of a fixed nature is integral to the kind of things that we are. This is indeed the way some commentators understand it (e.g., Catalano, *Commentary*, 229; Cox, *Sartre*, 161 n2; Warnock, 'Freedom in the Early Philosophy of J.-P. Sartre', throughout).

But this reading seems to be in tension with the idea that bad faith is a contingent condition of our culture that might be overcome. Sartre's theory of bad faith, he has told us earlier in the book, 'does not mean that we cannot radically escape bad faith': such an escape is indeed possible but presupposes the 'self-recovery of being that was previously corrupted' that Sartre calls 'authenticity' (B&N: 94 n9). How can this be possible if bad faith is a necessary or inevitable aspect of our being? How could authenticity be possible if 'man fundamentally is the desire to be God'?

The problem might seem to be resolved by distinguishing between aiming to achieve a fixed nature, on the one hand, and pretending to already have one, on the other. It might be argued that the desire to be God is part of the structure of our being, that we are perpetually striving to achieve an impossible combination of consciousness and a fixed nature, and that bad faith is the denial of this striving and the pretence that we already have a fixed nature. On such a picture, authenticity would be perfectly compatible with the desire to be God: the authentic person would simply recognise that our being is one of striving for a fixed nature that we do not and cannot possess (see Warnock, 'Freedom in the Early Philosophy of J.-P. Sartre', 14).

In abandoning the idea that bad faith and the desire to be God have the same aim, however, this attempt to resolve the problem makes the relation between the two unintelligible. A fundamental project is a project pursued through the pursuit of all of one's other projects. So if this account of the relation between bad faith and the desire to be God requires the former project to be a way of pursuing the latter, bad faith would be a way of attempting to literally change oneself into something with a fixed nature. But the project of bad faith is pursued through behaving as though my actions flow from a fixed character and seeing actions in general as flowing from people's fixed characters. How could behaving as though my character were not under my control and seeing behaviour in general as emanating from fixed characters be aimed at providing me with a fixed nature that I lack?

In order to resolve the problem, we need to bear in mind the point made in chapter 4 that Sartrean projects do not necessarily have objectives that can be achieved at some specific time. The project of staying alive is just the project of continuing to be alive. The inferiority project, moreover, is not the project of making it the case that at some point, when the project is complete, I am inferior, but rather the project of continually trying to make myself and other people believe that I am inferior. The desire to be God need not be the desire to bring about some fixed nature that I do not currently have, therefore, but could rather be the desire to continually make it seem as though I do have a fixed nature. Wanting a fixed nature should be understood as manifested not in the attempt to gain one, but in the attempt to make it seem as though I have one and to cover over the fact that I lack one. Understood in this way, the desire to be God is not a necessary structure of human existence in Sartre's scheme, but a way of describing bad faith that highlights the contradiction in the pretence that we are conscious but unchanging.

If this is right, then the passage in which Sartre seems to say that the desire to be God follows from the structure of being-for-itself cannot really be saying that at all and must instead be saying that it is the fundamental project of people in bad faith. 'The for-itself arises as the nihilation of the in-itself', Sartre writes, 'and this nihilation is defined as the project towards the in-itself' (B&N: 586). The 'nihilation' in question is our awareness of the mass of being-in-itself that makes up our material bodies and surroundings, an awareness that endows this mass of stuff with a sense or meaning according to the projects we pursue. The claim that this 'is defined as' a project towards being in-itself should be taken as a contingent claim about the way in which people currently are, a claim about bad faith, rather than an ontological claim about the structure of being-for-itself. Indeed, the phrase translated here as 'is defined as', *se définit comme*, is better translated here 'defines itself as': in bad faith, consciousness defines itself as a project aimed at having the solidity of being in-itself.

When Sartre concludes that 'human reality is the desire for being-in-itself' (B&N: 586), therefore, we should take 'human reality' to signify the empirical reality of human life in our culture rather than the ontological structure of our way of being. Distinguishing 'human reality' from 'being for-itself' in this way also allows us to make sense of his earlier claim that bad faith 'is essential to human reality' (B&N: 71) while also saying that 'consciousness conceals in itself a permanent risk of bad faith' (B&N: 94) and that this risk can be avoided (B&N: 94 n9). Bad faith might be essential to the empirical reality of the way people are, but it is not an ontological necessity, and it can be escaped in favour of an authentic attitude to existence.

This reading of the relation between bad faith and the desire to be God is confirmed when Sartre returns to this theme in the concluding chapter of the book. Here he tells us that conscious being 'is *in fact* a project of . . . attaining to the dignity of the in-itself-for-itself' and goes on to explain that this emphasised 'in fact' indicates that we cannot conclude that the desire to be God is part of the ontological structure of being-for-itself, only that it is part of the empirical reality of human life (B&N: 640). Were it part of the ontology of being-for-itself, it would be a necessary part of our existence, but since we cannot show this to be the case, it could be merely a contingent social fact. A few pages later, Sartre declares that it is indeed merely contingent when he proclaims that 'existential psychoanalysis is going to acquaint man with his passion', with the desire to be God, and in keeping with the religious analogy he describes this acquaintance as 'a means of deliverance and salvation' (B&N: 646).

Sartre then closes *Being and Nothingness* with a series of questions concerning this deliverance and salvation in a passage reminiscent of the endings of so many television shows where the viewers are asked to wonder whether the hero will free himself in time or whether the villain will succeed in his nefarious master plan and are then implored to stay tuned for the next enthralling episode. But of course they know full well that, as always, the hero will win out and the villain will be thwarted. Sartre asks us to stay tuned for the forthcoming volume on ethics, which he never published, to find out what will happen once people have become aware through existential psychoanalysis that their lives are structured by the pretence that we have the impossible existence of a conscious person with a fixed nature. Can bad faith be abandoned? Is authenticity possible? And of course, we already know the answers to these questions from what he has already said about bad faith. Sartre also asks more specific questions here, whose answers can be worked out to some extent from what he has already said. We will return to these in chapter 10.

In aiming to uncover the fundamental project pursued by a given individual, existential psychoanalysis aims to ascertain whether this individual is indeed in bad faith and if so precisely what kind of fixed nature that individual wants to seem to possess. The inferiority project, for example, is a form of bad faith in which one aims to present oneself as having an inferior nature. Sartre considers racial hatred, as we shall shortly see, to be a form of bad faith in which one identifies with a nature one takes to be determined by one's membership of some national or ethnic group. The ultimate level of the explanation of behaviour, for Sartre, is one's attitude towards the human condition: does one deny it in bad faith, pretending instead that people have fixed natures, or does one embrace it in authenticity? If one does the former, then there is the further question of what kind of nature one considers oneself to possess.

God and the Useless Passion 111

Sartre is happy to use the term 'fundamental project' to mean either the desire to be God or the specific form of this desire, such as presenting oneself as having an inferior nature or the nature of a Frenchman or whatever, and perhaps this ambivalence can be justified on the grounds that the desire to be God has to take some specific form in any given individual. We can now see clearly why Sartre thinks that all of the projects pursued by a given individual are unified by one single fundamental project. This has seemed puzzling to those commentators who understand the fundamental project to be something like the choice of career or image (see, e.g., McInerney, 'Self-Determination and the Project', 667–8; Morris, *Sartre's Concept of a Person*, 125–6). But if the fundamental project is one's attitude to one's own condition, whether one accepts it or hides from it in bad faith by pretending to have some specific nature, then the generality and profundity of this attitude explain why all of one's other enterprises occur within its confines.

Identifying the desire to be God with bad faith, however, does raise a further puzzle. Sartre claims that the desire to be God is the fundamental project we all pursue, although we may pursue different fixed natures from one another, which means that we must consider bad faith to be not simply a project that some people pursue but the fundamental project that we all (or at least those of us who have yet to be delivered and saved by understanding all of this) pursue and that thereby affects our entire outlook and everything that we do. It is claimed to be, as mentioned before, a pervasive social phenomenon. But this might not seem consistent with what Sartre has said about bad faith earlier on in the book. In particular, it might not seem to be consistent with the claim that bad faith is motivated by anguish, which is the realisation of the freedom we actually have over our characters and over the way the world seems to us and the way we respond to it.

This problem concerns the very idea that there is a motivation for bad faith at all. As we have seen in chapters 3 and 4, Sartre considers motivations to result from the projects that we pursue, so adopting the project of bad faith could be motivated only with reference to some value rooted in some other project. We saw in chapter 5 that Sartre thinks that projects can be adopted, and for that matter abandoned, without any motivation at all without thereby being unchosen. But we also saw there that we do not need to accept this in order to accept the rest of his existentialism: we can instead argue that projects can be chosen only in relation to values we already hold. Either way, we can accept that the values that motivate the adoption or abandonment of a project need not be rooted in a project at a deeper level: the position of a project in the hierarchy of determinables and determinations does not, of itself, restrict the levels in that hierarchy that can be revised on the basis of values rooted in that project.

But this is not enough to solve the problem of the motivation for bad faith. For if bad faith is motivated by anguish that results from another project somewhere else in one's hierarchy of projects, then either there is some other project that all or most people pursue or have pursued which engenders this anguish or there is a diversity of such projects. If there is one, then there should be some explanation of why all or most people adopt that project, which leaves us where we started. If there are many, then we need to know why such a plurality of projects all lead to anguish and why all or most people pursue at least one of these projects.

Rather than follow this route, we could instead question the need to understand the adoption of bad faith as motivated at all. McCulloch points out that bad faith might be better understood as an honest mistake, a simple confusion over the subtle details of our existence, 'a non-self-deceiving muddle' (*Using Sartre*, 64). After all, Sartre gives a particularly complicated and nuanced account of our kind of being, and although it is part of his theory that we have some dim, unconceptualised awareness of the true nature of our own existence, it seems perfectly possible that we can make errors when we try to translate this awareness into conceptual thought. So we might agree with Sartre that most people pursue the project of trying to present themselves as having some specific fixed nature or other but consider this to be based on the erroneous but nonetheless honestly acquired belief that people have fixed natures.

Given our emphasis on the social dimension of bad faith, moreover, we can see how such a belief might be honestly acquired: seeing the world as though people generally have fixed natures is precisely what we should expect of someone brought up in a culture in which people present themselves as having fixed natures and in which people treat one another as though they have fixed natures. Sartre's theory should lead us to expect, that is, that people brought up in an atmosphere of bad faith are likely to adopt that bad faith themselves, just as people brought up within a particular religious faith are likely to adopt that faith until they reach an age at which they begin to question it. What is more, we might think that people are unlikely to question the faith they are brought up with unless they are exposed to ideas contrary to it and that if Sartre is right about the pervasiveness of bad faith, then the attitudes of the people around one are likely to reinforce one's belief in fixed natures far more often than they challenge it.

From within Sartre's own theory of bad faith, therefore, we can see good reasons why people might just drift into this attitude as a result of confusion, socialisation, or both. Sartre's view that everyone, or almost everyone, in our culture is pursuing the desire to be God, the fundamental project of bad faith, can be explained by socialisation into the belief that people have fixed natures, a belief strengthened by the difficulty of unravelling the subtle detail of the true structure of character. Different people pursue this fundamental project in different ways, of course, but this can be explained by some people trying to find their true inner natures, others trying to present themselves as having some specific desirable inner nature, and still others doing both.

God and the Useless Passion 113

This is not to deny, however, that anguish has a role to play in the motivation of bad faith. It is rather to provide a place for anguish within Sartre's system and an explanation for its motivating role. Sartre's claim that motivations must be rooted in projects can be made compatible with the idea that anguish motivates the fundamental project of bad faith by understanding anguish as motivating the *retention* rather than initial *adoption* of that fundamental project. We can construe anguish, that is to say, as itself a motivation rooted in the project of bad faith. Anguish, according to Sartre, is awareness of our own freedom over our character. What makes this awareness unpleasant, what makes it anguish, is that it conflicts with the fundamental project, which involves seeing people as having fixed natures. Its unpleasant character reinforces the attractiveness of seeing people as having fixed natures and motivates conduct that removes the threat to this fundamental project by distracting oneself from this contrary evidence, perhaps by enacting evidence of one's fixed nature in its place.

Although Sartre does not explicitly make this point about anguish, it follows from what he does say about preferences generally. 'Generally speaking', he writes, 'there is no irreducible taste or inclination' since every preference 'represent[s] a certain appropriative choice of being' (B&N: 636). This claim is preceded by an extended discussion of the dislike of sliminess, an aesthetic distaste that Sartre considers to be universal, or at least very common, and which he argues is a manifestation of the fundamental project of wanting to have a fixed nature while also being a conscious, personal being (B&N: 630–2). If we consider this discussion of sliminess in detail, we can see more clearly how it also applies to his understanding of anguish.

Slimy things are repulsive, even horrifying, he claims, because their very sliminess symbolises the impossibility of having both the solidity of things and the dynamism of consciousness, of having a fixed nature while still being a person, of being in-itself-for-itself. It presents an image of consciousness, itself symbolised by fluidity, congealed by being mingled with the solid being in-itself, so that the movement of consciousness becomes constrained and then dominated by this being. Sliminess always symbolises this, he argues, because we all have a 'pre-ontological comprehension' of the different modes of being of consciousness and things, and find water to symbolise consciousness and solidity to express being-in-itself. We have no difficulty with these symbolic meanings of liquidity and solidity except when we encounter their combination in the slimy, which itself manifests the impossibility of combining the two while retaining their defining characteristics.

The desire to be God aims at understanding ourselves as combining consciousness with a fixed nature, possessed by being-in-itself, without either of these being altered or degraded by this combination. As we saw in chapter 5, Sartre holds that in pursuing a project we thereby value the goal of that project. The desire to be God therefore involves valuing the combination of consciousness with a fixed nature. What sliminess symbolises is that the combination of these things can occur only at the expense of their structures, and particularly that the dynamism of consciousness cannot be combined with the fixed nature of being-in-itself. Sliminess thereby symbolises the impossibility of the goal of the desire to be God by presenting the true outcome of mixing liquidity with solidity, dynamism with permanence, consciousness with a fixed nature. In showing the impossibility of something that we value, sliminess presents what Sartre calls an 'antivalue' (B&N: 631).

The general claim here is that we have aversive reactions to things that conflict with the values that are generated by our pursuit of projects. We find sliminess repulsive because it conflicts with the value generated by the project of bad faith. Conversely, anything that presents or supports that value will be attractive. Sartre thinks that this theory is valid not only for preferences that seem common to all or most people, such as an aversion to slimy things, but also to those preferences that differ from person to person. He takes these to vary with the projects that differ from person to person. 'It is not a matter of indifference whether we like oysters or clams, snails or shrimp', he claims, and one of the aims of psychoanalysis should be 'to unravel the existential significance of these foods' (B&N: 636).

There are two further aspects of this theory of tastes and preferences that we need to clarify in order to understand how it applies to anguish. One is that where sliminess symbolises something that is an antivalue because it conflicts with the aim of our projects, this is not the only way in which something can be an antivalue: another way is for our project to explicitly disvalue it. The second is that where sliminess merely symbolises something that is an antivalue, we can have aversive reactions to disvalued things themselves as well as to symbols of them. These two points are well illustrated by Sartre's theory of the nature of anti-Semitism, an account that he claims can be generalised to all forms of racial hatred (see A&J: part 1).

This theory holds that racial hatred is rooted in the project of seeing oneself as having a certain kind of fixed nature, bestowed upon one by one's membership of a certain national or ethnic group. This nature is seen as superior to those of other nationalities or ethnicities that neighbour or are integrated among the group one identifies with. What is more, membership of that superior group, possession of that superior nature, is seen as bringing with it certain birthrights, such as a right to the land and prosperity associated with that group and the right to certain social and cultural positions within that group. Racial hatred is first and foremost a proud identification of oneself with a particular group of people, a fundamental project of seeing oneself as having a fixed nature determined by one's membership of that group and seeing everyone else as having fixed natures determined by their membership of their groups.

Racial hatred is then generated when aspects of this purported birthright, this claimed national or ethnic heritage, are seen to benefit members of some other group rather than members of one's own. People identifying with a particular group in this way can thereby see themselves as dispossessed, as the victims of an objective wrong. They can suffer this position in an attitude of passive resentment of members of other groups, or of some specific other group, that they consider to have perpetrated this wrong, or they can take up violence on the grounds that this is required to restore the rightful possession of certain goods by their group of people. Either way, they explain their outlook and their actions with reference to the kind of natures they, like all members of their group, have and the situation their group finds itself in. 'The anti-Semite', Sartre writes, 'is a man who wishes to be a pitiless stone, a furious torrent, a devastating thunderbolt—anything except a man' (A&J: 54).

Sartre presents this as an account of the kind of anti-Semitism that leads people to genuinely find Jewish people viscerally disgusting and even to contaminate the air they breathe, but only when they know that these people are Jewish (A&J: 10–11, 33–4, 50–1). This is a deep-rooted hatred, one that involves an aversive physiological reaction to people known to belong to the hated group. This disgust, however, results only from the fundamental project of identifying oneself as having an elite nature in common with all members of one's elite group. Members of the hated group are disvalued precisely because of the value this project bestows on one's own group in contradistinction to them. The aversive reaction is to those people themselves, not to something that they symbolise. It occurs, moreover, not because those people in some way threaten or contradict one's fundamental project, in the way that Sartre thinks that sliminess threatens the desire to be God, but precisely because disvaluing those people is part of one's fundamental project.

This theory of repulsion is a development of the theory presented in the earlier work, *Sketch for a Theory of the Emotions*. Sartre there argues that emotions are responses to the relation between the way the world is and the way we would like it to be. When our projects are frustrated, we may become angry. When they are threatened, we may become frightened. When we are about to get something that we want, we may dance with joy as a kind of mime enacting that happy future event (see STE: part III). This theory has evolved not only in that the later version encompasses tastes and preferences, such as liking the taste of garlic or being disgusted by snails, but also in that the responses it explains are directly related not to changes we would like to bring about in the world but rather to the values and antivalues generated by our projects. Through this change, however, Sartre is claiming only that these feelings result from the relation between the way the world is and our projects, not that we think about this relation and decide how to respond. Sartre does not hold that each emotional response is reflectively chosen in response to the particular circumstances, even though some commentators seem to read him this way (see, e.g., Heter, *Sartre's Ethics of Engagement*, 28–9).

Sartre intends this theory of attraction and repulsion as manifestations of the projects one pursues, the kind of life one chooses to lead, to cover all tastes and preferences, including the foods one prefers and those one cannot abide. My utter dislike of celery, for example, should not be explained by some fact about my genes that has determined my taste and smell receptors to react in certain ways to celery, according to Sartre, but rather by the relation between the life I have chosen to live and the antivalue that celery presents or symbolises as a result. But we do not need to agree that gustatory taste requires psychoanalytic explanation in order to accept the Sartrean approach to explaining why people develop passionate dislikes of certain identifiable groups of people. Quite how far we should accept Sartre's account of preferences as extending, if indeed we should accept it as covering any of our preferences at all, is an interesting question. Should sexual preferences, for example, be explained by the form of life one has adopted or by genetic determinism? This is an issue we will return to in chapter 11.

What matters for present purposes is not whether Sartre is right about the origins of tastes and preferences, or about the origins of some range of these, but rather that this theory allows us to understand the relation between anguish and bad faith in his existentialism. Anguish, like disgust, is an aversive awareness of some feature of the world. We feel anguish, according to Sartre, whenever we are presented with evidence that our cherished belief in fixed natures is in fact false, whenever we are aware for whatever reason that people do have freedom over their characters and can change the way the world seems to them and the ways in which they respond to this. Anguish can be the aversion we feel to anything that symbolises or manifests this freedom. The desire to be God, the project of bad faith, bestows a positive value on the seeing humans as possessing fixed natures, and hence anything that suggests or indicates the opposite of this is disvalued to an extent that one feels an aversion to it, which leads to avoiding or ignoring anything presenting this antivalue. Anguish results from bad faith.

We should not understand Sartrean existentialism as claiming that we are *necessarily* averse to accepting our freedom over our characters and the responsibility it brings with it, therefore, but rather as attempting to diagnose the sickness underlying this aversion. Sartre understands bad faith, as we have seen, as a sickness affecting society in general rather than just some of its members. He wants to liberate us from the alienation from ourselves that this social sickness brings about. His aim is to point out the errors of the worldview that, as individuals, we have simply drifted into as a result of social conditioning but then reinforced in order to avoid the anguish produced as a result of this worldview. Sartre's theory is not pessimistic, but rather optimistic and liberationist. The alienation arises from our pursuit of the fundamental project of seeing people as having fixed natures, and since we can abandon any project and replace it with a different one, we can abandon bad faith in favour of an authentic acceptance and indeed affirmation of the way we really are.

God and the Useless Passion 117

Quite why we might want to abandon bad faith, or the desire to be God, and replace it with such an authentic attitude is an issue to which we will return in chapter 10. But this account of the relation between bad faith and anguish helps to explain one aspect of Sartre's recommendation of authenticity that might otherwise seem puzzling. If the true structure of our existence, our freedom over and responsibility for the way we see the world and the way we respond to it, is genuinely so unpleasant for us that anguish is the response we feel to anything that even so much as suggests or symbolises it, then authenticity hardly seems an attractive prospect. There might seem to be something strangely macho, that is, about the recommendation that we live in the recognition and acceptance of this unpleasant truth rather than under a comforting illusion: why should the truth be more important than our happiness?

Since anguish is a product of bad faith, this question is misplaced. The recommendation is not that we live a life of anguished acceptance of the truth. It is rather that we abandon the outlook that generates anguish in the first place, since this anguish is nothing but an aversion to evidence of the falsity of that outlook. Far from being a feature of the authentic life, according to Sartre, anguish is exclusively a feature of the inauthentic life of bad faith. This is not to say, of course, that a conversion to authenticity must mark the immediate end of anguish. Old habits die hard, attitudes harder still. Perhaps the road to authenticity is a difficult one, but nonetheless Sartre's recommendation is certainly one of a life in which anguish will not arise. This is not yet to say, of course, that authenticity is preferable to bad faith. Perhaps the life of bad faith has advantages over the authentic life, particularly if Sartre is right that bad faith dominates society. Perhaps the occasional bout of anguish is a price worth paying. In the next couple of chapters, we will see why Sartre thinks otherwise.

9 One Another

'Conflict is the original meaning of being-for-others' (B&N: 386). This striking sentence summarises one of the most famous aspects of Sartrean existentialism, the theory of the structure of relations between people. It is generally taken to be equivalent to the snappier and more quotable line from Sartre's play *Huis Clos*, 'Hell is . . . other people!' (223). But these phrases are usually misunderstood. They are usually taken to express a pessimistic account of interpersonal and social relations as necessarily conflictual, a theory that we can only misunderstand one another and must inevitably struggle to dominate one another. This is not, in fact, Sartre's view. His discussion of relations between people in *Being and Nothingness* is rather concerned with the way in which bad faith distorts our interactions with one another. He is attempting to identify the underlying cause of interpersonal and social problems. Within the context of his existentialism, moreover, we might take this effect of bad faith to provide us with a motivation to abandon it in favour of authenticity.

Part of the reason why readers of *Being and Nothingness* misunderstand this as making a claim about the way we necessarily relate to one another is the tendency to see the book as a series of theories about different aspects of our existence, perhaps with a common theme, rather than as a progressively broadening and deepening investigation of a single theory. It is not that Sartre presents an account of our bad faith about our own existence and then a separate account of the distinct issue of our relations with one another, but rather that the account of bad faith early in the book sets the framework within which the discussion of relations between people is conducted.

This misunderstanding of the book's structure also has the converse effect, which we have already seen in chapter 6, that readers often overlook the social dimension of bad faith that is clearly present in Sartre's examples of the waiter's clientele, the woman on a date, and the champion of sincerity. The later discussion of relations between people is intended to detail a theory already sketched in these passages. Indeed, at one point in the later discussion, Sartre refers back to the earlier discussion, saying that one way in which we mistreat one another is by reducing people to their social roles: in this attitude, 'the ticket-collector is only the function of collecting tickets; the café waiter is nothing but the function of serving the customers' (B&N: 402–3). The earlier discussion, moreover, prefigures the later one when Sartre claims that any attempt to objectify another person, such as the champion of sincerity's attempt to ascribe a homosexual nature to his friend, is 'offensive to the Other' as well as 'reassuring for me' (B&N: 88).

Sartre does not signal the structure of the book with sufficient clarity to avoid this misunderstanding, but the structure of the discussion of interpersonal relations itself also contributes to the problem. This is because Sartre discusses relations between people alongside the problem of solipsism, one's awareness of one's own character, and the role of the body in one's public image, among other things. Since this complicated discussion is conducted in the language of sartrais, whose terminology embodies various fine distinctions as we have seen throughout this book, it is not always clear exactly what Sartre is saying or even precisely which topic he is discussing. In this chapter, we will concentrate on the two central ideas of the core section of this discussion, the section entitled 'The Look' (*Le regard*), in which Sartre uses visual terminology to encapsulate his theory of the ways in which we think about people, the ways in which we see one another (see B&N: 281–2).

One central idea is that we see other people as having fixed natures and, since we are other people to those others, they think of us as having fixed natures. This generates a conflict between ourselves and others. William Ralph Schroeder summarises well, and indeed endorses, the sense in which these claims are usually taken when he writes in his book-length study of Sartre's account of interpersonal relations, *Sartre and His Predecessors*, that 'Sartre draws sweeping conclusions about the *necessary failure* of all *possible* human relationships', and hence we 'must interpret his claims to be about the *necessary* features of interpersonal experience' (179, emphasis original; see also, e.g., Catalano, *Commentary*, 180–1; Cox, *Sartre*, 46; Fox, *The New Sartre*, 54–6; Heter, *Sartre's Ethics of Engagement*, esp. 27). In this chapter, we will see that Sartre does not hold the pessimistic view that all human relationships are necessarily doomed to failure, but is rather aiming to describe the features of interpersonal experience within bad faith.

He does often sound as though he thinks conflict is inevitable, but this is because he is only discussing relations between people in bad faith and he thinks conflict is indeed inevitable between them. 'These considerations do not exclude an ethics of deliverance and salvation', he points out in a footnote to the subsequent discussion of how this conflict is played out in our culture, but 'this can be achieved only after a radical conversion which we cannot discuss here' (B&N: 434 n13). Sartre here echoes the footnote with which he closes his lengthy discussion of the nature and structure of bad faith, where he proclaims that his discussion 'does not mean that we cannot radically escape bad faith' and that such an escape 'presupposes a self-recovery of being which . . . we shall call authenticity, the description of which has no place here' (B&N: 94 n9).

Authenticity is, as we have seen, something to be fully described in the promised work on ethics, but is basically the fundamental project that Sartre recommends in place of bad faith. The conversion to authenticity would be 'radical' because it would be a change in the deepest roots of our behaviour: the fundamental project, the attitude we take towards our existence as beings lacking fixed natures. In using the term 'conversion' and describing authenticity as 'an ethics of deliverance and salvation', Sartre alludes to the religious analogy he uses to describe the combination of bad faith with the wish to remain a conscious person, the 'desire to be God' discussed in the last chapter. The central aim of existential psychoanalysis, he tells us at the end of the book, is to show us that our fundamental project is the desire to be God, in order to provide us with 'a means of deliverance and salvation': a route to authenticity (B&N: 646). We will consider authenticity in more detail in the next chapter.

Sartre presents his account of the basis of relations between people, his theory of the 'the look', as involving two 'moments', or aspects: one in which I become aware that the other person has formed an opinion of me; one in which I form an opinion of that other person. Either could occur first, the other following as a reaction to the alienation it causes, and the ensuing to-and-fro sequence could continue indefinitely (see B&N: 320). But to simplify matters, Sartre presents examples in which the other person thinks of me in a certain way, as a result of which I think of them in a certain way. The views that are formed, however, are always opinions concerning someone's nature: the other sees me as having certain fixed character traits, which I find alienating and therefore attempt to undermine by considering that person to have certain fixed character traits. Thus it is that 'my constant concern is to contain the Other within his objectivity and my relations with the Other-as-object are essentially made up of ruses designed to make him an object' (B&N: 320). The other person is, of course, just like me in this respect, with the result that interpersonal relations are fraught with alienation and objectification.

Those who read this as a theory of the necessary failure of human relationships therefore take Sartre to be saying two things: that we cannot think of other people except in terms of their possession of specific fixed traits; and that when somebody forms such an opinion of us, we cannot help but respond in a way designed to undermine that opinion. We will see that Sartre should rather be read, as Barnes and Cooper read him, as saying that *in bad faith* we see other people as having fixed traits, and *in bad faith* we cannot accept the nature ascribed to us by another person, so we seek to undermine their view of us by ascribing certain fixed traits to them (see Barnes, *Sartre*, ch. 5; Cooper, *Existentialism*, 186). It is within the context of a culture of bad faith that we should understand Sartre's discussion of the basis of relations between people.

Sartre introduces this theory by presenting an extended narrative example that is also intended to illustrate his response to the problem of solipsism and an aspect of his theory of self-consciousness. While looking through a keyhole, spying on the scene behind the door, I hear footsteps in the hall and immediately feel ashamed. This shame is the awareness that another person has seen me and categorised me as a snoop or a voyeur, or at least might well have done so (B&N: 282–5). The feeling itself is an awareness that I am indeed the person that the other is categorising in some way: 'my shame is a confession' (B&N: 285). What is more, it is an awareness of being ascribed some unpleasant character trait, such as being a snoop or a voyeur, as though this trait is a fixed aspect of my character, a part of my inner nature: 'for the Other, *I am leaning over* the keyhole as this tree *is bent* by the wind' (B&N: 286).

Being categorised in this way, being objectified by another person, is something that we find alienating, according to Sartre. We want to resist this categorisation. But it is not obvious why we should always want this, since some categorisations might have positive benefits for us, as Heter points out (*Sartre's Ethics of Engagement*, 41–2). Sartre muddies the waters somewhat by his use of the term 'shame' (*la honte*). This can make it seem as though we object to being categorised in negative terms. But Sartre rather thinks that we reject *any* objectification of us by another person, even one in seemingly positive terms: 'the alienation of myself', he tells us, 'is the fact of being-looked-at' (B&N: 287).

Sartre uses the term 'shame' in two distinct senses. He uses it in the ordinary sense to denote feeling ashamed of the kind of person one is seen as being, a reaction to being categorised in negative terms. But he also uses it in a more general sense—which he sometimes calls 'pure', 'original, or 'fundamental' shame—to denote the feeling of being objectified by another person at all. 'Pure shame is not a feeling of being this or that guilty object but in general of being *an* object', he writes, 'that is, of recognizing myself in this degraded, fixed, and dependent being which I am for the Other' (B&N: 312). There are therefore two basic forms of this fundamental shame: the one that we ordinarily call 'shame'; and another that involves identifying with the positive image that some other person has of one, which Sartre claims encompasses both pride and vanity (see B&N: 314–15).

Sartre considers fundamental shame itself to be unpleasant, regardless of which of these two forms it takes. This has sometimes been understood as the claim that we find it unpleasant when other people treat us as though we are mere things and thereby deny our freedom. One version of this reading takes the desire to be God as the desire to be something that combines freedom with a fixed nature, and hence takes objectification by other people to be alienating because it denies our freedom even though it ascribes to us a fixed nature (see, e.g., Barnes, *Sartre*, 45, 63). Another version is rooted in the idea that bad faith can take the form of identifying with one's freedom in order to dissociate oneself from the essence one in fact possesses, and hence claims that being objectified by another person is alienating for people in this form of bad faith because it denies their freedom (see, e.g., Bell, *Sartre's Ethics of Authenticity*, 75; Reisman, *Sartre's Phenomenology*, 123, 127).

We have seen in chapters 6 and 8, however, that Sartre considers there to be only one project of bad faith, which is the attempt to deny freedom and see oneself and people in general as having fixed natures, and that the desire to be God is the project of seeing oneself as possessing consciousness, not freedom, as well as a fixed nature. He considers this bad faith, this desire to be God, to be the fundamental project that we all, or most of us, pursue. The alienation of the look should be understood in a way that is consistent with this.

Some of Sartre's comments on this alienation do seem to refer to a desire for freedom, it is true, such as his claim that alienation arises because 'my nature is—over there, outside my lived freedom—as a given attribute of this being which I am for the Other' (B&N: 286). The language of freedom, moreover, thoroughly pervades his later discussion of the ways in which this alienation plays out in our culture (B&N: part III ch. 3). But this should be understood as another example of Sartre's failure to distinguish clearly between intensional and extensional senses of psychological terminology, a failure we considered in detail in chapter 6. He considers the terms 'consciousness', 'subjectivity', and 'freedom' to be coextensive, since they refer to all and only the same existents and do so for the same reason: freedom is a necessary aspect of being a conscious subject. Sartre has a habit of using these terms interchangeably in order to emphasise that they are coextensive.

This is misleading because we ordinarily use psychological vocabulary in an intensional way, which aims to capture not just what our beliefs and desires are about, but also how the things they are about seem to us, and hence the roles those beliefs and desires play in our mental lives. Whether or not Sartre is right that freedom is coextensive with consciousness, we can want the latter while not wanting the former, so long as we do not see the inconsistency this involves. Indeed, Sartre's theory of the desire to be God holds our desires to be inconsistent in precisely this way. It might be objected at this point that if Sartre is happy to recognise that people can have inconsistent desires, which anyway seems to be something that is empirically true, then why should we not interpret his theory of the look as involving a desire for freedom? This criticism might also be levelled at the discussion of bad faith in chapter 6: might we not simply have inconsistent desires with respect to our own freedom, wanting it in some respects or at some times, wanting not to have it in other respects or at other times?

This criticism overlooks the nature of our denial of our own freedom. It is not simply that we have a desire not to be free which, though long-standing, is only occasionally manifested in our thoughts and actions. It is rather that the denial of our freedom over our characters is an ongoing project that colours the way the world seems to us and flavours the way we behave, even to the extent that we mould certain aspects of the world in a way that helps us in this denial. Sartre understands bad faith, moreover, as a fundamental project that is manifested in all our other projects. It is responsible for the anguish we feel whenever we are confronted with anything that indicates or symbolises the freedom we prefer to deny. This theory is simply not compatible with the idea that we dislike it when other people deny our freedom. Indeed, the theory of bad faith might lead us to expect that we would positively enjoy being objectified.

So what is it, then, that Sartre thinks is so alienating about being objectified by other people? He claims that 'I accept and wish that others should confer upon me a being which I recognize' (B&N: 286). This might seem to suggest that what we find objectionable about the other person's view of us is that it clashes with our own view of ourselves. My fundamental project of presenting myself to myself and to others as having a certain kind of fixed nature, one including the virtues of honesty and integrity perhaps, might seem to be challenged by the other person's view of me as a snoop or a voyeur once they have witnessed my spying through a keyhole. Any traits of which I would be ashamed are traits that conflict with the nature I prefer to ascribe to myself, on this reading, so the view the other person has of me is alienating in the sense that it is a view of me other than the one I prefer everyone, including myself, to have.

This reading might seem to be supported by some of Sartre's fiction. It might seem that Garcin, the lead character in the play *Huis Clos*, finds Hell to be other people because, as we saw in chapter 4, he was executed for desertion from the army and therefore seems to other people to be a coward, which conflicts with his self-image as a courageous hero. A similar point might be made about Daniel in the 'Roads to Freedom' trilogy. His failed attempt to drown his cats, which we considered in chapter 5, is part of his larger project of seeing and presenting himself as having a nature that is at odds with the prevailing morality of the society around him. Other people often see him as a pleasant and caring person, which conflicts with the image he wants to project. This leads him, in the second novel, *The Reprieve*, to take up Catholicism on the grounds that God is always watching him and correctly judging his inner nature: 'he had been conscious of God's presence and he had felt like Cain: Here I am, as thou hast made me, cowardly, futile, and a pederast' (168; see also 178, 344–6). Far from finding his objectification alienating, Daniel positively seeks it out: he ascribes to God the view of him as having precisely the fixed nature he wants to think of himself as having.

This interpretation assumes that the look is alienating only when the nature the other person ascribes to me is different from the one I would ascribe to myself. But, as we have seen, Sartre thinks alienation arises simply from 'the fact of being-looked-at' (B&N: 287). The feeling of alienation is shame in the broader sense in which he uses that word, not the narrower: it is the recognition that the other person is ascribing a fixed nature to me, whatever that nature is. This is why Sartre has been understood to be saying that alienation is the feeling of a lack of control over the nature that is ascribed to one. 'The function of every concrete attitude toward Others', writes Schroeder, 'is to gain control of the dimension of oneself that Others have created' (*Sartre and His Predecessors*, 9; see also 255–6). Sartre does emphasise this lack of control. Indeed, he even points out that the problem is worse than a lack of control: I even lack knowledge of precisely how other people see me. 'Shame—like pride—is the apprehension of myself as a nature', he writes, 'although that very nature escapes me and is unknowable as such' (B&N: 286).

We might object that other people's views of us are not always quite so mysterious. If we know someone well enough to tell when they are being honest with us, then we might at times be able to see quite clearly what they think of us. Perhaps we could not predict every detail of the character sketch they would produce if asked, but we might nonetheless know its central points. In the case of pride, we might then ask what would be so alienating about knowing that someone else thinks highly of me and considers me to possess character traits that I consider myself to possess and that I want others to see me as possessing. Sartre does provide a careful analysis of pride (*la fierté*), one which answers this question and which does so in a way that differs significantly from his account of the alienation involved in what we ordinarily call shame.

Pride is, Sartre tells us, an 'ambiguous feeling' (B&N: 314). We all have a dim awareness that the value of someone else's admiration depends on it being freely given rather than being the necessary outcome of their fixed nature, he thinks. The feeling of pride is therefore uneasy. On the one hand, it is of course pleasant to be seen as possessing some positive trait, especially if this is a trait that we consider to be a part of our fixed nature. On the other hand, this feeling contains within it a suggestion that the other person does not or might not have a fixed nature. This is threatening to my fundamental project since this project involves seeing people as having fixed natures (see B&N: 314–15). We should understand this within the context of Sartre's notion of an 'antivalue', discussed in the last chapter: this is the idea that we have negative feelings in response to anything that presents, indicates, or symbolises something that is either explicitly disvalued by our projects or that conflicts with the values generated by our projects. We feel anguish whenever we are aware of anything that manifests, suggests, or symbolises the freedom people have over their characters, over the way the world seems to them and the way they respond to it.

Our awareness that we can only really enjoy admiration that does not flow from the fixed properties of a person therefore incorporates anguish into the feeling of pride. This is the 'ambiguity' of the feeling: it is at once positive, since we identify with the lauded traits, and negative, since it involves anguish. Our response to this anguish is to see the other person as having fixed character traits after all, to see their admiration for us as flowing from their very nature. But 'this is to kill the hen that lays the golden eggs': we can no longer feel genuinely proud in response to admiration that comes about so mechanically (B&N: 314). Our negative response to being objectified by others is therefore not always a response to our loss of control over our image. In the case of pride, it is a response to the inconsistency of this pride with our bad faith.

We are now in a position to see just what is alienating about being objectified by other people. In the case where we feel ashamed, we are ascribed a nature that conflicts with the one that we prefer to consider ourselves as possessing. In the case of pride, we are ascribed a nature that concurs with our self-image, but the feeling of pride itself conflicts with the very idea that we have a fixed nature at all. While we can describe bad faith, or the desire to be God, as the fundamental project that all or most of us pursue, we could also say that we pursue a wide range of different fundamental projects: although we all pursue the project of pretending to have a fixed nature, we each pretend to have a specific fixed nature, and this differs from person to person. This individualised fundamental project generates the values of having a fixed nature and of having certain character traits as part of that nature.

Someone else's objectification of me, my feeling of shame in the general sense, can therefore be alienating in either of two ways: it can present or suggest an antivalue conflicting with the value of possessing the particular traits I identify with; or it can present or suggest an antivalue conflicting with the value of possessing a fixed nature. If someone ascribes to me traits I do not identify with, this presents the former type of antivalue. If someone ascribes to me traits I do identify with, my resultant pride presents me with the latter kind of antivalue. The unpleasant feeling involved in awareness of either of these antivalues can be escaped only by thinking of the other person as having some fixed nature or other. This is why 'my making an object out of the Other must be the second moment in my relation to him' (B&N: 310). 'My defensive reaction to my object-state will cause the Other to appear before me in the capacity of *this* or *that object*' (B&N: 319).

If the other person is seen as naturally suspicious or base, for example, then this undermines the validity of their view of me as a snoop or a voyeur. If the unpleasant feeling results from the awareness that the other person might not have a fixed nature, on the other hand, then it is obvious that I can escape this by categorising them as the sort of person who naturally lauds certain kinds of traits or who interprets behaviour in a certain kind of way, although this is at the cost of undermining the positive value their positive judgements might have for me. This explains why Daniel seeks solace in religion. God can play the role of seeing him as depraved by nature where people cannot, not because Daniel can manipulate the view he thinks God has of him more easily than he can manipulate the view other people seem to have of him, but because the affirmation of his self-image provided by God's view of him does not threaten to undermine his view of people as having fixed natures: God's views can be seen as freely formed without undermining the idea that people lack such freedom.

Having a fixed nature ascribed to one by someone else is therefore alienating because, one way or another, it inevitably involves presenting one with an antivalue that is threatening to one's pursuit of the fundamental project of bad faith. But such threats can be neutralised by seeing the other person as having some fixed nature or other, a strategy that harmonises perfectly with the aims of bad faith. This is a unified account of what Sartre thinks is alienating about being categorised in terms of fixed traits by another person and why he thinks that the inevitable response is to categorise that other person in terms of fixed traits. That is, the reason why it is alienating to be the object of another person's look itself explains why the inevitable response is to return the look. But this does not yet account for all of Sartre's theory, since we might yet ask why it is that the other person should categorise me in terms of fixed traits at all. To put the question another way, if I catch you looking through a keyhole, why must I understand you as having the fixed trait of being a snoop or a voyeur, rather than as having some such revisable trait, perhaps rooted in the projects that you are pursuing?

Much of what Sartre says about this does seem to suggest that we categorise others in terms of fixed properties, that we objectify them in the sense that we think of them in ways appropriate to thinking of objects, simply because we cannot do otherwise: for some reason, our thoughts about others necessarily objectify those others. He tells us, for example, that 'the Other-as-subject can in no way be known or even conceived as such' (B&N: 317). Sentences such as these can seem to indicate the idea that there is something about the structure of consciousness that constrains us to see one another in the way that is only appropriate for categorising mere chunks of being in-itself: as having fixed defining properties. He sometimes seems to endorse the idea, that is, that since consciousness is always intentionally directed towards an object, anything that we are conscious of will seem to be an object.

If we pay attention to another person, Sartre tells us, then 'this could only be as to objects, for attention is an intentional direction towards objects' (B&N: 292). A couple of pages later, Sartre tells us that 'as a pure subject', the other person is something 'which by definition I am unable to know—i.e. to posit as an object' (B&N: 294). In these passages, however, Sartre is not describing the necessity of categorising the other person in terms of fixed properties. If this were his topic, these claims would involve an equivocation. They would derive the conclusion that we can only treat other people as though they are *metaphysical objects*, things that possess fixed properties, from the premise that we cannot be aware of them except as *intentional objects*, targets of our awareness. The notions of intentional object and metaphysical object are logically independent of one another within Sartre's philosophy, as well as generally: an intentional object need not be a metaphysical object and a metaphysical object need not be an intentional object, though the same thing could be both sorts of object, or indeed something could exist that is neither a metaphysical object nor an intentional object.

It is clear from the context, however, that Sartre does not make such an elementary blunder as to conflate these two clearly distinct concepts. In these passages, he is not concerned with the ways in which we categorise one another, but rather with a related problem that he discusses alongside this issue, that of how it is that we are aware that other people are metaphysical subjects at all. He is addressing, that is, a question concerning our awareness that other bodies are conscious people. His claim is that this awareness is implied by our awareness of ourselves as objects of their consciousness: pure, fundamental, original shame implies the subjectivity of some other person who is aware of us, he claims. 'Thus for me the Other is first the being for whom I am an object: that is, the being *through whom* I gain my objectness' (B&N: 294).

His point is that this awareness cannot motivate focusing attention on the other person to make their subjectivity, their consciousness, the explicit direct object of my awareness. Another person's consciousness cannot be an intentional object of my awareness, because their consciousness is nothing but the appearing of intentional objects to them. Sartre even goes so far as to say that the other person's consciousness 'is not even conceivable', because to think of consciousness is always to think of consciousness from within and therefore is always to think of one's own consciousness (see B&N: 320). This is a central aspect of his response to the problem of solipsism: our experience makes us aware that there are other conscious subjects, but we cannot formulate any explicit thought about or direct conscious attention to the subjectivity of other people (see B&N: 257–9).

Although Sartre is clearly not equivocating on the notion of 'object', however, he might nonetheless seem to be arguing on the basis of this impossibility of explicit knowledge of the subjectivity of another person that we therefore cannot know or treat other people as free subjects. He does seem to draw such a connection when he writes, '*that other* consciousness and *that other* freedom are never *given* to me; for if they were, they would be *known* and would therefore be an object' (B&N: 295). But even if we take this at face value as the claim that we can never know another person's freedom, whatever that claim might mean, this would not imply that we are forever constrained to treating other people as if they have no freedom over their characters or as though their actions flow from their natures just as the behaviour of inanimate objects is determined by their properties. Sartre does not claim that we cannot think of and treat other people as conscious subjects, for example, and it would be ridiculous to make such a claim given that we clearly do think of and treat one another this way. The claim that we cannot have explicit knowledge of another person's freedom therefore does not entail that we cannot acknowledge that they do not have fixed natures. Which is just as well, of course, for if it were impossible to think of people except as having fixed natures, then there would seem to have been no point whatsoever in writing *Being and Nothingness* and no point in reading it, since this is a book aimed at persuading us that people do not have fixed natures. We might even wonder whether it would even be possible to have written a book arguing for a theory that is literally unthinkable.

What is more, such a theory of our views of the actions of other people would not sit well with Sartre's account of our views of our own experiences and actions. Although we generally consider ourselves to have fixed natures from which these flow, according to Sartre, we are capable of seeing ourselves as we really are, as having changeable characters manifested in our experience and behaviour. Our reflection on our own experiences and actions, that is, is usually 'impure' because, like all experience, it is coloured by our project of bad faith. As we saw in chapter 7, however, Sartre does not think that reflection must be misleading in this way: a 'pure' reflection is possible, he tells us, and this will bring about a kind of 'katharsis'. 'This is not the place to describe the motivation and structure of this katharsis', he adds (B&N: 182). Pure reflection is part of the authentic attitude towards our existence, and the katharsis in question is part of the radical conversion to authenticity, and as we have already seen in this chapter, Sartre refuses to say much at all about authenticity or the conversion in *Being and Nothingness*, leaving these topics for the future work on ethics (B&N: 647).

It is our bad faith that makes us see other people as having fixed natures, just as it makes us see ourselves in that way. To see ourselves as we genuinely are requires us to abandon the project of bad faith and replace it with a project of authenticity, according to Sartre, and it would seem that the same is true of our views of one another. That the other person categorises me as having a fixed nature, therefore, is not inevitable but rather a product of bad faith. This connection between the alienating look of another person, the uncomfortable categorisation of myself as having some specific fixed character, and bad faith is mentioned early on in *Being and Nothingness* in the example of the unhappy homosexual and the champion of sincerity. 'Who cannot see how offensive to the Other', Sartre asks, 'and how reassuring for me is a statement such as, "He is just a pederast", which removes a disturbing freedom from a trait and which aims at henceforth constituting all the acts of the Other as consequences following strictly from his essence' (B&N: 88). The champion of sincerity is motivated by bad faith: he wants to deny that his friend has any freedom over his character in order to affirm that people generally, including himself, have fixed natures. This is offensive to his friend not because his friend wants to affirm his freedom but because he wants to see his own fixed nature differently.

Sartre is therefore describing an aspect of the social dimension of bad faith. But the theory can be applied even in cases where the other person is not in fact ascribing to me a fixed nature, or indeed is not even looking at me. All that matters is that I assume that they are doing so. This is an assumption that I will make if my worldview is coloured by the project of bad faith: whatever they think of me, they think it in terms of my nature, I will think, since everyone knows that actions flow from fixed natures. So although Sartre does mean to be presenting a theory of the relations between people in bad faith, this is really a theory of the social relations to which an individual is condemned by bad faith regardless of whether or not other people are also pursuing the project of bad faith. It is because Sartre takes bad faith to be a pervasive social phenomenon that he does not make this very clear, though he does emphasise, as we have seen, that we do not in fact know precisely how other people categorise us and that this does not matter to his theory.

Not only does the theory of bad faith as a project explain why we categorise one another in terms of fixed properties, why we see other people as having natures, therefore, but it also explains why people in bad faith will assume that they are being categorised by other people in terms of their having this or that nature. My bad faith makes me assume that other people will see me as '*seated* as this inkwell *is on* the table' or as '*leaning over* the keyhole as this tree *is bent* by the wind' (B&N: 286). The conflictual relations that Sartre describes in *Being and Nothingness*, that is to say, do not actually require both parties to be in bad faith: an individual in bad faith is condemned to this alienation felt in the presence of other people and to respond to this alienation by objectifying the other person in whatever way will end the feeling of alienation, regardless of whether or not anyone else is in bad faith. We will return to this point in the next chapter, when we consider why someone might be motivated to abandon bad faith in favour of authenticity and whether it would be a good idea to do so.

We can see from this analysis of Sartre's account of the look, moreover, that the characters in the play *Huis Clos* are not locked into quite the same battle as Sartre thinks that people in bad faith lock themselves into. The much-quoted punch-line of the play, 'Hell is . . . other people!' (HC: 223), is often taken to summarise his idea that we necessarily misunderstand and seek to dominate one another (see, e.g., Heter, *Sartre's Ethics of Engagement*, 35). Not only does Sartre not think that this conflict is necessary, however, but this play does not even dramatise the theory that he does propound, as we shall see.

The crucial difference between the characters in the play and ourselves, of course, is that we are alive and they have died. Because their lives have ended, there is nothing they can do to add to the sequence of actions on the basis of which they will be categorised and judged. Death robs us of the ability to give meaning to our own past behaviour by our present actions (B&N: 561). Were Garcin still alive, he could strive to make his desertion seem, to himself and to other people, to be an act of courage required for him to take a stand against the war, though were he to just cower in hiding until the war is over his desertion would seem very much like an act of cowardice. Being shot for this desertion, however, has robbed him of the chance to choose between these and other possible projects, and hence of the ability to show his desertion in one light or another. The meaning of his life is now entirely a matter of the views people take on the record of events. An ended life, as Sartre puts it, 'is a life of which the Other makes himself the guardian' (B&N: 562). It 'remains in the hands of the Other like a coat which I leave to him after my disappearance' (B&N: 565).

Garcin sees the people he has left behind talk about and reinterpret his life in ways he can no longer influence until all memory of him fades away. The peculiarity of his position, of remaining conscious of his life and those of his Hell-mates even though he is dead, means that his life will never be entirely forgotten: there are three eternal witnesses to it. But this is not enough. Garcin does not simply want his life to be remembered. It matters to him that he is remembered in a particular way, as a courageous and tough person, not as a coward. He is uncertain about the meanings of his own actions, about whether he genuinely was courageous or cowardly, as we saw in chapter 4, and this uncertainty means that he recognises that his life can be interpreted either way. This is what tortures him: not that some people see his life differently to the way he would like it to be seen, but that the evidence is ambiguous between his having been cowardly and his having been courageous. Since he can no longer add to the record, of course, what he recognises is that this evidence will always be ambiguous. Inez insists that he really was a coward and Estelle dithers to suit her purposes, but this serves only to remind him of the real problem, which is not that anyone in fact sees his life as cowardly but that the evidence does not preclude anyone from doing so.

Garcin faces a problem very different from the one that Daniel grapples with in the 'Roads to Freedom' trilogy, therefore. Daniel is in bad faith. He sees people as having fixed natures and wants to see himself as having a particular kind of fixed nature. His problem is that other people do not see him this way. Their looks 'always stopped short at my skin', he complains (TR: 169). His own view of himself is lacking in significance without confirmation provided by someone else: 'I *am* a paederast—he uttered the words, and words too they remained, they passed him by' (TR: 113). Were he to find someone who agreed with his self-image, however, he would have to see this as issuing from their fixed natures and hence as worthlessly mechanical. Hence his recourse to God, whom he can see as freely confirming his self-image without this undermining the idea that people have fixed natures. Garcin, on the other hand, is concerned not with how people see what he is now, the character he has in Hell, but rather with the way they see the record of his life, the actions he has committed. Once one has died, Sartre claims, one's life becomes an object with fixed properties (B&N: 321). Garcin may of course think that his life manifests his fixed nature, but this is not the fulcrum on which his difficulty rests. He is not condemned to Hell by bad faith. He cannot evade his sentence by converting to an authentic recognition of the freedom people have over their characters. There really is no way out.

What the play has in common with the theory of relations between living people, of course, is the visual metaphor of the look. The characters in *Huis Clos* find that they have had their eyelids removed and that the only reflective surfaces in which they can see themselves are, appropriately enough, one another's eyes (HC: 182–4, 197–9). They cannot help but look at one another, and they cannot look at themselves except as they are reflected in each other's eyes. They are not looking at one another's characters, however, but at one another's pasts, the closed ledgers of their lives (see B&N: 559). It is what they have done, not who they now are, that is being judged. All that they can find problematic, therefore, is the difference between the ways in which this is seen, or could be seen, and the way in which they would like it to be seen.

Whereas for living people, on the other hand, it is our characters that are under scrutiny, and this causes an additional problem. Not only do we want others to see us as having certain traits and not other ones. If we are pursuing the project of bad faith, we are also averse to any evidence that people have freedom over their characters. We want to be seen as having certain fixed traits, but we do not want to recognise that other people are free to see us in this way or that. For this reason, according to Sartre, bad faith condemns the living individual to unpleasant relations with other people. As we will see in the next chapter, this gives us good reason not to live in bad faith.

10 The Virtue of Authenticity

If there are values only because they are generated by the projects we pursue, as Sartre thinks is the case, then what implications does this have for ethics? Does it restrict the arena of valid moral theorising to those relativist theories that allow moral value to depend solely on individual preferences? Does it go even further and require us to accept the nihilist view that nothing really matters at all? Sartre has often been understood as committed to either relativism or nihilism in ethics. It is certainly true, as we have seen, that he thinks that all values, positive and negative, depend on the goals of our projects and on the means to achieving those goals: considered apart from our projects, in his view, reality consists only of brute being-in-itself devoid of value. 'Thus it amounts to the same thing whether one gets drunk alone or is the leader of nations', he is often quoted as saying (B&N: 646–7).

The liberationist tenor of *Being and Nothingness*, however, makes abundantly clear that Sartre does not accept either relativism or nihilism in ethics, but rather believes bad faith to be an objectively bad thing and authenticity an objectively good thing. The line comparing leading nations to drinking alone should not be taken out of context. It is not true that in this passage, as one commentator puts it, 'Sartre affirms that all actions are equivalent' (Bell, *Sartre's Ethics of Authenticity*, 154). The line is rather intended to encapsulate the attitude of those who recognise that people in our culture can be understood in terms of the fixed nature that they are pretending to have, but who nonetheless fail to recognise that this project can be abandoned in favour of an authentic attitude to our existence. This attitude, which Sartre calls 'despair', is one that 'still shares in the spirit of seriousness' because it involves taking the futile desire to be God as 'written in things' rather than as a contingent project (B&N: 646). This is to be contrasted with the correct understanding of the desire to be God as not only futile but contingent, and therefore seeing that it can be replaced with authenticity. Sartre then raises questions about where this correct understanding should lead and promises to address them in a future book on ethics (B&N: 647).

It is not enough, of course, to simply proclaim that authenticity is the attitude that we all should adopt. What is required is a reason why we should accept this claim. Such a reason cannot appeal to any value that is independent of the particular projects that individuals pursue, since Sartre denies that there are any such values, and cannot appeal to any value that is contingent on our pursuing certain projects, since the recommendation of authenticity is supposed to be objective and universal. But without such a reason, we seem to be left with two problems: in the normative sphere, we seem to be left with relativism and nihilism to choose from; and as a matter of psychology, it seems that people pursuing the fundamental project of bad faith cannot discover any motivation for abandoning it in favour of authenticity. Sartrean existentialism therefore faces these questions: how can it be a matter of universal normativity that we should embrace authenticity instead of bad faith, and how can there be a universally available motivation for doing so? In short, what is so good about authenticity?

Answering the metaethical question concerning the recommendation of authenticity would not be enough to rule out all forms of ethical relativism, however. For although it would show that there is at least one objectively binding norm, that of being authentic, it would not of itself show that there were any more. Why should there be any restrictions on the way an authentic person, someone who recognises the true nature of human existence, behaves towards other people? Perhaps authenticity is compatible, as some people have charged, with a complete disregard for the dignity and welfare of other people. Discussions of the ethical implications of Sartrean existentialism usually focus on this normative issue, but the metaethical question is the more fundamental. We will see in this chapter that there is a way of answering this more fundamental question within the confines of Sartre's theory of character and that Sartre does indicate his intention to provide this kind of answer. Our analysis will also delimit the possible responses Sartre can make to the normative question of whether authenticity requires respect for the dignity or welfare of others. The ethics of authenticity itself, however, is a matter outside the scope of this book.

Sartre's famous lecture *Existentialism Is A Humanism*, delivered in an overcrowded room to an overexcited audience in Paris in 1945, was aimed at rebutting the criticism that his existentialism ruled out any objective ethics. It should not be taken as a definitive statement of Sartre's approach to this issue, however, not only because of its brevity but also because Sartre points out in the discussion that expressing his philosophy for a general audience inevitably involves distorting it, or at least 'diluting' it (EH: 55). The major work on ethics promised at the end of *Being and Nothingness* never appeared, moreover, so there is no definitive statement of an ethical theory of Sartre's. The preparatory notes for the promised book have been collated, edited, and published since Sartre's death and are available in English under the title *Notebooks for an Ethics*, but we will not be concerned with this text, because we can find all we need to resolve our issue in the works that Sartre himself published.

In the popular lecture, Sartre presents two reasons for preferring authenticity to bad faith. First, he claims that bad faith is 'an error' or, more strongly, 'a lie' and can therefore be judged negatively as untruthful (EH: 47). This should be understood in the context of other comments he makes in that lecture about the truth of human existence. At some time in the future, he points out, it may be that society becomes ordered along fascist lines. 'Fascism will then become the truth of humanity' (*la vérité humaine*), he tells us, 'and so much the worse for us' (EH: 36). This might seem to be the claim that truth itself is not objective but rather relative to the society one lives in. Far from securing the objective value of authenticity, therefore, the claim that authenticity reflects the truth might seem to be a way in which Sartre endorses a form of ethical relativism, though one in which value is relative not to individuals directly but to the societies within which individuals formulate and pursue their projects.

Sartre distinguishes, however, two levels of truth about humanity. The empirical truth about humanity differs from society to society and from age to age because there is no common human nature that helps to explain our practices, just the sets of projects we pursue. There is, nonetheless, a deeper underlying truth that unites all of humanity, the universal human condition (EH: 42–3). This matches the distinction that we saw in chapter 8 between the sartrais terms 'human reality' and 'being for-itself' as they are used in *Being and Nothingness*: the former signifies the empirical facts about human life in our culture, the latter the structure of our existence. This is made clear in the parallel distinction he draws between two forms of humanism: one that lauds the empirical reality of humanity by taking the achievements of actual human beings to be indicative of some kind of human nature, and one that recognises and values the underlying structure of what it is to be human, the kind of existence we have. Sartre rejects the former on the grounds that there is no underlying nature that accounts for these 'admirable deeds of certain men' (EH: 51–2). He recommends the latter and calls it 'existentialist humanism', or 'existentialism' for short (EH: 52–3).

To say that authenticity recognises the truth about the kind of existence we have, however, is not yet to say that it is valuable. What is required is a reason to value the truth in general or at least this truth in particular. We might think that truth is less valuable than comforting illusions, for example, or at least that it is in this case. If values are dependent on projects, then there could be individuals whose projects determine for them a set of values that excludes truth, or this particular truth, or at least subordinates it to other concerns. The problem we started with remains: if all values are dependent on projects, there seems to be neither universal motivation nor universal justification for preferring the truthfulness of authenticity to the untruthfulness of bad faith.

Sartre immediately follows his point about authenticity recognising the truth of human existence with the more complicated argument that since values stem from my freely chosen projects, it is logically inconsistent to value anything while denying the freedom in which that valuing is grounded (EH: 48). But this argument seems to involve a sleight of hand, for Sartre's theory of the nature of values is that they are generated by the pursuit of projects, and this does not in itself seem to require that we have any freedom over those projects. Were our projects fixed facts about us, then could it not still be the case that values are generated solely by this pursuit of goals? Some commentators understand Sartre to claim that we are all, due to the structure of our existence, pursuing the goal of being the God-like being-in-itself-for-itself. Although we have seen that this is not in fact Sartre's view, we can also see that if it were Sartre's view, he could still hold that our valuing that impossible state results from this structure of our existence.

The argument that it is inconsistent to value anything while denying freedom, however, can be understood as relying on a claim about values that we have seen Sartre make in another context. In his discussion of pride, as we saw in the last chapter, Sartre appeals to the idea that being admired by someone is only enjoyable if we understand that admiration not to follow mechanically from that person's fixed nature but rather to embody an evaluation they freely make (B&N: 314–5). Sartre seems to think, that is, that a simple causal process cannot bestow value. There is a hint of this view in his example of the champion of sincerity. This character wants his friend to admit to being homosexual by nature since this admission will show that his sexual attraction to men is not a matter of his values and he will therefore not be judged for it. This thought implicitly appeals to the idea that values can only result from free choices, that a mechanical attraction does not involve any evaluation of the attractive object. This is why Sartre says that the champion of sincerity 'makes use of' human freedom in his attempt to deny it: he makes use of the connection between valuing and freedom in order to argue for something that he clearly values (B&N: 87–8; see also B&N: 433).

We need not consider the merits of this claim about values, or even consider in detail precisely how it should be understood, however, because the argument that implicitly appeals to it in order to show that authenticity is objectively preferable to bad faith is one that is flawed for a simpler reason. Just as the argument that appealed to the truthfulness of authenticity required the value of truth, the argument that appeals to the logical inconsistency of bad faith requires that we value logical consistency. If values are dependent on projects, then there seems no reason why someone cannot have a value system that subordinates logical consistency to other concerns and therefore be perfectly happy with an incoherent but comforting illusion. There seems to be neither universal motivation nor universal justification for preferring the consistency of authenticity to the inconsistency of bad faith.

An objective reason for preferring authenticity over bad faith, one that can both justify and motivate this preference for everyone regardless of the projects they pursue, can be identified only by showing that bad faith necessarily conflicts with our values in at least one area of life. Since bad faith is a fundamental project, the other projects of the person in bad faith must manifest it in some way. If it can be shown that the underlying project of bad faith must prevent the success of these other projects, at least in some important domain of life, then the values generated by those other projects would provide both justification and potential motivation for abandoning bad faith. Just as the inferiority project prevents the person from achieving the goals set by those projects pursued as a way of pursuing inferiority, as we saw in chapter 4, bad faith might conflict with the values generated by projects pursued as ways of pursuing that project of bad faith. So long as the relevant domain is central to our lives and highly important to us, this would mean that anyone in bad faith is better off abandoning it in favour of authenticity, and anyone who understood this could have the motivation to do so.

This is one of the purposes of Sartre's discussion of our relations with one another. Within the project of bad faith, our relations with other people can only be projects that aim to achieve some valued goal that cannot be achieved. There is only a narrow range of attitudes available, none of which can be maintained for long, and we must switch between them interminably, forever failing to achieve whatever it is that we are trying to achieve. Our relations with other people are hamstrung by the framework of bad faith within which they are conducted. The emphasis on truth and consistency in *Existentialism Is A Humanism* might perhaps have been intended as an imprecise, or 'diluted', presentation of this kind of reasoning. Truth and consistency need not be understood as valuable themselves, that is, so long as we allow that false or inconsistent views of ourselves and other people stymie our relations with one another and thereby conflict with the values those relations involve.

Spelling out this argument precisely and assessing its ethical significance are tasks outside the scope of this book, but in order to show that Sartrean existentialism does have some hope of embracing an ethical position other than relativism or nihilism and in order to see how such a position might fit into contemporary ethical debate, we need to look more closely at Sartre's discussion of our concrete relations with one another. That Sartre intends this passage to play this role in recommending authenticity is obscured by three major shortcomings of *Being and Nothingness* that we have already encountered. One is Sartre's general failure to make the structure of the book sufficiently clear. Another is his insistence on discussing these aspects of social and interpersonal relations alongside the related but distinct concerns of the problem of solipsism and the role of the body in relations with others. The third is his failure to distinguish clearly between intensional and extensional senses of psychological terms. That Sartre does intend his discussion this way is nevertheless indicated by his claim that the relationships he discusses can be escaped only by 'a radical conversion' to 'an ethics of deliverance and salvation' (B&N: 434 n13), which we saw in the last chapter to be a description of the project of authenticity.

Sartre begins his discussion of concrete relations with others, relations that embody the abstract relation of 'the look' discussed in the last chapter, by claiming that they embody two distinct basic attitudes towards another person. In one, I attempt to get the other person to affirm that I do indeed have a fixed nature, which Sartre describes as an attempt to 'assimilate' the other to my project of seeing myself in a certain way; and in the other attitude, I focus attention on the other person and see them as having a fixed nature. Within the project of bad faith, my relationship with another person, according to Sartre, will continually oscillate between these two basic attitudes, looking at them and allowing myself to be looked at by them, each attitude being 'enriched by the failure of the other' (B&N: 385).

Sartre goes on to subdivide these two basic attitudes. There are, he tells us, two forms of the appropriation of the other person's perspective for my own objectification: love and masochism. There are, on the other hand, four forms of the objectification of the other person: indifference, sexual desire, sadism, and hatred. But the discussion of these more specific attitudes seems inconsistent, as James Giles points out ('Sartre, Sexual Desire and Relations with Others', 158–9). Having defined love and masochism as the two forms of appropriation or assimilation of another person, for example, Sartre goes on to describe these two attitudes as opposites: love involves 'absorbing' the other person, whereas masochism is 'causing myself to be absorbed' by the other person (B&N: 399). Although hatred is initially defined as one way of reducing the other person to an object, furthermore, Sartre later describes it as an attempt to destroy the other person altogether (B&N: 432).

Giles suggests responding to the first of these difficulties by understanding masochism as a third basic attitude towards others, that of 'trying to make oneself part of the other', and by responding to the second either by adding hate as the fourth basic attitude of 'trying to destroy the other' or by 'stretching the description' of the second basic form to 'the attempt to get rid of the other person's consciousness' (159). But such responses are less than satisfactory, he adds, because 'the clarity of the simple two-attitude system becomes obscured and the relations between the various attitudes become more difficult to explain' (159).

They are also unsatisfactory for a deeper reason. Sartre wants to show that these attitudes all manifest the fundamental project of seeing oneself as having certain fixed character traits. Another person can seem like an ally in this project, since their view can affirm one's own. But as we saw in the last chapter, awareness of another person can also threaten this project in either of two ways. If the other person sees one differently from how one would like to be seen, this impugns one's self-image. If the other person sees one how one would like to be seen, the value this has for one conflicts with the view of all people as having fixed natures that determine their thoughts and behaviour. Sartre wants to divide our attitudes to other people into two categories according to these two broad relationships we can have to other people's views of us. One kind of attitude aims at reinforcing our self-image through the view the other person has of one. The other kind of attitude aims at neutralising any threat they might present to our self-image. If Sartre cannot make the various attitudes he describes fit this dichotomy, then either his account of the project of bad faith, the desire to be God, will need revision, or he will need to abandon the idea that this is the fundamental project manifested in all of our other projects.

The account of love (*l'amour*) that Sartre offers is based on the contentious claim that loving someone is the project aimed at being loved by that person (B&N: 388). But we need not understand all love in this way. It seems perfectly possible to have a particularly high regard and strong affection for someone without necessarily wanting this to be reciprocated. Such love from afar, however, does not present a substantial problem, since we can understand Sartre to be discussing just the kind of love, common enough and central to our lives, that does involve a desire for reciprocation. This wanting to be loved, he goes on, is wanting the other person not only to see one as having a particular nature that is admirable, or even loveable, but also to value one in such a way that no other value could weigh more heavily with them (B&N: 391).

This desire is unstable because of the relation we all understand to hold between value and freedom. We do not want to be 'the object of a passion that flows forth mechanically', claims Sartre: the lover 'does not want to possess an automaton, and if we want to humiliate him, we need only try to persuade him that the beloved's passion is the result of a psychological determinism' (B&N: 389). Here we see again Sartre's view that we already understand that unless something is valued freely, it is not really valued at all. To discover that the other person's love for you follows strictly from their psychological make-up is, according to Sartre, to no longer feel truly loved at all. The feeling of being loved, therefore, like the feeling of pride, contains within it the suggestion that people do not, or might not, really have fixed natures. This is one way in which bad faith is stultifying: it conflicts with the value of being loved. The desire to be loved, moreover, is one way in which we try to pursue the project of bad faith, as it is one way in which we try to reassure ourselves of our fixed natures.

Being loved is therefore alienating. In the sartrais introduced in the last chapter, the feeling of being loved involves an antivalue within the context of the project of bad faith. For this reason, this kind of love degenerates, according to Sartre, into masochism (*le masochisme*). Rather than aiming to fascinate the other person, to absorb their attention and become a supremely valuable object, in this project one aims rather to become simply one object among others, aiming to be desired simply as 'an instrument to be used' (B&N: 400). Where the desire to be loved involves the value of being seen to have some particular nature unsurpassable in value, masochism involves the more modest value of simply being seen as an object with a fixed nature. The label 'masochism' might make this project seem rather exotic, but the humdrum reality of a passionless but functional relationship can also fit the bill.

We can now see that the first apparent inconsistency that Giles points out in Sartre's discussion is not really an inconsistency at all. Love and masochism have in common the use of the other person to bolster one's view of oneself as having a particular fixed nature. They both involve appropriating the other person for my purposes. The difference is that in love the emphasis is on the details of the character that I want the other person to ascribe to me, whereas in masochism the emphasis is on their seeing my character as fixed. Sartre complicates this by exploiting the ambiguity of the verb 'to absorb' (*absorber*) to draw the distinction, saying that wanting to be loved is attempting to absorb the other person's attention, whereas masochism is attempting to be absorbed into the other person's worldview as an object (B&N: 399).

The project of masochism, however, is no more stable than the project of being loved, since one no longer has control, or even knowledge, of the way in which the other person sees one: 'this alienated Me', Sartre writes, 'remains in principle inapprehensible' (B&N: 400). Their view of one's character might therefore be quite different from one's own, which undermines one's confident ascription of a particular fixed nature to oneself. The project of bad faith even conflicts with the value involved in masochism, therefore. For this reason, whether in the form of love or of masochism, the general aim of using other people to objectify oneself leads to alienation.

The strategy for escaping this alienation is to categorise the other person as having some specific fixed nature, as we saw in the last chapter, thereby either denying that their admiration is freely given or undermining the validity of their view of us. The objectified person then 'possesses a pure and simple image of me which is nothing but one of his objective affects and which no longer touches me' (B&N: 402). Although this attitude can be motivated as a response to alienation, Sartre denies that it need be: the ordering of these basic attitudes as first and second is just an expository device, he claims; either can be motivated by the failure of the other, either can occur first without any such motivation.

The simplest form of this basic attitude is what Sartre calls 'indifference' (*indifférence*) or 'blindness' (*cécité*) to the status of other people as other subjects with characters and perspectives on the world. We can treat other people as tools and obstacles in our world, just like the inanimate objects they move between, he claims, learning how to operate them in order to get what we want and to avoid them when that better suits our purposes. This point of view 'can be maintained for a long time', even 'for a whole life', except for 'brief and terrifying flashes of illumination' (B&N: 403). It is in this perspective that 'the café waiter is nothing but the function of serving the customers' (B&N: 402–3). Sartre is not making the implausible claim that there is a common attitude of explicitly denying that other human beings have subjective lives, but is rather claiming that we often treat other people just as we would if we thought they were mere fleshy machines. 'Of course they have some knowledge of me, but this knowledge does not touch me. It is a matter of pure modifications of their being' (B&N: 402). Their views of us are not treated as valid opinions about the kind of people we are, in this attitude, but rather as facts about them that contribute to their being useful to us or being obstacles to be avoided.

Although this is a relatively stable attitude, the aims of bad faith are not entirely achieved through it. Understanding that people do indeed have views of me, just as I have views of them, leads to an uneasiness (*malaise*) or anxiety (*inquiétude*) even when I do not pay any attention to what those views are: indifference 'is accompanied by the consciousness of a "wandering and inapprehensible" look, and I am in danger of its alienating me behind my back' (B&N: 404). Pinning people down to their positions within the world as it is organised by my enterprises and concerns, that is, does not quite remove the nagging sense that they see me as having certain characteristics and that these may include traits other than those that make up my preferred self-image. Their views of me are not neutralised: 'everything happens as if I wished to get hold of a man who runs away and leaves only his coat in my hands' (B&N: 415).

Alongside this way of objectifying people in general, Sartre claims, sexual desire (*le désir sexuel*) and sadism (*le sadisme*) are ways in which we try to objectify particular people close to us. The goal of sexual desire, he claims, is the incarnation of the other person's subjectivity in their body, so that there is no more to them than can be manipulated through touching their skin. The 'profound meaning' of this aim is to prevent the other person from forming views of me, or indeed from thinking or experiencing anything, that is beyond my understanding and control (B&N: 415–16). Incarnation renders the subjectivity of the other person 'enclosed within the limits of an object' and 'because of this very fact, I shall be able to touch it, feel it, possess it' (B&N: 417). But this project must fail, because this incarnation lasts only so long as one caresses the other person. Wherever this activity leads, however it comes to an end, the other person's awareness ceases to be absorbed by my caresses and so disappears from my control (B&N: 419–20). The goal of sexual desire, therefore, can only be achieved temporarily.

This failure of sexual desire can lead to adopting either the masochistic approach we have already considered, the aim of which is to present myself to the other person as having some particular nature, or the sadistic attitude of treating the other person as incarnated and malleable without aiming to manipulate their view of me (B&N: 419–420, 426). We have already seen that masochism fails because it leaves open the possibility that the other person's view of oneself diverges significantly from one's preferred self-image. Sadism fails for the same reason. After all, sadism totally abandons the project of manipulating the other person's image of oneself, settling instead for merely perpetuating their incarnation. Sadists therefore fail to escape the alienation that results from the other person holding views of them that are beyond their own knowledge and control (B&N: 427).

The most extreme way of attempting to neutralise the threat another person might present to one's self-image is hatred (*la haine*), which is not an attitude towards 'this appearance, this fault, this particular action', Sartre claims, but rather comes about when the individual wants 'to get rid of its inapprehensible being-as-object-for-the-Other and to abolish its dimension of alienation' (B&N: 432). Instead of aiming to appropriate the other person's view of oneself for one's own ends, this attitude 'wishes to destroy this object in order by the same stroke to overcome the transcendence which haunts it' (B&N: 432). Hatred is the desire to be rid of the other person, and hence rid of their ability to see one in ways other than the way one wants to be seen. Were this desire fulfilled, however, this would not end the alienation but rather cement it. Once the other person is destroyed, their view of me slips into the past and becomes 'an irremediable dimension of myself' (B&N: 434). Just as death deprives me of the ability to act in ways that might alter the view others have of me, the death of another person deprives me of the ability to try to manipulate their view of me. Hatred is therefore a reaction to alienation, but one that cannot remove it.

Returning to the objections Giles makes to this taxonomy of attitudes towards others, we can see that he is right to complain that Sartre's account of hatred does not really fit with the description of the second basic attitude as one of objectifying the other person. We need not, however, take either of the routes Giles recommends for solving this problem. Another solution is available, one that can best be seen if we also consider a third objection Giles presents. Having first introduced sexual desire as one species of the second attitude, Sartre goes on to proclaim that all interactions between individuals 'include as their skeleton—so to speak—sexual relations' (B&N: 428). He soon adds that Love and Desire, newly capitalised, are 'in fact integrated into *all* attitudes' towards other people, and are therefore the 'original' attitudes (B&N: 429). Giles sees in this discussion just blatant inconsistency, resulting perhaps from confusion, and generating myriad problems that ultimately require us to abandon the Sartrean account of sexuality and interpersonal relations ('Sartre, Sexual Desire and Relations With Others', 159–166).

The inconsistencies in this passage, however, simply come about because Sartre wants to address two separate issues using the same distinction and is unable to do so. He wants to distinguish two kinds of attitude one can have towards the objectification of oneself in the eyes of another, and he wants to use this analysis to uncover the grain of truth in the idea, common in psychoanalysis, that all interpersonal interaction is suffused with sexuality. The first goal requires a distinction between identifying with the other person's view of oneself and attempting to undermine it, the second a distinction between objectifying oneself and objectifying the other person. These distinctions do not line up: the claim about sexuality concerns personal relations with specific individuals rather than one's attitudes towards people at large, so indifference is irrelevant; and hatred simply does not fit the distinction between objectifying oneself and objectifying the other, as Sartre readily admits (B&N: 428).

Sartre's claim that sexuality underpins personal relations between individuals is neither as implausible nor as interesting as it might seem, moreover, since Sartre refuses to define sexuality in terms of a particular kind of pleasure (B&N: 406–7). He takes sexuality to be concerned with objectification: the desire to be loved and its degraded form of masochism aim at one's own objectification, the desire for sexual interaction and its degraded form of sadism aim at the objectification of the other person. Within the project of bad faith, he thinks, these basic aims govern our relations with one another, when we are neither indifferent to nor hating one another. Interpersonal relations involving sexual pleasure manifest these basic structures, Love and Desire, he thinks, just as most interpersonal relations do. This is not really the claim that sexuality is involved in all interpersonal relations, however, but rather the claim that sexual relations involve the same basic structures as most other interpersonal relations.

The acceptability of Sartre's view of sexuality is not our concern here: we are concerned with the other claim of this passage, that our relations with other people are governed by our attempt to either control or undermine the views they have of us. We need not even agree with this claim, moreover, or with the taxonomy of the species of these attitudes that Sartre offers. What is important for our purposes is that this discussion has clarified the structure of Sartre's reasoning in favour of authenticity. It is not simply that bad faith leads to conflictual relations with one another, and that this makes us all unhappy, since such an argument would have to appeal to the universal value of happiness. It is rather that within the fundamental project of bad faith we can only pursue certain types of relationships with one another and these will always fail by their own lights because they will always value goals that cannot be achieved. 'At whatever moment a person is considered, he is in one or other of these attitudes— unsatisfied by the one as by the other' (B&N: 430).

Sartrean existentialism can in principle meet the challenge of showing that authenticity is preferable to bad faith for everyone regardless of the projects they pursue and hence regardless of the values they hold, therefore. If bad faith unavoidably involves the frustration of our projects, it conflicts with the values that we hold as a matter of having those projects, even if we would not have precisely those projects and therefore those values were it not for our bad faith. Justification for authenticity would come from the very values had by those in bad faith, and recognising this would provide the motivation for abandoning bad faith. Should such an argument for authenticity be constructed in a persuasive form, which is something that we cannot investigate further here, however, this would not be sufficient to clear Sartrean existentialism of the charge of moral relativism. There is a second hurdle, as we have already seen: there also needs to be substantial restriction on one's behaviour towards other people.

In his discussion of this normative ethical question, Sartre sometimes sounds as though he endorses the view that anything goes so long as it is consistent with the authentic recognition of our freedom over our characters. 'Nowhere is it written that good exists', he proclaims in his popular lecture, 'that we must be honest or must not lie' and as a result 'everything is permissible' (EH: 28–9). Because moral theories are 'always too broad in scope to apply to the specific and concrete case under consideration', moreover, 'we have no choice but to rely on our instincts' (EH: 32). Authenticity must have a social dimension, of course, just as bad faith has a social dimension: if one truly understands and accepts that, as a matter of human existence, one has control over the ways in which one sees the world and the ways in which one responds to it, then one will see all people in this way. But this is not yet to respect those people or care about their welfare. Oppression and exploitation do not require a mistaken view of their victims, and might well be all the more efficient without it.

Despite sometimes sounding as though he thinks that anything goes, of course, Sartre wants to show that his existentialism demands a respect for the dignity of other people and the promotion of their welfare, which he conceives in terms of their opportunities for the expression of their freedom. There are no specific kinds of actions, such as lying or cheating, that are impermissible by their very nature, he thinks. We may invent any course of action we choose, so long as this 'invention is made in the name of freedom' (EH: 50). In the language of contemporary ethical theory, Sartre is expounding here a form of virtue ethics according to which actions are to be assessed in terms of whether or not they manifest the character trait of respecting and promoting freedom (see EH: 50–1). Those who genuinely possess this trait can rely on their 'instincts' in deciding what to do, he thinks. But why, we may ask, should authenticity should bring this trait with it?

Throughout *Being and Nothingness*, Sartre appears to think of bad faith in the way in which Christianity traditionally conceives of original sin: he implies that bad faith underpins our ethical failings by distorting our vision of the world and other people, and that all that is required for virtue is the removal of this distorting influence. He even, albeit somewhat briefly, claims that what Christianity conceives as guilt is the alienation caused by other people's views of oneself, and that original sin is therefore the state responsible for this alienation (B&N: 431–2). Authenticity cleanses us of this original sin and is therefore 'an ethics of deliverance and salvation' (B&N: 434 n13). Given his avowed atheism, it is not clear what to make of Sartre's liberal use of concepts derived from Christian theology, as Sarah Richmond points out in her introduction to *The Transcendence of the Ego*. But it does seem that he is not simply borrowing language, nor is he only trying to give a sceptical naturalistic picture of the origin of such thinking.

In his picture of bad faith at least, he seems genuinely influenced by central aspects of Christianity. Regardless of the fidelity of his reading of theology, it is not difficult to see why Sartre was attracted to seeing bad faith as a blight whose removal would restore us to moral health, given his view of its influence over our relations with one another.

By the time of the popular lecture, however, Sartre seems to have become aware of the inadequacies of this picture. Central to his discussion is a brief account of the relation between authenticity and respect for the freedom of other people. First he claims that 'once a man realises, in his state of abandonment, that it is he who imposes values, he can will but one thing: freedom as the foundation of all values' (EH: 48). Recognising the true structure of our existence brings with it the aim of promoting 'freedom for freedom's sake' (EH: 48). The reason for this seems to be that my own freedom 'depends entirely on the freedom of others' (EH: 48). 'I cannot set my own freedom as a goal', he tells us, 'without also setting the freedom of others as a goal' (EH: 49). It is quite unclear, however, why the recognition of my freedom over my character should require me to 'set my own freedom as a goal'. Sartre does tell us that this 'will to freedom' is 'implied by freedom itself', but that hardly helps (EH: 49). Equally unclear is the purported relation between my freedom and that of other people: is this merely a point about logical consistency, in which case we might ask why authenticity should require us to value that, or is it the seemingly false claim that I cannot subjugate others in order to achieve my goals?

Perhaps we should understand this discussion as a 'diluted' form of an argument parallel to the reasoning in favour of authenticity uncovered in this chapter. Perhaps we should see Sartre's claim that authenticity requires respect for the freedom of others as grounded in the same way as his claim that authenticity is objectively better than bad faith. This would require that we find reason to believe that treating other people in ways that does not respect their freedom prevents us from achieving the things that, within the fundamental project of authenticity, we value as the goals of our projects or the means to those ends. Given the ontology of values involved in Sartrean existentialism, of course, this would seem to be the only possible way of showing that respect for the freedom of other people is universally good, the only way of providing an objective justification and an objective motivation for treating others in ways that respect their dignity and promote their welfare. What needs to be shown, that is, if there is to be a substantial ethics grounded in the virtue of authenticity, is that exploitation and oppression are necessarily at odds with the values available to the authentic person, at least within some key area of life.

Such an argument might be based on the role that other people play in constructing my public identity, just like the argument for authenticity itself. Some commentators read Sartre in precisely this way: Sartrean ethics is based on the 'recognition' of the other person, they claim, because the authentic person cannot aim to present a particular public image without recognising the freedom of other people that is required for their part in the construction of that public image. 'To be authentic I must respect others because others make me who I am', as one commentator succinctly puts it (Heter, *Sartre's Ethics of Engagement*, 75; see also Carney, *Rethinking Sartre*, esp. ch. 5). But this argument is unconvincing. Recognising someone's freedom is not the same as respecting it. Respecting the freedom of enough people to secure one's own image, moreover, seems compatible with exploiting and oppressing many more. The descriptive claim that my public persona is partly constructed by other free beings, therefore, does not entail a general obligation to respect other people, despite what some commentators claim (see esp. Carney, *Rethinking Sartre*, 89; Heter, *Sartre's Ethics of Engagement*, 86).

There may, however, be some sophisticated reasoning linking authenticity to respect for other people in general, parallel to the subtleties of the argument that bad faith constrains us to valuing goals in our relations with other people that we simply cannot achieve. But it is not an aim of this book to see whether Sartre succeeds in providing such reasoning in his published and unpublished works subsequent to *Being and Nothingness*, or indeed whether one can be provided for him, significant though these tasks are. Whether or not authenticity can ground any substantial ethics within Sartre's account of the nature of value, therefore, is an issue we will leave unresolved. It is not necessary, however, to accept Sartre's account of the ontology of values in order to agree that authenticity is a virtue. A variety of metaethical theories are compatible with the idea that it is better to recognise the way people really are than to mistake them for something else. The recommendation of such recognition could be made, moreover, from within any normative ethical theory.

Sartre's discussion of the problems with bad faith in *Being and Nothingness* is interesting within moral thought not only for the idea of a cardinal virtue of authenticity, but also for its argument that authenticity is valuable regardless of one's projects because its absence condemns one to valuing goals that cannot be achieved. The thought here is that moral imperatives can be universally binding without being grounded in normatively binding religion or rationality and can be universally motivating in the absence of any universally held goals or beliefs. Values can be objective without being written in the heavens: their universal importance can be written instead in the frustration necessarily involved in trying to live without them.

Sartre's form of this argument is rooted in his theory of character as consisting in the projects we pursue and which thereby form the world as we experience it and the ways in which we react to that experience. This theory of character has been the central topic of this book, and for good reason: it has the potential to make a major contribution to moral psychology, to present a strong alternative to the Aristotelian consensus that character consists in rationally guided habits, and thereby to challenge any approach to practical normative ethics that assumes the consensus theory. So the final chapter of this book is devoted to making more explicit the distinctive nature and strengths of this alternative account of character.

11 Being One Self

By far the most influential understanding of character is the one Aristotle articulates in *Nicomachean Ethics*: the patterns we can discern in the way an individual sees things, thinks and feels about them, and behaves in response to them, on this view, are ultimately rooted in our habits. Reflective rational consideration has some role to play in developing and refining our character traits, but practice is crucial, not only for training or programming ourselves but also for learning to enjoy the particular pleasures to be had from certain ways of seeing things, thinking about them, feeling about them, and responding to them. We can reason about which traits we would prefer to have, and we can reason about how to go about forming them if we lack them or refining them if we possess them imperfectly, but in order for our preferred traits to become and remain genuine parts of our character, we must incorporate them into our habits and learn to find pleasure in exercising them (see esp. 1103a14–1104b3).

This picture differs markedly from Sartre's theory that character consists in projects. If we accept the Aristotelian view, then the only advice we can give to someone unhappy with some aspect of their personality is to try to get out of the troubling habit. But if the Sartrean account is right, then this advice may well prove useless: the unhappy person should rather work out which projects of theirs are responsible for whatever is troubling them, decide whether or not the value of that project makes their difficulty worth while, and if it does not then abandon that project. For if the Sartrean account is right and the troubled person merely works hard at breaking a certain habit, then they may well replace it with a new one that is just as troubling or perhaps even worse. The new habit, that is to say, may be just another way of pursuing the same project, and if it is the project itself that is causing the problem, then the new habit will be no better than the old.

What is more, as we have seen, the Sartrean account allows for the thought that what an individual needs to change in order to become a happier or a better person need not be obvious to them. Although this theory of character is opposed to the idea that our perceptions, thoughts, feelings, and behaviour can be caused by unconscious drives and impulses, it leaves room for the possibility that some of the projects that a person is pursuing might be not only deep but buried. Sartre criticises psychoanalytic theories that postulate sex drives and nervous temperaments, for example, as basic causes of our behaviour. He claims that these are described as basic purely because of a 'refusal to push the analysis further' (B&N: 581). We have seen that he thinks of sexuality as manifesting the projects that the individual pursues, and he would say the same about levels of confidence. We should not understand ourselves as made up of collections of diverse inclinations, unconscious or otherwise, but rather as a 'totality', an integrated hierarchy of our projects (see B&N: 584). Some of the projects lower down this hierarchy are ones we may be unaware of, either because they are not obvious from our more immediate projects, or because pursuing them requires that we hide from ourselves this very pursuit. Bad faith and the inferiority project are good examples of this second kind of reason, as we have seen in chapters 4 and 7.

The aim of this chapter is to show that this Sartrean picture of character as consisting in a holistic network of projects is preferable to both the Aristotelian view of character and the view that behaviour is rooted in certain basic drives and impulses. We can approach this topic by first considering an aspect of Sartre's discussions of character that might seem particularly controversial. This is his belief that sexuality is a matter of the projects one pursues. 'Is it not rather that some people find themselves attracted to men, some to women, and some to both?', asks McCulloch (*Using Sartre*, 67). To clarify the problem, it is worth bearing in mind that Sartre does not hold the implausible view that each trait is itself a project, as though one could not be jealous or mean without aiming to be precisely that. His view is rather that the patterns in our behaviour that are described by our characterological language result from the projects we pursue. But this is not in itself enough to make his account of sexuality seem plausible: sexual orientation does not seem to result from choices at all.

We could respond to this criticism by denying that sexual orientation is a matter of character. While many aspects of your sexual behaviour may well manifest character, orientation itself, we might argue, is not part of your character but rather part of the way your body is, like your metabolism or your natural hair colour. This would preserve the idea that character consists in one's projects: sexual orientation would not be covered by this claim in the first place. The problem with this move, however, is that it stands in tension with the functional definition of character involved in the theory it is meant to defend. The argument for identifying each person's character with their set of projects, as we saw in chapters 2 and 3, rests on the idea that character trait terms pick out whatever properties of a person explain the noticeable patterns in that person's perceptions, thoughts, feelings, and actions. Since sexual orientation is manifested in those patterns, excluding it from our character seems somewhat arbitrary, with the result that opponents of the Sartrean approach to explaining behaviour can just insist that all manner of other aspects of those patterns are external to our character as well.

Rather than taking this route, we could understand sexual orientation as an aspect of ourselves that is integrated into our character even though we have no control over it. If we understand character in the Aristotelian way, then this integration is a matter of the kinds of habits that we have developed in relation to our sexual orientation, the ways in which we think about it, and the kinds of pleasures that we seek in expressing or suppressing it. If we understand character in the Sartrean way, on the other hand, then this integration is simply a matter of the projects we pursue that involve our sexual orientation in one way or another. We saw in the last chapter that in *Being and Nothingness* Sartre argues that bad faith constrains our relations with other people, including our sexual relations, to follow certain basic formulas. The project of bad faith is pursued in all of our activity, he thinks, including the expression of our sexual orientation. This sexual orientation might not itself be part of our character, on this view, but the precise ways in which it influences our perceptions, thoughts, feelings, and actions are a matter of our character, and result from the projects that we pursue.

Other potential counterexamples to Sartre's account of our control over our character might help to illuminate this point. Drug addiction, for example, is a state of an individual that accounts for some aspects of their experience and behaviour. An ex-smoker might crave nicotine at the slightest smell of tobacco smoke, where another person might not. We can agree that the disposition towards craving is not itself part of that person's character, even though it may have been caused by past behaviour that did manifest their character, and still maintain that the craving is never felt just as a craving for nicotine. It is rather experienced as a craving to be resisted, a craving that might win out, a craving that justifies relenting, and so on. Quite how the nicotine addiction is manifested in thought and action is a matter of character, therefore.

Hunger provides a universally recognisable example. The facts that human bodies require food and that this need is manifested in hunger are certainly aspects of ourselves that influence the ways in which we perceive, think, feel, and act, but are neither parts of our character nor under our control. Among people who have sufficient access to nourishment, however, the way in which hunger is manifested in experience varies widely: we can take great pleasure in good meals, treat food as a mere source of necessary sustenance, or seek some sort of virtue in hardly eating at all. These different attitudes to food, and many more besides, express different characters and are present in different ways of seeing the world, thinking and feeling about it, and acting in it.

Sexuality is not simply a matter of sexual orientation. Just like the need for food in all of our lives and the addiction to nicotine in the lives of some, we can think of sexual orientation as a standing fact about a person which impacts on their experiences and actions only insofar as it is integrated into their character, whether this be a matter of their habits or their projects or anything else, and the individual's overall sexuality as formed by this integration. Sexual orientation differs from these other examples, of course, in that it is available in a variety of flavours, but this need make no difference to its relation to character. Such a view of sexuality contrasts markedly with the Freudian account of basic animal drives lurking in the nonrational and unconscious darkness and aiming to express themselves in experience and action whether openly or in disguise. This alternative view, outlined by Sartre but transferable to the Aristotelian theory of character, denies that sexuality is beyond our control, seeing it as part and parcel of the character we have built up and can alter rather than some alien if inner force that occasionally erupts into our daily lives.

Saying that sexual orientation itself is not a matter of character does not imply that it is not really part of oneself. For we can understand character as the aspect of oneself that explains the way one perceives, thinks, feels, and behaves while allowing that there may be further aspects of oneself that this character draws upon. If we accept the Sartrean picture of character, then we can say that sexual orientation itself is not part of character: it never features in experience and action on its own, but only in the way in which it is integrated into projects. The projects it is integrated into form our character, on this view, and we can add that one takes ownership of one's orientation by this integration. Ownership does not require acceptance or affirmation: even those who try to resist, suppress, or deny their sexual orientation thereby integrate that orientation into these projects.

Quite what ownership of unconscious drives and impulses could amount to is a question we will address later in this chapter. First we will sharpen the issue of ownership by comparing this Sartrean account with the Aristotelian view of character, according to which we could understand ownership as a matter of integration into the habits one has developed, the rational control over those habits, and the pleasures one seeks through those habits. Nothing that has been said so far in this chapter gives us reason to choose between this and the Sartrean theory. At this stage, it seems that both are equally capable of understanding ownership of desires in terms of their integration into character, rather than in terms of their emanating from character, and both thereby allow us to see character as the unifying aspect of the self. But we shall now see that only on the Sartrean account can this connection between ownership and character be maintained in the face of a certain sort of objection.

We can bring this objection sharply into focus by considering two examples introduced by Harry Frankfurt in his work on freedom of action, work that has been central to discussions of the notion of autonomy and the nature of action in anglophone philosophy over the last few decades. The first concerns an unwilling drug addict who has a desire to take a certain drug, resulting from the addiction, but also a desire not to take the drug.

Both of these desires are what Frankfurt calls 'first-order': they are desires that are not directly concerned with other desires. This addict may also have second-order desires, desires that are directly concerned with first-order desires. Unwilling addicts may have the second-order desire not to have the first-order desire to take the drug: as well as wanting to avoid taking it, they might also want to stop wanting to take it. Frankfurt reserves the term 'second-order volition' for a particular kind of second-order desire: it is the desire that a particular first-order desire is the one that issues in action. So the unwilling addict has the second-order volition to act on the first-order desire not to take the drug.

Such an unwilling addict, claims Frankfurt, might yet take the drug or might not. The second-order volition may prove ineffective, or it might prove effective. Through the second-order volition, the addict identifies with the desire not to take the drug and puts the competing desire at a distance. This identification with the desire not to take the drug, according to Frankfurt, allows the addict to 'meaningfully make the analytically puzzling statements that the force moving him to take the drug is a force other than his own' and that it is 'against his will that this force moves him to take it' ('Freedom of the Will and the Concept of a Person', § 2). Second-order volitions, on this view, determine which of one's first-order desires are truly one's own. It might be objected that if one's addictive desires result, as they usually do, from a past course of behaviour freely entered into, then one cannot disown them in this way. But with the distinction we have already drawn between character and ownership, we can retain the spirit of Frankfurt's example even if we disagree with his theory of ownership. By integrating the addictive desire into a habit or project, even one of resisting it, one makes the desire one's own. But if it is integrated into one's character only through the attempt to resist it, and one acts on it nonetheless, then one can truly deny that taking the drug was a result of one's character.

Central to Frankfurt's own account, however, is the idea that an unwilling addict might take the drug despite having no second-order desire to act on the first-order desire for the drug. In such a case, according to Frankfurt, the addict does not really act: taking the drug is not something this addict does. This is quite an influential claim. J. David Velleman, for example, writes that Frankfurt's example shows that 'an agent's desires and beliefs can cause a corresponding intention despite him, and hence without his participation' ('What Happens When Someone Acts?', 463/125). Velleman therefore follows Frankfurt in thinking that the key issue in understanding autonomous action is understanding the difference between ordinary behaviour and 'cases in which human behaviour proceeds without the agent as its cause' ('What Happens When Someone Acts?', 470/132). This idea of behaviour that the agent does not perform, however, certainly seems questionable. We need not accept, that is to say, the idea that an unwilling addict might take a drug despite the second-order desire not to act on the addictive desire and in the absence of any countervailing second-order desire.

To see just what is so unintuitive about this, consider an example Philippa Foot gives of behaviour that happens to someone rather than being something they do. 'One can imagine the scene: he is sitting quietly in his chair and has said that he is going to go on reading his book', she writes, when 'suddenly he cries "Good heavens, I can't control my legs!" and as he moves across the room, he hangs on to the furniture or asks someone else to hold him' ('Free Will As Involving Determinism', 441/64). When unwilling addicts take their drugs, this is not because they have literally lost control over their bodies, and neither does it seem that way to them. As any ex-smoker will tell you, the moment of weakness that leads to lighting up is not one in which the residual desire to smoke, activated perhaps by the smell of nearby smoking or other environmental factors, takes over and controls the body, but rather the moment at which one caves in and replaces the second-order volition to act on the desire not to smoke with a new second-order volition to, just this once, act on the desire to smoke. Second-order volitions need not be consistent over time. One can usually prefer to act on the desire not to smoke but occasionally prefer to act on the competing desire. (Frankfurt himself makes this point about inconsistent second-order volitions in his later paper 'The Faintest Passion', §§ 4–5, but insists nonetheless that unwilling addicts may take their drugs in the absence of second-order desires to act on their first-order desires for the drug.)

It seems more plausible that a first-order desire can issue in action only with the blessing of a second-order desire, however temporary it may be. But this is not to say that it can be integrated into one's character only through such endorsement. For desires can also be part of your character if you consistently suppress them: the addict who succeeds in never again taking the drug is nonetheless someone for whom the desire to take the drug is part of their character, since it is part of the trait of resisting that temptation. The addict who successfully resists taking the drug for some time, but occasionally relents, acts out of character only in the sense that the actions are unusual: we can still understand such actions as reflecting some character trait, such as weakness under certain unusual circumstances. But herein lies a problem. The theory that a desire is genuinely one's own only if it is integrated into one's habits or projects, and thereby becomes part of one's character insofar as it is integrated into these habits or projects, requires an answer to this question: what makes a habit or a project genuinely one's own?

We can see this problem more clearly if we consider the second of the examples we are taking from Frankfurt. What if someone acts on a desire that they only had because it was implanted in them, through neurosurgery, perhaps, or magic, or hypnosis, by somebody else? Frankfurt uses this kind of example to argue against a certain view of moral responsibility (see 'Alternate Possibilities and Moral Responsibility', § 4). But we can adapt it to our purposes. We should say, of course, that the implanted desire is not one that the person really owns. If someone manages to induce in you the desire to smoke through one of these unusual ways, when you have never had this desire, then this desire is not really yours. This kind of example can be used against Frankfurt's account of ownership. Consider the slightly different case where I hypnotise you into forming both the first-order desire to smoke and the second-order volition to act on that desire. Neither the desire nor the volition, it seems, are genuinely your own.

Frankfurt's theory of the ownership of desires needs to be supplemented by an account of the ownership of second-order volitions, therefore, because it needs to be able to define which possible second-order volitions account for the ownership of first-order desires and which do not. We could hardly claim that a second-order desire is genuinely one's own only if there is a third-order desire about it, of course: what would make this third-order desire one's own? Frankfurt might seem to be addressing this problem in 'Identification and Wholeheartedness', where he points out that his previous writings on these topics leave a question concerning 'what account to give of the distinction between volitional elements that are integrated into a person and those that remain in some relevant sense external to him' (§ 5). When one formulates a higher-order volition, he argues in this paper, one is deciding how to resolve a conflict between that and at least one other desire, which involves judging that one will, all things considered, want to stick to this decision (§ 4).

This does not answer the question we are asking, however, and neither is it intended to. Frankfurt is not here attempting to define desires that we own in a way that would distinguish them from desires that have been implanted in us. He is rather discussing how we in fact draw the line between those of our desires with which we identify and those that we intend to banish from our lives or at least struggle against as inner but alien forces. He is concerned with how we go about trying to make ordered and harmonious selves out of the incoherent and unruly desires we find within us, with what it is to accept a desire as one's own or to reject it (see §§ 5–7). We can take from this discussion, however, the insight that ownership is not a matter of causal origins, but rather a matter of incorporation into oneself as constitutive of one's identity and outlook, even though neither the Aristotelian nor the Sartrean theory we are considering requires that this incorporation involves accepting the desire.

We are left, then, with the question of just how these theories should understand this incorporation. On the Aristotelian view of character that we are considering, of course, implanted desires could become genuinely one's own through their relation to rationally guided habits and their associated pleasures, and they would become aspects of one's character according to just how they were integrated into these habits. Almost the same account is available on the Sartrean view, except that the desires need to be integrated into projects rather than habits. But these responses to the question of ownership just push the issue back a stage. What accounts for the ownership of habits or projects? How should proponents of these theories understand a scenario in which the relevant habit or project was also implanted by neurosurgery, hypnosis, or magic? Ownership cannot be a matter of wholehearted endorsement, since people are not that consistent. Frankfurt might well be right that our reflective decisions concerning our desires aim for some kind of harmony between them, that is to say, but such harmony is unfortunately not a descriptive fact about ourselves and our characters.

What is more, we cannot account for the ownership of projects or habits purely in terms of an ongoing rational acceptance of them. It might seem, that is, that if one accepted an implanted project or habit as one's own, then its causal origins would no longer be relevant. Frankfurt argues for this kind of theory in 'The Faintest Passion': so long as reflective consideration of a desire has not yielded any further desire to change it, then we can say that the agent is satisfied with possessing it and has therefore taken ownership of it (§§ 7–8). What this overlooks, however, is that we can imagine scenarios in which the reflective thought leading to this acceptance is itself skewed by further desires or values that have also been implanted. It is not enough, that is to say, to point out that both the Aristotelian and the Sartrean views of character recognise the role of critical consideration of one's own behaviour patterns and attempts to change them, so that an implanted project or habit becomes truly one's own by being endorsed, at least sometimes if not consistently. Hypnotising you into habitually wanting a cigarette whenever you are drinking beer, for example, I could implant with the habit a strong sense that this is indeed good and desirable. So the question just becomes more complicated: when are one's reflective considerations of one's own behaviour patterns genuinely one's own?

The holism of the Sartrean philosophy of character provides a ready solution to these problems: ownership of a project or of a value, like ownership of a desire, is a matter of its integration into one's overall set of projects. Projects can be related to one another as determinables and their determinations, as we saw in chapter 4, and this allows them to be integrated with one another in a complex hierarchy. Some projects are ways of pursuing others. Projects can motivate the adoption or rejection of other projects. Some 'projects towards more restricted possibilities' are embedded 'within the compass' of deeper underlying projects (B&N: 484). One's projects are not merely a collection of distinct aims but rather an 'organic totality' (B&N: 476). Sartre holds, as we saw in chapter 8, that there is one fundamental project at the root of each individual's character, and that this is usually a project of bad faith, but we do not need to accept this aspect of his theory in order to accept the idea that the projects in which one's character consists form an integrated holistic network related by motivation as well as endorsement.

This aspect of the Sartrean account is unavailable on the Aristotelian picture of character as consisting in a set of habits, since habits are not related to one another as determinable and determination and do not motivate one another. Habits simply lack the teleology that underpins these relations between projects. The question of ownership cannot be properly answered on the Aristotelian picture, therefore: if it is possible to implant a desire in someone, then it seems possible to implant the disposition that grounds a habit, and indeed the value that will guarantee that this habit is endorsed on rational reflection. Conceptualising character in this way does not allow us to distinguish those aspects of the explanation of someone's behaviour patterns that are genuinely parts of that person, and perhaps also parts of that person's character, from alien forces that might be implanted in one way or another.

Were a project implanted into someone, on the other hand, and were we to accept the Sartrean theory of character, then we could distinguish this from a project genuinely owned by that person on the grounds that only the latter fits into the individual's network of projects in the right way: ownership is a matter of either being motivated by some deeper project or by being at least part of what unifies one's projects at the most fundamental level. Implanting a desire into you would not result in a desire you genuinely possess, because this desire would not be motivated by projects you already pursue. Implanting a project or two to avoid this problem would only be implanting projects that are not genuinely your own, because they are not motivated by projects that you pursue. It might seem that this leads to an infinite regress, just like the view that owning a desire means owning some higher-order desire to have that desire. But this objection would miss the point of the distinction between orders of desire and levels in a hierarchy of projects.

In order to provide the relevant motivation for the implanted desire, one would have to implant the project that motivated it, and the project that motivated that project, and so on until one reached a fundamental and therefore unmotivated project. At each level, the newly implanted project could conflict with other projects at its own and at other levels in ways that would lead to its rejection. Ensuring that the newly introduced desire became properly integrated into someone's set of projects, therefore, would require making wholesale revisions to their character. Far from introducing an aspect of the person's character that fits the theory's criteria for ownership yet is intuitively alien to that person, this enterprise would seem to leave us with someone who might no longer be the same person at all. The resulting psychological framework could be described as the artificially altered mindset of the same person, of course, but it seems equally plausible to say that such an extreme and abrupt change in outlook is the beginning of a new person possessing a new character. This is not to say that we must accept that psychological continuity is necessary for personal identity over time, but only to say that it is not intuitively obvious that one person can exist through such a large-scale psychological discontinuity. Even if we agree that the person does remain the same, it is not obvious that we should deny that they genuinely own the projects that now make up their character.

The criticism that we raised against Frankfurt's theory of the ownership of desires, then, was that it fails to distinguish between those desires that are genuinely one's own and those that might have been induced somehow from outside. There is an intuitive difference between these, as we can see from thinking about the possibility of having desires implanted by neurosurgery, hypnosis, or magic, and Frankfurt's theory fails to respect this intuitive difference. We have also seen that a more complicated version of the same argument can present problems for the Aristotelian view of character. Since habits, or at least the dispositions in which they consist, can be implanted, the argument runs, the Aristotelian view of character does not really allow us to distinguish between character traits actually owned by an individual and habits that might be induced from elsewhere.

But this argument cannot be run against the Sartrean account, because the holistic nature of a network of teleological states such as projects means that the implantation required for the argument is no longer one that clearly gives us the same person as beforehand but with alien traits alongside those they genuinely own. We can make a similar point about behaviour. Your actions are not merely ones that proceed from desires or habits of yours, since these could have been implanted in a way that leads us to deny that they themselves are genuinely yours. For an action to be yours, for you to be responsible for it, it must proceed from some aspect of your psychological make-up that is genuinely yours.

Similar reasoning can be used to show that the Sartrean approach to explaining behaviour is preferable to the traditional psychoanalytic theory that experiences and actions often result from drives and impulses that are genuinely parts of ourselves but which are unconscious and beyond our reflective control. Such theories need to give criteria for the ownership of these purported drives and impulses so that they can be distinguished from other drives and impulses that might be artificially implanted in the unconscious by a neurosurgeon, a hypnotist, or a magician. Unless they are to be understood as a holistic teleological network, motivating one another, some being forms of other ones, and so on, then it would seem that this kind of framework for understanding behaviour is subject to the same kind of argument as Frankfurt's account of the ownership of desires and the Aristotelian theory of character: we can always make up a scenario in which this theory fails to distinguish someone's own drives and impulses from others that influence their experiences and actions.

If we understand the unconscious drives and impulses as forming a teleological totality of projects, on the other hand, then we depart significantly from the Freudian picture of them as blind and nonrational. Pursuing a project requires sensitivity to environmental details and to the requirements of the other projects being pursued. The determinable-determination relation between projects described in chapter 4, moreover, is a rational means-end relation: one project is selected as a way of pursuing another. What is more, the Freudian idea that unconscious drives aim to be expressed in experience and action even if only symbolically seems incompatible with understanding them as goal-directed projects. Kleptomania might symbolically express the Oedipus complex, for example, because it breaks a social taboo and enacts illicit possession, but it can hardly be said to be a way of pursuing an oedipal project.

Understanding unconscious drives and impulses as nested sets of projects moves a long way, therefore, from the Freudian account of a functional division of mental activities, and instead presents us at best with the view that each of us is divided between the self we consider our own and another that also inhabits our body and pursues its own set of projects. In the absence of significant evidence of such an inner alien self, it seems that we cannot save the classical psychoanalytic theory of unconscious drives and impulses by understanding them as forming hierarchies of projects. Sartrean existentialism is therefore superior to the classic psychoanalytic theory of the mind for the same reason that it is superior to Frankfurt's approach to ownership of desires and to the Aristotelian theory of character: it alone among these options can provide us with satisfactory accounts of selfhood and of character.

Contrasting the Sartrean account of character with Frankfurt's moral psychology in this way, however, downplays the similarities between them. Frankfurt wants to understand freedom of action in terms of the control one has over the desires one manifests, abandoning the traditional emphasis on the ability to have done otherwise, and this is very much in keeping with Sartre's approach to freedom. Sartre holds, of course, that we have a kind of freedom over our projects that is incompatible with any kind of determinism. He is an incompatibilist, where Frankfurt aims to present a form of compatibilism. As we saw in chapter 5, however, this can be removed from the Sartrean picture without making significant alterations to the rest of it and the Sartrean picture is probably better off without it.

The remaining view, though not in all details Sartre's own, is the Sartrean theory that character consists in projects over which we have the freedom of reflective control. Although most of our changes to our characters over time may be piecemeal, we can nonetheless be motivated to change even our most fundamental project, and far-reaching changes to our character may come with such a change in its deepest root. Putting this in the language developed by Frankfurt, we can say that on the Sartrean picture of character any project can yield second-order volitions concerning the first-order desires involved in any other project. McInerney is therefore mistaken to argue against Sartre's theory of freedom that its denial that desires are enduring aspects of ourselves precludes our having reflective control over them ('Self-Determination and the Project', 676–7). It is precisely *because* Sartre thinks of desires as the products of our contingent projects that he can claim that we have control over them: we have control over those projects. The holistic approach to character and selfhood, therefore, can ground an approach to freedom quite similar to Frankfurt's.

Although the Sartrean theory of character was contrasted with the Aristotelian one in this chapter and claimed to be superior to it, this does not rule out the possibility that the correct account is some hybrid of the two. Perhaps some traits are rooted in our projects while others are simply habits. Perhaps the way a given project is pursued is determined, or partly determined, or at least can be, by habits that span across such projects, such as habits of thinking along certain lines or seeking immediate rather than long-term goals. Perhaps habit has a role to play in explaining how our projects become engrained, if indeed they do, so that any account of how we can change our projects needs to take account of the force of habit. There may be still further ways in which projects and habits combine in the production of behaviour patterns. As well as distinguishing a broadly Sartrean picture of character from Sartre's own theory, therefore, we can identify a broadly Sartrean contribution to the understanding of character: the very idea that the patterns in our behaviour may be rooted not just in the inertia brought about by repetition, but by traits that are inherently purposive and goal-directed. This contribution will be enhanced by further investigation and elaboration of this idea.

Sartrean existentialism involves many similarities to and echoes of the philosophy Aristotle propounds in *Nicomachean Ethics*. The emphasis on authenticity as a central value can be seen as a form of naturalist eudaimonism: where Aristotle thought that the central human good was well-being or flourishing as a person, which involves excelling in the rational capacities that define human being, Sartre thinks that it is the well-being or flourishing consequent upon recognising and promoting the freedom that defines our existence. But the centrality Sartre accords to freedom in his early writings is not strictly required by his theory of character or his further theory that we live in a culture of bad faith about the nature of our existence. If authenticity is just the acceptance of the true nature of our existence, and opposition to anything that distorts or represses it, then it seems that the human flourishing promoted by the authentic attitude should not be understood solely in terms of human freedom but should instead be understood in terms of all aspects of human existence and the human condition. After the works that we have considered in this book, Sartre's ethical thought developed into a more general eudaimonism in precisely this way. But the core of the account of human existence involved in this ethical outlook remained the theory that character consists in the projects we pursue and need not pursue.

There is a second way in which Sartre's thought echoes Aristotle's, one that aligns it with a movement in current moral philosophy that emphasises character and virtue more than rational thoughts and emotional responses. At the heart of this movement is the idea that ethical thought can and should penetrate deeper into the person than do theories that simply tell us how we should go about thinking about moral problems or that analyse our moral judgements in terms of emotional responses and stop there. Participants in the ethical discussion about character and virtue want to understand why different people think in the different ways in which they do, what grounds our emotional responses to the situations we confront, and what explains the different ways in which different people perceive the world. The interest is not simply in how we should respond, but in how we should train ourselves to be, whether this is to help us to respond in the right ways or just because ethics should be primarily concerned with the kinds of people we are. Like Aristotle and his recent followers in this movement, Sartre is concerned to explain how our perceptions, thoughts, and emotions are grounded, and so his work should be of interest in these areas of debate.

All of this might seem to presuppose, however, that there is anything of value in the theory that Sartre has constructed. It returns us, that is to say, to a question that was raised in chapter 1. Is it legitimate to base theories of perception, thought, emotion, and behaviour on the kinds of observations and analyses that Sartre used to develop his theory of character? While it may have been acceptable for Sartre, should we not rather abandon this whole approach and base our views on the findings of scientific psychological experiments? This question involves a misunderstanding of the relation between theory construction and experimental evidence. Experimental results do not interpret themselves: they are significant only in relation to the theories that are being tested. What is more, there can be theoretical as well as evidential reasons to prefer one theory over another. Considerations such as the predictive power of a theory or the way in which it fits with our other best theories can be reasons to prefer it over its rivals. We have seen that the Sartrean theory of character scores important theoretical points over other theories central to these debates. That should be reason enough to take it seriously.

But this is not to say, of course, that there is no place for experimental evidence in assessing this theory. Perhaps scientific data will show that we must reject it after all. Perhaps we will find that it needs to be refined in important ways if it is to be acceptable. The theory does aim to be an account of the actual construction of character and indeed of the ways in which we are aware of and interact with the world. So we can in principle design ways of testing it empirically: the theory will predict certain results rather than other ones from experiments that are sufficiently carefully designed. There are two major areas of current intellectual enquiry that will be most obviously useful here. One is social psychology: since this is, after all, a theory of character, it should be possible to test it by testing the ways in which people see certain situations, the ways in which they think and feel about them, and the ways in which they behave in response to them. Social psychologists have discovered a wide variety of ingenious ways of measuring these things, although as was mentioned in chapter 1 there are logistical and ethical constraints on the ways in which these tests can be administered and these constraints may turn out to be restrictive in important ways.

The other relevant area of intellectual enquiry is cognitive science: since this is a theory of perception, thought, and emotion as well as action, it can be evaluated against the backdrop of current scientific enquiry into these areas. One major area of debate at the moment, for example, concerns the role that our understanding of our own bodies and the ways in which it can act plays in the construction of our visual experience of the world around us. Discussion in this area clearly bears upon the acceptability or otherwise of Sartre's account of the way we see the world as partly determined by our goals. The nature of cognition and emotion, the relations between them, and their relations to action are all areas of extensive and vigorous scientific debate, much of which may bear on whether we can accept the Sartrean picture of character, or indeed any other picture of character available to us.

Just as we need to understand theories of character with due attention to their details, so too we should guard against drawing conclusions too hastily from experimental literature. There are many ways in which philosophers interested in the findings of scientific psychology can go wrong. Sufficient care needs to be taken to ensure that the experiments under consideration are indeed representative of literature currently well regarded among professionals in its own field, for example, and that their results really do bear on the issue at hand rather than only on some related but distinct issue of interest to the original authors. Such pitfalls are best avoided through interdisciplinary work in which experiments are designed expressly to test the empirical commitments of philosophical theories of character, though this is not the only way to avoid them. But avoid them we must if we are to reap the benefits this research has to offer our theories of the nature and knowledge of character. Our understanding of ourselves and one another lies at the heart of many of our personal, moral, social, and political concerns, and is employed in all of our attempts to address them. It is only through careful theoretical and empirical reflection that this understanding can mature into a detailed and responsible picture free of ideology and superstition.

Bibliography

Aristotle. *Nicomachean Ethics*. Translated by Christopher Rowe. Commentary by Sarah Broadie. Oxford: Oxford University Press, 2002.
Barnes, Hazel E. *Sartre*. London: Quartet, 1974.
Barnes, Hazel E. Sartre's Ontology: The Revealing and Making of Being. In *The Cambridge Companion to Sartre*, edited by Christina Howells, pp. 13–38. Cambridge: Cambridge University Press, 1992.
Bell, Linda A. *Sartre's Ethics of Authenticity*. Tuscaloosa: University of Alabama Press, 1984.
Bernasconi, Robert. *How To Read Sartre*. London: Granta, 2006.
Carney, John C. *Rethinking Sartre: A Political Reading*. Lanham: University Press of America, 2007.
Catalano, Joseph S. *A Commentary on Jean-Paul Sartre's Being and Nothingness*. Chicago: University of Chicago Press, 1974.
———. Successfully Lying to Oneself. *Philosophy and Phenomenological Research* 50, no. 4 (June 1990): 673–693.
Cooper, David E. *Existentialism: A Reconstruction*. Second edition. Oxford: Blackwell, 1999.
Cox, Gary. *Sartre: A Guide for the Perplexed*. London: Continuum, 2006.
Danto, Arthur C. *Sartre*. Second edition. London: Fontana, 1991.
Doris, John. *Lack of Character: Personality and Moral Behaviour*. Cambridge: Cambridge University Press, 2002.
Føllesdal, Dagfinn. Sartre on Freedom. In *The Philosophy of Jean-Paul Sartre*, edited by Paul Arthur Schlipp, pp. 392–407. La Salle: Open Court, 1981.
Foot, Philippa. Free Will as Involving Determinism. *The Philosophical Review* 66, no. 4 (October 1957): 439–450. Reprinted in *Virtues and Vices and Other Essays in Moral Philosophy*, second edition, by Philippa Foot, pp. 62–73. Oxford: Clarendon, 2002.
Fox, Nik Farrell. *The New Sartre*. London: Continuum, 2003.
Frankfurt, Harry G. Alternate Possibilities and Moral Responsibility. *The Journal of Philosophy* 66, no. 23 (December 1969): 829–839. Reprinted in *The Importance of What We Care About*, by Harry G. Frankfurt, pp. 1–10. Cambridge: Cambridge University Press, 1988.
———. Freedom of the Will and the Concept of a Person. *The Journal of Philosophy* 68, no. 1 (January 1971): 5–20. Reprinted in *The Importance of What We Care About*, by Harry G. Frankfurt, pp. 11–25. Cambridge: Cambridge University Press, 1988.
———. Identification and Wholeheartedness. In *Responsibility, Character, and the Emotions: New Essays in Moral Psychology*, edited by Ferdinand David Schoeman, pp. 27–45. Reprinted in *The Importance of What We Care About*,

Bibliography

by Harry G. Frankfurt, pp. 159–176. Cambridge: Cambridge University Press, 1988.

———. The Faintest Passion. *Proceedings and Addresses of the American Philosophical Association* 66, no. 3 (November 1992): 5–16. Reprinted in *Necessity, Volition, and Love*, by Harry G. Frankfurt, pp. 95–107. Cambridge: Cambridge University Press, 1998.

Gilbert, Daniel T., and Patrick S. Malone. The Correspondence Bias. *Psychological Bulletin* 117, no. 1 (January 1995): 21–38.

Giles, James. Sartre, Sexual Desire and Relations with Others. In *French Existentialism: Consciousness, Ethics and Relations with Others*, edited by James Giles, pp. 155–174. Amsterdam: Rodopi, 1999.

Harman, Gilbert. The Nonexistence of Character Traits. *Proceedings of the Aristotelian Society* 100, no. 2 (2000): 223–226.

Heter, T. Storm. *Sartre's Ethics of Engagement: Authenticity and Civic Virtue*. London: Continuum, 2006.

Howells, Christina. Conclusion: Sartre and the Deconstruction of the Subject. In *The Cambridge Companion to Sartre*, edited by Christina Howells, pp. 318–352. Cambridge: Cambridge University Press, 1992.

Hume, David. *A Treatise of Human Nature*. Edited by David Fate Norton and Mary J. Norton. Oxford: Clarendon, 2007. First published in three volumes, 1739–1740.

———. *An Enquiry Concerning Human Understanding*. Edited by Tom L. Beauchamp. Oxford: Clarendon, 2006. First published in 1748.

Husserl, Edmund. *Cartesian Meditations: An Introduction to Phenomenology*. Translated by Dorion Cairns, The Hague: Martinus Nijhoff, 1950. Originally written in German, but first published in French translation, in 1931. First German edition published in 1950.

Jopling, David A. Sartre's Moral Psychology. In *The Cambridge Companion to Sartre*, edited by Christina Howells, pp. 103–139. Cambridge: Cambridge University Press, 1992.

Leak, Andrew. *Jean-Paul Sartre*. London: Reaktion Books, 2006.

Manser, Anthony. A New Look At Bad Faith. In *Sartre: An Investigation of Some Major Themes*, edited by Simon Glynn, pp. 55–70. Aldershot: Avebury Press, 1987.

McCulloch, Gregory. *Using Sartre: An Analytical Introduction to Early Sartrean Themes*. London: Routledge, 1994.

McDowell, John. Virtue and Reason. *Monist* 62, no. 3 (July 1979): 331–350. Reprinted in *Mind, Value, and Reality*, by John McDowell, pp. 50–73. Cambridge: Harvard University Press, 1998.

McInerney, Peter K. Self-Determination and the Project. *The Journal of Philosophy* 76, no. 11 (November 1979): 663–677.

Milgram, Stanley. *Obedience to Authority: An Experimental View*. New York: Harper and Row, 1974.

Morris, Phyllis Sutton. *Sartre's Concept of a Person: An Analytic Approach*. Amherst: University of Massachusetts Press, 1976.

———. Self-Deception: Sartre's Resolution of the Paradox. In *Jean-Paul Sartre: Contemporary Approaches to His Philosophy*, edited by Hugh J. Silverman and Frederick A. Elliston, pp. 30–49. Brighton: The Harvester Press, 1980.

———. Sartre on the Transcendence of the Ego. *Philosophy and Phenomenological Research* 46, no. 2 (December 1985): 179–198.

Reisman, David. *Sartre's Phenomenology*. London: Continuum, 2007.

Richmond, Sarah. Introduction. In *The Transcendence of the Ego*, by Jean-Paul Sartre, pp. vii–xxviii. London and New York: Routledge, 2004

Ross, Lee. The Intuitive Psychologist and His Shortcomings: Distortions in the Attribution Process. In *Advances in Experimental Social Psychology*, volume 10, edited by L. Berkowitz, pp. 173–220. New York: Academic Press, 1977.
Santoni, Ronald. *Bad Faith, Good Faith, and Authenticity in Sartre's Early Philosophy*. Philadelphia: Temple University Press, 1995.
Sartre, Jean-Paul. [TE] *The Transcendence of the Ego: A Sketch for a Phenomenological Description*. Translated by Andrew Brown. London and New York: Routledge, 2004. Translation of *La Transcendance de l'Ego: Esquisse d'une Description Phénoménologique*, Paris: Vrin, 1988. First published in 1936.
———. [STE] *Sketch for a Theory of the Emotions*. Translated by Philip Mairet. Second edition. London and New York: Routledge, 2002. Translation of *Esquisse d'une Théorie des Emotions*, Paris: Hermann, 1939.
———. [IPPI] *The Imaginary: A Phenomenological Psychology of the Imagination*. Translated by Jonathan Webber. London and New York: Routledge, 2004. Translation of *L'Imaginaire: Psychologie Phénoménologique de l'Imagination*, revised by Arlette Elkaïm-Sartre, Paris: Gallimard, 1986. Original edition published in 1940.
———. [B&N] *Being and Nothingness: An Essay in Phenomenological Ontology*. Translated by Hazel E. Barnes. Revised edition. London and New York: Routledge, 2003. Translation of *L'Être et le Néant: Essai d'Ontologie Phenomenologique*, revised by Arlette Elkaïm-Sartre, Paris: Gallimard, 1994. Original edition published in 1943.
———. [HC] Huis Clos. Translated by Stuart Gilbert. In *Huis Clos and Other Plays*, by Jean-Paul Sartre, pp. 177–223, London: Penguin, 2000. Translation of *Huis Clos*, Paris: Gallimard, 1944.
———. [AR] *The Age of Reason*. Translated by Eric Sutton. Harmondsworth: Penguin, 1986. Translation of *L'Âge de Raison*, Paris: Gallimard, 1945.
———. [TR] *The Reprieve*. Translated by Eric Sutton. Harmondsworth: Penguin, 1986. Translation of *Le Sursis*, Paris: Gallimard, 1945.
———. [EH] *Existentialism Is A Humanism*. Translated by Carol Macomber. New Haven and London: Yale University Press, 2007. Translation of *L'Existentialisme est une Humanisme*, revised by Arlette Elkaïm-Sartre, Paris: Gallimard, 1996. Original edition published in 1946.
———. [B] *Baudelaire*. Translated by Martin Turnell. New York: New Directions, 1950. Translation of *Baudelaire*, Paris: Gallimard, 1946.
———. [A&J] *Anti-Semite and Jew*. Translated by George J. Becker, New York: Schocken Books, 1976. Translation of *Réflexions sur la Question Juive*, Paris: Morihien, 1946.
———. [IS] *Iron in the Soul*. Translated by Eric Sutton. Harmondsworth: Penguin, 1986. Translation of *Le Mort Dans l'Âme*, Paris: Gallimard, 1949.
———. [IT] Itinerary of a Thought. Interview in *New Left Review* I/58 (November-December 1969): 43–66. Reprinted in Jean-Paul Sartre, *Between Existentialism and Marxism*, New Left Books: 1974.
Schrift, Alan D. *Twentieth-Century French Philosophy: Key Themes and Thinkers*. Oxford: Blackwell, 2006.
Schroeder, William Ralph. *Sartre and His Predecessors: The Self and the Other*. London: Routledge and Kegan Paul, 1984.
Solomon, Robert C. True To Oneself: Sartre's Bad Faith and Freedom. In *Dark Feelings, Grim Thoughts: Experience and Reflection in Camus and Sartre*, by Robert C. Solomon, pp. 131–176. Oxford: Oxford University Press, 2006.
Velleman, J. David. What Happens When Someone Acts? *Mind* 101, no. 403 (July 1992): 461–481. Reprinted in *The Possibility of Practical Reason*, by J. David Velleman, pp. 123–143. Oxford: Clarendon, 2000.

Warnock, Mary. Freedom in the Early Philosophy of J.-P. Sartre. In *Essays on the Freedom of Action*, edited by Ted Honderich, pp. 3–14. London: Routledge and Kegan Paul, 1973.

Webber, Jonathan. Sartre's Theory of Character. *European Journal of Philosophy* 14, no. 1 (April 2006): 94–116.

———. Virtue, Character and Situation. *Journal of Moral Philosophy* 3, no. 2 (July 2006): 193–213.

———. Character, Common-Sense, and Expertise. *Ethical Theory and Moral Practice* 10, no. 1 (February 2007): 89–104.

———. Character, Global and Local. *Utilitas* 19, no. 4 (December 2007): 430–434.

Wider, Kathleen. *The Bodily Nature of Consciousness: Sartre and Contemporary Philosophy of Mind*. Ithica: Cornell University Press, 1997.

Index

A

actions: 51–53, 56–58, 61–62, 149–151, 155.
addiction: 148, 149–151.
Age of Reason, The: 42, 63–64, 69, 123.
alienation: 116, 120–126, 128–129, 138–142, 143.
anguish: 66–67, 72, 74, 82, 85, 105, 107, 111–113, 116–117, 123, 124.
Anti-Semite and Jew: 6, 49–50, 55, 98, 114–115. *See also* ethnicity; racism.
antivalue: 113–115, 124–125, 138. *See also* discomfort.
anxiety: 140.
Aristotle: 3, 5, 15, 146–149, 152–158.
attraction: 39–41, 135. *See also* repulsion.
authenticity: 5, 10, 46, 108, 110, 116–117, 119–120, 127–129, 131, 132–145, 157.

B

bad faith: 4–5, 9–10, 16, 22, 45–46, 48, 71–72, 74–87, 88–102, 105–113, 116–117, 118–126, 128–131, 132–142, 157; content and structure: 91; restricted and general content: 74–75, 91; attitude towards evidence in structure: 93–98; diagram of different senses of the phrase: 96. *See also* seriousness.
Barnes, Hazel: 23, 107, 120, 121.
Baudelaire: 6, 10.
Being and Nothingness: throughout; structure of: 118–119.
being-for-itself: 49, 108–110, 134.
being-for-others. *See* interpersonal relations.
being-in-itself: 24, 26, 31–32, 34, 39, 49, 68, 77, 86, 107–110, 113–114, 126, 132.
Bell, Linda: 122, 132.
Bernasconi, Robert: 77.
blindness: 139.
body, the: 21, 76, 84–85, 119, 136, 147.
buried projects: 54, 71, 100, 147.

C

candour: 74, 79. *See also* sincerity.
Carney, John: 145.
Catalano, Joseph: 20–21, 22, 23, 45, 80–81, 86, 94–95, 108, 119.
celery: 116.
censorship: 89–90.
champion of sincerity: 80–81, 83–84, 86, 92, 93, 95, 118–119, 128, 135. *See also* sincerity; unhappy homosexual.
chance: 60–61, 64–66, 72–73, 104, 105. *See also* indeterminism.
choice: 9, 22, 29, 34–35, 38, 41, 48, 50, 53–54, 62–63, 65–66, 67, 69, 71, 77–78, 107, 113, 135.
Christianity: 107, 143–144. *See also* God.
compatibilism: 69, 72, 87, 104–105, 156. *See also* determinism; incompatibilism; indeterminism.
conflict. *See* interpersonal relations.
consciousness: 19–20, 23–24, 44–49, 50, 104, 106–109, 113–114, 122, 126–127.
consistency, logical: 85, 122, 125, 135–136, 144.

constitution: 24–25, 31–33, 37, 39, 59, 63–64, 82, 92–93, 95, 97, 99, 109, 111, 128.
conversion: 42–43, 57, 62, 64–66, 71, 119–120, 128, 136, 142.
Cooper, David: 44, 120.
Cox, Gary: 20–21, 77, 80–81, 85–86, 108, 119.

D

Daniel: 63–64, 65, 69, 70, 123, 125–126, 130.
Danto, Arthur: 45.
death: 129–130, 141.
deliberation: 28, 33–34.
deliverance. *See* salvation.
desire to be God. *See* God.
desire, sexual. *See* sexuality.
despair: 132.
determinism: 7, 21–23, 28–29, 32, 36, 42, 45–49, 53, 57, 60–61, 67, 69, 74–75, 78–79, 81–82, 85, 104–105, 138. *See also* compatibilism; incompatibilism; indeterminism.
discomfort: 84–86, 93, 124, 128. *See also* anguish; antivalue; anxiety; uneasiness.
disgust. *See* repulsion.
displeasure. *See* antivalue.
distraction: 90–91, 93, 99.
Doris, John: 8, 17.
Dostoyevsky, Fyodor: 11, 64.
dreaming: 101.

E

education: 3.
ego: 19–20, 23–27, 29, 41.
Elkaïm-Sartre, Arlette: 31.
emotion: 19, 30–31, 32–33, 34–35, 36–38, 41, 50–51, 100, 115, 157–159. *See also* feelings.
essence: 8–9, 20–22, 43, 46, 59, 75, 76, 79, 121–122, 128. *See also* nature.
ethics: 2–3, 110, 119–120, 128, 132–145, 157–159.
ethnicity: 3–4. *See also* racism; *Anti-Semite and Jew*.
eudaimonism: 157.
existentialism: *throughout*; Sartre's definition: 134.
Existentialism Is A Humanism: 8–9, 59, 133–136, 143–144.
experimental psychology. *See* scientific psychology.

exploitation: 143–145.
extensional and intensional meanings: 75, 82–83, 84, 92, 102, 122, 136.

F

facticity: 19–23, 45, 47, 75–76, 80–82, 86.
faith: 93–96, 99, 112.
fatalism: 104–105.
feelings: 18, 23, 25, 28, 34, 39, 40, 50, 67, 115, 124, 146–147, 148. *See also* disgust; emotion.
Føllesdal, Dagfinn: 63–64, 66.
Foot, Philippa: 151.
Fox, Nik Farrell: 20, 119.
Frankfurt, Harry: 149–157.
free will: 60–61. *See also* libertarianism; liberty of indifference.
freedom: 7–9, 22, 29, 47, 59–73, 74–88, 93, 98–99, 101, 104–105, 107, 111, 113, 116–117, 121–123, 124, 127–128, 134–135, 138, 143–145, 149–150, 156–157.
Freud, Sigmund: 11, 89–90, 102–103, 149, 155–6.
fundamental project: 28, 54–58, 70–72, 87, 107–116, 120, 122–123, 124, 125–126, 133, 135–136, 137–138, 142, 144, 153.

G

Garcin: 51–52, 53, 56, 100, 123, 129–131.
Gide, André: 64.
Gilbert, Daniel: 13–14.
Giles, James: 137, 139, 141.
God: 106–114, 115–116, 120, 121–122, 123, 125–126, 132, 135, 137–138. *See also* Christianity.
good faith: 77, 93–95, 96, 97.
guilt: 143.

H

habits: 20, 25, 35, 41, 145, 146–149, 152–155, 157.
happiness: 2, 70, 117, 142.
Harman, Gilbert: 8, 13.
hatred: 25, 32, 38, 39, 49–50, 64, 110, 114–115, 137, 141–142.
Hegel, G. W. F.: 44–45.
Heter, T. Storm: 20–21, 38, 68, 81, 86, 115, 119, 121, 129, 145.

homosexual. *See* unhappy homosexual.
Howells, Christina: 23.
Huis Clos: 51–52, 100, 118, 123, 129–131.
human reality: 21, 22, 36, 107–110, 134.
humanism: 134.
Hume, David: 15, 60–62, 64–65, 69, 72, 104–105.
Husserl, Edmund: 23.

I
Imaginary, The: 38–42, 101, 104–105.
imagination: 19, 23–25, 36–37, 38–42, 43, 84, 101.
impure reflection. *See* reflection.
incarnation: 140.
incompatibilism: 67, 104–105, 156. *See* compatibilism; determinism; indeterminism.
incorporation. *See* selfhood.
indeterminism: 60–62, 64–67, 69, 72, 87, 104–105.
indifference: 137, 139–140, 142. *See* liberty of indifference.
Inez: 51, 130.
inferiority project: 54, 55–56, 57–58, 68, 69, 70–72, 102, 107–108, 109, 110–111, 136, 147.
initial project: 54, 55, 62, 71. *See also* fundamental project.
intensional: *See* extensional and intensional meanings.
intentionality: 126–127.
interpersonal relations: 1, 5, 9–10, 118–131, 136–142.
Iron in the Soul: 42–43, 59.
Itinerary of a Thought, The (interview): 7, 9.

J
Jopling, David: 23, 56.

K
Kant, Immanuel: 15.
kleptomania: 102, 156.
Kojève, Alexandre: 44–45.

L
Leak, Andrew: 42.
libertarianism: 60–61. *See also* free will; liberty of indifference.
liberty of indifference: 60–62, 65, 114. *See also* libertarianism; free will.

look, the: 119–120, 122–123, 126, 129, 131, 137. *See also* interpersonal relations.
love: 38, 39, 137, 138–139, 141–142.

M
magic: 32–33, 36–38.
Malone, Patrick: 13–14.
Manser, Anthony: 77, 80–81, 85–86, 94–95.
masochism: 137, 138–139, 140, 142.
Mathieu: 42–43.
McCulloch, Gregory: 20–23, 45, 54, 63, 66, 80–81, 86, 112, 147.
McDowell, John: 19, 35.
McInerney, Peter: 20–21, 54, 56, 66, 68, 111, 156.
melodies: 20, 24–25.
metamorphosis. *See* conversion.
metaphysics: 7, 24, 47, 49, 126–127. *See also* ontology.
metastable: 101–102.
Milgram experiment: 12–14, 17–18.
Milgram, Stanley: 12–14, 17–18.
mobile: 30–31, 34, 59, 60–61, 62, 70, 92–93. *See also* motif.
moral psychology: 11–15, 105, 145.
morality. *See* ethics.
Morris, Phyllis Sutton: 20–21, 27–28, 56–57, 81, 111.
motif: 30–31, 33, 34, 59, 60–61, 70, 71, 92–93. *See also* mobile.

N
nature 8–10, 20–22, 28–29, 45–46, 74–79, 80–86, 88, 89, 91–94, 95, 97, 98–101, 105–116, 119–131, 132, 134, 135, 137–140, 143. *See also* bad faith; essence.
negation: 48, 68. *See also* nothingness.
négitaté. *See* nothingness.
nihilation: 18, 108–109.
nihilism: 132, 136.
nonbeing. *See* nothingness.
non-persuasive evidence: 93–98, 99.
non-positional awareness: 50, 83. *See also* non-thetic awareness.
non-thetic awareness: 18, 50, 83, 92, 93, 100, 102–103.
nothingness: 47, 49, 67–69, 72.

O
objects: 126–127.
obsessive-compulsive disorder: 41.

Oedipus: 104.
Oedipus complex: 102, 156.
ontology: 7, 49, 67, 72, 144–145. See also metaphysics.
oppression: 143–145.
original sin: 143.
other people. See interpersonal relations.
ownership. See selfhood.

P

passion: 107, 100.
personal identity: 154–155.
Philoctetes: 64.
Pierre: 68.
politics: 3–4, 42.
positional awareness. See non-positional awareness; non-thetic awareness.
preferences. See tastes.
pre-judicative awareness: 83. See also non-thetic awareness.
pride: 121, 124–125, 135, 138.
projects 4, 28, 31, 32–33, 34–36, 38, 42, 43, 44, 47–58, 59–73, 87, 92–93, 99–103, 104–105, 107–109, 111–116, 122–123, 145, 146–149, 152–157; as hierarchy: see esp. 52–58. See also buried projects; fundamental project.
psychaesthenia. See obsessive-compulsive disorder.
psyche: 26–27, 29. See also ego.
psychoanalysis: 1, 55, 56, 70–71, 89–90, 102–103, 110, 114, 116, 120, 141, 146–147, 149, 155–156.
psychological determinism. See determinism.
psychology. See moral psychology; scientific psychology.
pure reflection. See reflection.

Q

qualities: 25–29, 32, 41, 43, 79, 81–82, 84–87, 103. See also ego; essence; nature.

R

racism: 4, 114–115. See also ethnicity; *Anti-Semite and Jew*.
radical: 62.
randomness. See chance.
Raskolnikov: 64.

rationality: 145, 155–156.
recognition: 144–145.
reflection: 23, 28, 38, 50, 74, 80, 82–83, 100–101, 102, 128; pure and impure: 100–101, 128.
Reisman, David: 26, 29, 80–81, 122.
relationships. See interpersonal relations.
relativism: 132–133, 134, 136, 142–143.
Reprieve, The: 42, 59, 123, 130.
repulsion: 39, 41, 113–116.
resistance: 24, 89.
responsibility: 7–9, 59–60, 74, 79, 88, 99, 116–117, 151.
Richmond, Sarah: 143.
Roads to Freedom trilogy: See *Age of Reason, The*; *Reprieve, The*; *Iron in the Soul*; Daniel; Mathieu.
Ross, Lee: 13.

S

sadism: 137, 140–141, 142.
salvation: 110, 119–120, 136, 143.
Santoni, Ronald: 44.
sartrais: 6, 21, 22, 24, 31, 32, 46, 76, 92, 95, 119, 134, 138; defined: 6.
Scheler, Max: 11.
schizophrenia: 40–41.
Schrift, Alan: 45.
Schroeder, William Ralph: 119, 124.
science: 94–95, 98, 159.
scientific psychology: 10–15, 158–159.
self. See ego.
self-awareness. See reflection; self-consciousness.
self-consciousness: 50–51, 53–54, 100–101, 120–121. See also reflection.
self-deception: 54, 77, 83–84, 87, 88–103, 112; paradoxes of: 88–89, 97, 103.
selfhood: 146–157.
seriousness: 91, 98–99, 132.
sexuality: 80, 116, 137, 140–142, 147–149. See also unhappy homosexual.
shame: 69, 70, 121–125, 127.
sin: 107, 143.
sincerity: 74, 75, 77, 79, 81–82, 84, 86, 95. See also champion of sincerity.
situation: 30–33.

Sketch for a Theory of the Emotions: 32, 36–38, 41, 90, 102, 115.
sliminess: 113–115.
social policy: 2, 3–4.
social psychology. *See* scientific psychology.
solipsism: 23, 119, 120–121, 127, 136.
Solomon, Robert: 101.
spirit of seriousness. *See* seriousness.
symbolism: 102, 113–116, 117, 123–124, 156.

T

tastes: 25, 56, 103, 113–116.
temporality: 27, 44–46.
thetic awareness. *See* non-thetic awareness.
ticket-collector: 118–119.
time. *See* temporality.
transcendence: 19–20, 22, 75–76, 80–81, 85–86.
Transcendence of the Ego, The: 23–28, 36–37, 41, 43, 66.
truth: 134, 136.

U

unconscious: 89–90, 102–103, 146–147, 149, 155–156.

uneasiness: 124, 140.
unhappy homosexual: 80–84, 85, 86–87, 92, 93, 95, 97, 128. *See also* champion of sincerity.

V

value: 34, 49, 68–69, 70–72, 77, 80, 91, 98–99, 111, 113–114, 115, 124–125, 132–139, 142, 144–145, 153–154, 157. *See also* antivalue.
vanity: 121.
Velleman, J. David: 150.
vertigo: 66. *See also* anguish.
vice: 2–3.
virtue: 2–3, 35, 143, 157–158.
voluntariness. *See* will, the.

W

waiter: 22, 76–79, 83–84, 86, 88, 92–93, 102, 105–106, 118–119, 139–140.
Warnock, Mary: 48, 68, 108.
Wider, Kathleen: 45, 48.
will, the: 33–34, 41, 149–151. *See also* selfhood.
woman on a date: 84–86, 92, 118.
world: 24, 31–33, 92–93.